BRINGING THE LAW TO TEXAS

For Les + ~~Janet~~ + Jenni

Merry Xmas

2002

BRINGING THE LAW TO TEXAS

CRIME AND VIOLENCE IN NINETEENTH CENTURY TEXAS

ALLEN G. HATLEY

CENTEX PRESS
LaGrange, Texas
2002

Manufactured in the United States of America

ISBN 0-9649416-1-9 (hardcover)
ISBN 0-9649416-2-7 [papercover]
LOC# 2002091128

cover design by David Timmons

cover painting *The Hold Up*, by Charles M. Russell
(30-1/8" x 48-1/8" oil on canvas, 1899),
courtesy of Amon Carter Museum,
Fort Worth, Texas. [1961.212]

Centex Press
1525 Post Oak Road
LaGrange, Texas 78945

TABLE OF CONTENTS

LIST OF ILLUSTRATIONS

ACKNOWLEDGMENTS

A number of people have helped me in this journey through an earlier and more violent Texas, but none so much as Janet Cave, who never failed to encourage, inspire and most important, make me laugh. Thanks to Chuck Parsons, Roy Young and Carolyn Edwards for reviewing the text and offering suggestions on how to make it better, to Bob McCubbin for those great photographs, and to Deborah Brothers for making it work. A special thanks to Ronald DeLord, President of "CLEAT," The Combined Law Enforcement Association of Texas, whose leadership in compiling and analyzing the data that has been so vital to the fulfillment of a Memorial in Austin to fallen lawmen. Because he and those who worked with him shared that data, many of those on the Memorial are a part of this book.

As I travelled around the state a number of people helped me to compile the data cited in this book. They include Jan Brown, District Clerk in Brown County, Kathy Barrow, District Clerk in Burnet County, Bill Stein, Director of the Nesbitt Memorial Library in Colorado County, Terri Cox, District Clerk in Lampasas County, Jeff Jackson in Lampasas County, Debbie Honig, District Clerk in Llano County, Beatrice Langehenning, County & District Clerk in Mason County, Cheri Hawkins, County & District Clerk in Shackelford County, JoAnn Lackey, District Clerk in Taylor County and Carolyn Collins, District Clerk in Young County. Special thanks go to Pam Nickel and Lori Kirk at the Department of Public Safety in Austin and the staff of the Texas State Library and Archives Commission who always give of their time and talents in solving a researchers problems.

INTRODUCTION

This book describes how lawmen and the courts in what was sometimes a violent, dirty and savage land, worked to bring law and order to Texas during the first 55 years of the Lone Star State. It is not always a heroic story of good vanquishing evil, but it is an accurate and comprehensive account of the never ending effort to establish the rule of law in Texas. But this is more than just a retelling of the traditional chronicles of outlaws versus lawmen, or crime and the courts. This story looks past the obvious history of lawlessness that is often portrayed, in an effort to help uncover and understand the causes and motivations behind some of the more violent periods, places and men in early Texas history.

At the time of its entry into the Union in December of 1845, Texas had a population of almost 200,000 people and covered an area of more than 260,000 square miles. Most Texans lived in the 36 organized counties in the eastern half of the state and less than 7,000 of those lived in any type of town or urban setting. The size of the individual counties varied greatly. One of the largest was almost 16,000 square miles in size, making it near to impossible for locally elected lawmen to provide any protection to many of its residents. Within months after annexation and the new sense of security it offered, another thirty-one counties were organized. Despite the growth, or perhaps partially because of it, the State of Texas during its early years was a surprisingly peaceful land, except for its frontier, that strip of land just partially settled and on the edge of civilization, where Texans lived daily with the threat of Indian raids and the heightened expectation of violence.

The primary goal in writing this account was to provide an accurate, entertaining and sweeping story for general readers and for scholars alike about how ordinary men and women fought a never ending war to bring the rule of law to Texas. Such a story about crime, violence and the criminal justice system in nineteenth century Texas has never been written. One reason is that an accurate story cannot be limited only to tales about the Texas Rangers, as has too often happened. It was the elected and appointed lawmen scattered across the many different counties and municipalities in the Lone Star State, who were those most involved in establishing the rule of law. They were also the people who paid the highest price, for they made up some 75 percent of those who we know were killed in Texas during the nineteenth century while wearing a lawman's badge.

We also know that during the states first 55 years, Texas lawmen and ordinary citizens fought hostile Indians, Mexican bandits, cattle rustlers, horse thieves, bank robbers, just plain outlaws and occasionally each other. The most recent data available tells us that over 25O-lawmen died in the line of duty during that period. As the count continues, however, more names will surely be added. We also knew that Texas during the nineteenth century was a state that would long be dominated by its ever changing and more violent western frontier. It was a state that even until the middle of the twentieth century would still be dominated by its rural roots and rural population.

As the book progressed, it became obvious that for this story to be something more than just another look at the adventures of different cops and robbers, the criminal justice system needed to be examined from a somewhat larger and different perspective. That included reviewing much of what had been written before about crime in the Lone Star State, while examining hundreds of records dealing with the life, death and exploits of numerous lawmen and some of the outlaws. Court records in a number of counties were also examined in order to answer the question of just what crimes were committed and how violent Texas was at any time during its first 55 years as a state. It was a daunting task that occasionally left me reeling, but one key to the writing of this book was the ability for the first time to recognize a large number of lawmen who played active roles in upholding the law in nineteenth century Texas.

While there is little to admire about most career criminals, many Texas outlaws have gained a good deal of notoriety. Surprisingly little, however, has been written telling us much about individual Texas lawmen in the nineteenth century, except for a few of those serving with the Texas Rangers. One reason for the lack of this information has been the difficulty of unearthing most of those stories of individual lawmen. The recent efforts of the Peace Officers Memorial Foundation, Inc. and the Combined

Law Enforcement Associations of Texas (CLEAT), along with those others who have made the Peace Officers Memorial in Austin, Texas into a reality, have provided a most accurate roll call of those who gave their lives attempting to bring the rule of law to the Lone Star State. The ongoing work of compiling that list of fallen lawmen will make us all even more aware of their sacrifice.

Another factor contributing to the lack of information on individual peace officers in early Texas is that relatively few lawmen from that period appear to have considered law enforcement as a long term, much less a life-long career, as it has become for many in the twentieth century. As a result, most lawmen serving in their counties or in the towns of Texas, moved on to a new location or another line of work after a few years in law enforcement and many of their stories were lost.

Perhaps as a result, very few lawmen in Texas have reached the icon status that some of those almost mythical pistoleros have become who upheld the law in the Kansas trail towns and the boom towns like Tombstone and Denver, or even in some of the smaller Western mining towns. El Paso Town Marshal Dallas Stoudenmier, who may have killed as many as four men on his third day in office and then killed another about a week later, spent less than a year as that city's marshal. John Selman was elected Constable in El Paso's Precinct #1 a little over a decade later. He shot and killed two men during only three and one-half years on the job, before he was killed himself. Timothy "Longhaired Jim" Courtright was appointed City Marshal in Fort Worth in 1876. He kept the peace in that town's lively red-light district called Hell's Half Acre for three years without killing anyone. Ben Thompson served less than a year as Austin's City Marshal. All of the above are certainly among the better known Texas lawmen in the nineteenth century. But as a group their total tenure as Texas lawmen was only about eight years. They were by nature violent men and would collectively kill more than a dozen men during the more violent times in their lives, but only about a half dozen of those men were killed while they wore a badge.

State law enforcement was really little different, as most of the early rangers, the State Police and those serving in the Frontier Battalion usually spent only from a few months to a few years in those organizations. The exceptions were some of those in positions of command, but few spent enough time to ever formally retire from the State Troops, not even John B. Jones. One reason why more has been written about the Texas Rangers than other lawmen in Texas is the large amount of information available on the Ranger organization. Furthermore, most of the basic research on the activities of the state troops can be done at just two locations: the Texas State Library and Archives Commission located in Austin and The Texas Ranger Museum and Hall of Fame in Waco. On the other hand, records about Texas county and municipal law enforcement activities, the courts and the criminal justice system, are scattered throughout Texas' 254 counties.

To find that data, if it still exists, is often a major challenge. That job is not helped by the host of county histories that concentrate only on family histories. Some county courthouse records have also been lost through theft, in floods and fires, some of which were set to destroy the records of certain outlaw families and land frauds. Some records can also no longer be read simply because the ink has faded; but the vast majority of those surviving records were fortunately written by a multitude of clerks that excelled in penmanship. As a result, occasionally the reward of research in some counties is phenomenal.

I knew that there were already available a number of well-written and accurate books that allows us a look in some detail at many of the more famous individual outlaws. As a result, while I did not set out to rewrite those stories into a nineteenth century "Texas Most Wanted," no book on the criminal justice system would be complete without looking at some of the criminals who committed the crimes. So, I include the misadventures of a number of outlaws, primarily as a backdrop on which to give a sense of the times and to look at the commission of crimes and level of violence at any one time and place in Texas.

While many of the serious and violent crimes were committed by men and women with no roots in Texas communities, most of the identified serial killers of the day, including Cullen Montgomery Baker, John Wesley Hardin, Bill Longley, and Jim Miller were all the offsprings of decent men and women. Most had also been raised, if not born in the Lone Star State. An in-depth look at those men in the pages to follow, will quickly dispel the idea that murders committed by teenage boys are somehow a late twentieth century phenomena. All four of those murderers noted above, more than one-hundred and fifty years ago, killed their first and sometimes their second man while they were 17 years old. These were also far from the only young men to kill before they could legally vote. They were just the better known.

Those elected sheriffs and constables along with their deputies, the town marshals, and the members of numerous police departments in the growing Texas towns and cities, in contrast to those lawmen commissioned by the state, did not depend on a particular administration in Austin to pass appropriations before they could or would enforce the law. When an elected sheriff, a constable or their deputies walked out of their front door each day, they were "the law," and the trails they followed each day, and the streets they walked each night were lonely and often dangerous.

At the same time, this book does not ignore the efforts of those troops raised by the State of Texas. They served under a number of different organizations while protecting Texans from violence, usually on the frontier. Those efforts are woven into their appropriate places and times in this narrative. State troops at different times in Texas are represented by groups of armed men including the law enforcement activities of the controversial Texas State Police. In addition they include various groups of frontier militia, Texas Rangers and the Frontier Battalion. The primary purpose of the state militia and rangers was to defend against, to chase and to kill hostile Indians during those critical first three decades. They were very good at what they were organized to defend against, especially after revolving pistols and cartridge carbines became available. Then after 1874, in addition to still chasing Indians, the newly organized Frontier Battalion was instructed to aid and support local law enforcement and they first took on the role of peace officers.

Because of their duty as the primary Indian fighters and peace keepers on the Texas frontier, recognition of the role played by the U. S. Army is also a part of the larger story of murder and violence in nineteenth century Texas. All of these groups played major roles in the attempts to bring law and order to Texas and the accounts of each are often brought together for the first time in this story.

In addition, the prosecution of criminals arrested by any lawman depended on the workings of the various judges, prosecuting attorneys and the court system of Texas to complete that process. Yet, they are very often ignored in any story of frontier justice, so I also attempted to briefly examine the activities of the Texas court system. My purpose in doing this was not to write the court's history, but to find out just what type of crimes were committed, how violent the state really was, along with where and when it was the most violent. I did this by looking at and evaluating the only information that can complete the story, court records in selected counties. There was never any thought of looking at the records in more than just a few of the 254 counties; furthermore, not all Texas counties have a data base to permit such a study. As a result, a significant amount of time was required just to visit, examine and determine if a particular county was worth further effort. In a few cases information was available over the entire period examined, plus back into the republic. But in most cases, if it was there at all, court records covered an average of from 25 to 30 years of the 55 years examined in this book.

Unfortunately, many district, county or justice court records in Texas counties are really not good sources of accurate information, for I found few early court dockets and minute books indexed or easily understood. To determine just how many of those indicted of crimes were ever tried, convicted and sentenced to time in a jail or penitentiary, much less how much time they actually might have served, is an awesome undertaking in more than just a few courts. Also, some courts over 100 years ago decided to suddenly seal many grand jury indictments when a new judge or district attorney was elected. This may have made it easier to arrest some unknowing suspect, but 100 or more years later it makes it much more complicated and occasionally impractical for a historian to trace crime and many of the criminals involved in the records of such a court.

This book looks at a very different State of Texas than the one we live in today. My work indicates to me that there is abundant evidence that much of Texas was generally much more dangerous following the Civil War than some have believed. The sudden influx of sometimes embittered and desperate white and black men, made violence more likely for either the lone traveller, on an isolated farm, or among those new communities now formed by freed slaves. Changing times and different laws also make some comments necessary with regard to specific "crimes" in nineteenth century Texas. For example, fence cutting, abortion, failure to work on a public road, fornication, selling certain goods on Sunday and disturbing a religious service were all crimes at sometimes during the period we will examine.

Yet, not all of those acts constitute crimes today, or if they do some laws are seldom enforced. Slavery was no crime before the Civil War, so slaves that ran away and those who aided them in their flight were committing crimes in early Texas. The sale of liquor, dueling, various forms of gambling in public places and the unlawful carrying of a firearm have all been against the law at some time in the past and may still be today in some Texas communities. But laws are often an experiment and a new Texas law in 1887, in an effort to make the favorite meeting place of the day, the saloon, less violent and less of a den of inequity, prohibited saloons from employing any screen or similar device to obstruct the view through its entrance. Was the swinging saloon half-door, which soon became an icon for the thirsty and the adventurous, no more than just a way to circumvent that law?

Criminal homicide at the beginning of the twenty-first century is known by several names with somewhat different elements to those current crimes of murder, capital murder, manslaughter and criminally negligent homicide. In nineteenth century Texas and in this book, only the all inclusive term "murder" is used to describe the crime of intentionally, knowingly, recklessly, or with criminal negligence causing the death of an individual. In this book "to kill" or the act of "killing" someone, is a more general term and is used when a murder is committed, but that killing may have been in self-defense or an accident, and only the further description defines the criminal offense. Burglary, ordinary theft, arson, robbery, livestock theft, and other crimes discussed herein have elements similar, if not the same as those offenses today. The crime of "assault," in this book, however, includes aggravated assault, assault and battery, robbery, rape, assault with intent to kill and any other violent crime that intentionally, knowingly or recklessly causes bodily injury to another.

There is no special software program used to calculate the incidence of crime in this journey through nineteenth century Texas. This is because the data base is still too inexact and often biased to be able to do much more than to develop an accurate sense of the level, and type of crimes committed across Texas, plus identify some of the areas where and when certain crimes were being committed. That information and its analysis is part of this story and much of the data on the type of crimes committed, crime rates and a Uniform Crime Reporting analysis of nineteenth century Texas is contained in Appendix B. I suggest that this is only the first, but an important step toward trying to really understand crime and criminals in this state.

One part of the criminal justice system that I have spent very little time discussing in this book is the Texas prison system.

Prisons have been a part of the justice system in America since Colonial times. Some of the first American prisons were based on the principal of isolating and maintaining absolute silence among the inmates. There were no shared cells, nor were work, meals or exercise a time for prisoners to mingle. Isolation was practiced throughout a prisoner's sentence. Other prisons locked down at night behind high outer walls, but prisoners in the daytime labored together. Texas chose the second system.

Most of Texas lacked secure county jails in which to house prisoners up to fairly late in the nineteenth century. In the early days, a ring set in the floor with a large chain passing through held any number of prisoners shackled day and night to that chain. The first state prison with 266 regular cells was built near Huntsville, Texas, and the first prisoner did not arrive there until Oct. 1, 1849, only a few months short of four years after annexation. As in parts of the American South, early Texas relied more on fines, humiliation, shame, the whipping post, branding and the gallows to punish most of its offenders, rather than on large prisons or jails. The second state prison located near Rusk, Texas did not open until 1881, some 32 years later. By the end of the 188Os, there were just over 1,5OO prisoners held in these two penitentiaries.

My first efforts at writing about the criminal justice system in Texas is contained in a previous book, "Texas Constables, A Frontier Heritage," published by Texas Tech University Press in 1999. By design that book concentrated on just one group of almost forgotten lawmen, although a host of other peace officers and some court officials played a role in many of those stories. But, it was the first serious study of the 179-year old history of Texas Constables. I approached that first look at constables against the backdrop of the organization of the many Texas counties and in the context of local county government. That was because local government oftentimes dictated the workings of most county and precinct criminal justice systems, as much and sometimes more than the Texas Constitution or any law book.

Stephen F. Austin, the great Anglo-American colonizer of Mexican Texas, has sometimes been called the founder of the Texas criminal justice system. That is, at best, only partially correct. The truth is that the first Mexican Governor of Texas, Jose Felix Trespalacios, should actually get some of the credit for initially establishing the roots of the criminal justice system in Anglo-Texas. It was Governor Trespalacios, who in late 1822 while Austin was in Mexico City for over a year, created the first two judicial and militia districts (precincts) in Austin's Colony. He called upon the settlers to elect militia officers and an alcalde, or justice of the peace in each district. In addition, several Spanish and Mexican laws survived the revolution and are popular pieces of legislation even into this century.

Then on March 5, 1823, John Tumlinson Sr, the first elected alcalde, or justice of the peace in Austin's Colorado District, wrote Mexican government leader Baron de Bastrop in San Antonio de Bexar that he had on his own earlier, "appointed but one officer who acts in the capacity of constable to summon witnesses and bring offenders to justice." That constable, Thomas V. Alley, was the first law enforcement officer in Austin's Colony and in Anglo-Texas. It seemed a fitting event with which to begin our story of the criminal justice system in Chapter I.

In addition to the first foundations of the criminal justice system in Texas being in part Mexican in origin, the history of law enforcement in Texas differs significantly from many other areas in the American West. One major reason for that difference is that almost all other areas annexed by the United States west of the Mississippi River held territorial status for a number of years before they were recognized as states. Texas never went through that process. Texas was an independent nation for almost ten years prior to annexation, had an elected local and national government, plus already had a much larger population in the republic, than in most of the territories.

As a result, there were very few federal lands and only very, very small federal Indian Reservations within the state that have survived the passage of time. With almost no federal lands of any kind in Texas, the U. S. Marshal's Service in nineteenth century Texas had little jurisdiction over any crimes committed in the state. Except for the arrest of those who robbed the mails, who had outstanding federal warrants along with the service of federal civil and criminal papers, the U. S. Marshal played no more than a minor role in law enforcement in Texas. The U. S. Marshal was never as important a lawman in Texas as he was in New Mexico, Wyoming or Oklahoma, and current information indicates that no more than three deputy marshals were killed in the line of duty in Texas during the first 55 years. It was only the fees received for service of criminal and civil papers, and the ability to officially go across jurisdictional boundaries to chase outlaws for the rewards offered for their capture, that made being a U. S. marshal or his deputy a sought after job in Texas during the nineteenth century.

During the 16 years between annexation and secession the frontier moved westward more than 200 miles. Texas west of that changing line of army posts at any one time, however, was a vast, largely inhospitable, savage and vacant land. Except when well-armed groups banded together to occasionally cross that land, life in the wild was hard, brutal and usually short. That frontier was regularly visited by Indians. If they were not hostile when they arrived on the Texas frontier, they soon were. Throughout Texas history, most approaching Indians were usually viewed through the sights of a rifle, which could make the most peaceful Indian, suddenly hostile.

As I began to research and write this book about crime and violence in the state of Texas, the information available strongly indicated that with the exception of a much higher level of violence and murder along the state's frontier, anti-bellum Texas was a rather peaceful and largely non-violent land. While I found no reason to alter that first analysis across much of the state, there were certainly some long settled areas of Texas where violence played a significant part in the lives of some. The relatively few murders that were committed prior to secession in 1861 were also very personal acts. They were committed at close quarters, often by an act of violence such as a beating, knifing, strangling or a drowning. Except for the use of an occasional shotgun, a firearm was seldom used. Before the Civil War, a knife was often the weapon of choice.

No event in American history except possibly the attack on Pearl Harbor, had an impact on this nation like the Civil War and its immediate aftermath. The level of violence in Texas soon after the Confederacy's surrender does not appear to have jumped much higher, although the sudden availability and more familiarity with firearms after the war soon made Texas an armed camp. Firearms would, however, soon become the favored way with which to solve many disagreements, and after the Civil War, a revolver was quite accurately called "the great equalizer."

Post Civil War Texas proved to be as violent as many of the anecdotal accounts of that period remind us. I suggest that for a number of Texans, many areas of the state after the Civil War were actually more violent than has been thought, for a remarkable amount of the violence that took place went both unrecorded and unpunished. As a result, even looking at grand jury indictments does not always do justice to any analysis of crime. One reason for this was that much of that violence just after the Civil War was directed toward a large number of black freedmen. If not mistreated, many were uprooted and scattered across a less than friendly land. It did not end there. While a large number of black men were also killed by a host of white racists, a surprising number were also set upon and more were killed as the result of conflicts with other former slaves. But, unless that violence resulted in an arrest and a grand jury indictment, elected law enforcement and the Frontier Battalion largely ignored the problem.

The killing of most any stranger in a community by a respected local citizen was, where possible, usually chalked up to self-defense and also then went unpunished after a quick trial or hearing. Conflicts that resulted in any killing taking place along a lonely Texas road following the war might as well have happened on the moon, for few witnesses were around to inform the law regarding who committed such an offense. Few of those who helped lynch an accused murderer or suspected cattle thief were ever arrested or accused of murder themselves. For behind those masks they wore was usually a local lawman and more than one of the leading citizens of the community. As a result, I suggest that any calculation of murders and other violent crimes in nineteenth century Texas usually errs on the low and not on the high side.

Soon after the war ended, the increased number of people entering Texas and the opportunities presented for more public gambling and excessive drinking appear to have significantly increased the number of acts of violence in many areas across this state and throughout much of the West. Many Texas counties during Reconstruction and into the late 187Os would also experience an increasing number of murders. Depending on where you made your home in the Lone Star State, varying amounts of violence were a part of many communities until the mid-189Os. Much of that violence was initially due to the large number of faceless men and women-the grifters, hobos and drifters-who lived in or passed through Texas after the Civil War. Then in many areas of Texas by the late 187Os, more aggressive law enforcement was the rule, and as a result lawmen died just as often when arresting a drunk as when chasing a desperate bank robber.

While many of those who committed crimes soon after the war were former soldiers, not all of those sometimes desperate men and women were the product of the Civil War's aftermath. Texas did not live in total isolation. As a result, the large number of business failures, stock market losses and deflation, along with major lay-offs and high unemployment that occurred across the nation as a result of the Panic of 1873, would add significantly to the chaos, crime and violence of the 1870s. This was particularly true as those who had fallen on hard times arrived in Texas, or were scattered throughout the West.

As a result, that 10 year period from 1869 to 1878, was a time of unequalled violence across the state. At least 81 lawmen in Texas are known to have been murdered during those 10 deadly years. They were killed by outlaws, Indians and too often by nothing more than a fool or a drunk with a gun. In addition to the lawmen killed, a host of other citizens, some good and some bad and whether Black, white or brown, male or female, found themselves in situations where they were also caught up in the violence so prevalent during that decade of the 1870s.

When I first looked at data on crime in Texas, I was initially convinced that after about 1878, murders of lawmen and other citizens plus the incidence of some crime in Texas declined and stayed low during the next two decades. As I examined more information, much of it derived from various court records on crimes in a number of Texas counties, that information changed that view. This led me to the calculation of crime rates, based on the Uniform Crime Reporting procedures. As a result, I am now convinced that murder rates and the incidence of violence in Texas did decline for a few years after 1878. But, then for short periods during the 1880s and earliest 1890s, violence and crime did not go away, but sometimes actually exceeded the violent days during Reconstruction. The information developed in writing this book indicates that much of Texas was indeed a dangerous place to reside, with few exceptions from 1868 to 1900.

The causes of much of that crime and violence in Texas was about the same as in other areas of the Old West. There existed in Texas at the end of the Civil War, however, a set of conditions that exacerbated the sudden spread of violence. One of those circumstances was that Texas was the only state with any sizable population already fighting a life or death struggle along its frontier with hostile Indians to secede from the Union. As a result, it lost U. S. Army protection for the four years of the war. It was not long after the U. S. Army abandoned the frontier forts in Texas in 1861, before various groups of Indians understood how few guns there were between the Red and the Rio Grande Rivers, and they then came mostly after horses and cattle, killing those who stood in their way. Texas was also the only Western state after the Civil War that was occupied by the Union military for almost five years and controlled by a hated carpetbagger civil government for another four years. While the federal government reoccupied or built new forts to protect the frontier after 1865, nearly a decade of unpopular state government took its toll across all of Texas in respect for the law.

Texas was also the only state on the Western frontier with a large number of freed slaves after the Civil War, and racial strife in many parts of the state was soon rampant. The lack of any major Indian settlements within the state probably reduced that one cause of ethnic crime; however, hostile Indian attacks on isolated settlers, on travellers and the theft of livestock were still taking place by Indians raiding into Texas during the entire decade of the 187Os. A few hostile Indians were still active in West Texas even into the early 188Os. As a result, any Indian in Texas was assumed to be a hostile Indian and the U. S. Army and much of the Frontier Battalion were involved pretty much full-time in ridding the state of its most hated public enemy.

Adding to the increased violence in Texas after the Civil War were also a series of conflicts which arose between different interest groups as the state grew. Conflicts took place between cattlemen, sheepmen and homesteaders, between large and small ranchers. Those conflicts were over land, access to water and markets for various products, and for political and economic power. Various ethnic conflicts also contributed to crime and violence as newly arriving large numbers of Irish, Scandinavian, German and suddenly emancipated Blacks interacted with already established Mexican-American and Anglo-American settlers in Texas.

During the first 55 years of the Lone Star State, however, crime was not limited to Texas and the West. Documents available for most of that same period (1851 to 1885), indicate that in New York's largest penitentiary, Tombs Prison, there were 26 men executed. Eleven of those executions were performed in the period before the Civil War, two executions during the almost 4-1/2 years of the war and 13 in the two decades after the war. With regard to what were referred to as popular crimes, robbery took on a new meaning in 1862, when the first recorded bank robbery took place in New York City. During the remaining 3-1/2 years of the Civil War, 11 other local banks were robbed. Then in the next two decades, some 76 bank robberies took place in New York, with 31 of those robberies in the three years from 1868 to 1870. It is obvious, therefore, that the James and Younger boys did not invent robbing banks.

Crime in the North East portions of the nation sprung out of the many slums. In 1868 nearly 80,000 crimes of all types were reported in New York City alone, and in the 1870s there were reportedly 30,000 people making their living from some type of thievery, while some 2,000 gambling dens served the city. After the Civil War, the saloons, gambling dens, other types of vice and opium-smoking were flourishing industries in New York City, along with other largely non-violent crimes like forgery and bank sneak thievery. Beginning in the post-Civil War period, the majority of professional criminals in the North East were white, Anglo-Saxon and Protestant. It would not be long, however, before some of the newly arrived Irishmen, Sicilian longshoremen, Germans, Jews and a few Italians would begin their efforts to dominate crime along the East Coast of the United States, as more and more immigrants stepped off the boats at Ellis Island.

But that is another story, for another time. There is little doubt that during the last half of the nineteenth century, Texas proved to be violent enough for most who came looking. Where and when it was violent, what crimes were committed and how lawmen and the courts worked to establish the rule of law during those first 55 years of the Lone Star State, I hope you will find out as you read, "BRINGING THE LAW TO TEXAS, Crime & Violence In Nineteenth Century Texas."

CHAPTER I
COLONIAL TEXAS AND THE REPUBLIC

TEXAS BEFORE THE REVOLUTION:

In the decade before the Texas Revolution, with the exception of hostile Indian depredations, court records and other documents confirm that the incidence of any crime, particularly violent offenses in the first Anglo-American Colony, were extremely rare. This was mainly due to several factors, perhaps the most critical was the good fortune in attracting what has been called, The Old Three-Hundred, a remarkably law abiding group of early settlers in Stephen F. Austin's first colony. Another important factor was the establishment of the first civil and criminal court system in Austin's colony as early as December of 1822. A final but no small consideration, was Austin's long and personal leadership of the colony.

Contrary to what would happen in some frontier areas within the United States, the rule of law was, therefore, never really missing in the first Anglo-American settlements of Texas. In addition, the isolation in which most of those settlers lived also helped reduce the incidence of crime, except for the robbery and destruction of property and life by hostile Indians.

The justice system initially established in Austin's Colony in December of 1822 and during 1823, included the office of alcalde, in each of the first two districts. When initially implemented in the colony that was the equivalent of a justice of the peace. The alcalde had both judicial and administrative duties and applied Spanish/Mexican civil and criminal laws in Austin's colony. The first alcaldes then appointed a law enforcement officer, a Constable, "to summon witnesses and bring offenders to justice." The first sheriff, with initial jurisdiction throughout the colony was also appointed, but that would not take place until sometime later.[1]

The justice courts established in Austin's and the other Anglo-American colonies, plus the criminal justice system established later in the Republic, all relied upon a combination of Castellan and English Common Law as their basis of civil and criminal justice, for initially Mexico accepted many of the already established laws of New Spain. It would be some four years after the Texas Revolution, in 1840, before the Congress of the Republic of Texas would officially make English Common Law the law of the land. But over two centuries of Spanish and Mexican rule left their imprint on Texas law.[2]

The adoption of certain Spanish laws in Texas is particularly true with regard to land, or property, water and mineral rights, and family relationships. Adoption was unknown in English common Law, but as early as 1850 in Texas it was introduced by statute. The surviving Spanish laws most familiar and most cherished by many Texans even today, are those property rights, including ones introduced by Spanish civil law which are the basis for community marital property rights in Texas. This, and an act of the Mexican state legislature in 1829 recognizing a homestead-exemption law, were both later adopted by the Republic of Texas. Texas law also recognized the Mexican model of "protecting the home," by permitting a husband to kill his wife's lover without fear of legal consequences.[3]

As early as 1824, there were as many as several thousand settlers in the eastern part of Mexican Texas who were not authorized to enter the country and were squatting on land. Most were too isolated for the Mexican officials to bother with. Many of those same people were considered criminals by Austin and were sometimes accused of stealing horses, mules and cattle from his colonists. To Stephen F. Austin those people represented a population over which he had no control and that worried Austin.

Some have criticized the Anglo-American settlers in Austin's Colony for relying too much on civil trials, in contrast to the use of arbitration, which was popular with most Mexican jurists. This is, however, not a valid criticism, as arbitration was also used by the early alcaldes in Austin's colony to settle differences. A look at Austin's alcalde court dockets and other information as early as 1824, indicates small claims and civil proceedings resulting from arbitration, as well as from jury trials and court judgments. The lack of formal legal training of most Mexican jurists in Texas, whether Mexican-Texian or Tejano or Anglo-American, was one of the most likely reasons why many of those jurists favored arbitration.[4]

The business of the courts, through the service of civil and criminal writs, attachments, warrants and subpoenas, were all commonplace in Austin's and in the other Anglo-American Colonies in Texas during the period before the Texas Revolution. In Austin's Colony, there was also the use of speedy jury trials by the accused peers, the right of habeas corpus and bail bonds, along with sentences including fines, sometimes public lashings and the rare, but occasional sentence of banishment. Those rights of the accused were not available, however, in the rest of Mexico.[5]

As early as 1823, dissatisfaction with certain aspects of Mexican justice was strongly voiced among Austin's settlers. Those feelings first surfaced following an incident of pillaging and theft from newly arrived settlers on the seacoast in the Colony during the last months of 1822. Many considered theft, particularly on the frontier, on a par with murder. In that case of theft, colony leaders discovered some of the stolen goods and apprehended one of the three suspects who participated in the actual theft of some of the goods after the settlers were murdered, probably by Indians. That one suspect who was apprehended was Stephen A. Wilson.[6]

A trial was held, which was presided over by a magistrate, who along with a jury listened to the evidence and convicted Wilson as an accessory to the theft. Each member of the jury signed his name confirming his vote for conviction and in accordance with Mexican government orders, those documents were sent to Governor Jose Felix Trespalacios on March 5, 1823. Stephen Wilson was also transported to San Antonio on that date, for review of his sentence and the carrying out of punishment.[7]

Upon arrival in San Antonio, however, and much to the surprise and disgust of the Anglo-American settlers, the governor's only punishment was to banish Wilson from Texas. No public lashings, or other punishment was given, nor was there any restitution provided. The problem was that most Anglo-American settlers believed that banishment by itself in this case represented no punishment at all, but showed how unjust Mexican justice was in Texas. W. B. Dewees, who was a member of the escort to San Antonio, later alleged that Wilson had actually escaped from the jail in San Antonio and disappeared. Whether Stephen Wilson escaped or was banished, a great deal of resentment was felt by many of those first settlers in Austin's Colony. After that, whenever possible, Austin's justice courts would avoid sending prisoners to San Antonio de Bexar for judicial review and sentencing, for even by that early date, they had already lost some confidence in the system.[8]

By 1834, after more than a decade of intermittent unrest in Mexico following liberation from Spain, elements of the military led by General Antonio Lopez de Santa Anna overthrew the Federalist form of government and brought an end to rule under the popular Constitution of 1824. Many Mexican citizens in Texas and elsewhere felt betrayed, because only two years before most Tejano and Anglo-Texians had strongly supported Santa Anna when he initially declared for Federalism.

In several areas of Mexico, including Texas, great dissatisfaction was expressed over the imposition of what were now viewed as onerous new central government control and policies, which brought an effective end to representative government in Mexico. New laws also included increased import duties and taxes and brought on interference in commerce by newly established customs houses. An increased military presence was now visited on Texas, along with the imposition of military law in some areas. The combination of those acts caused great concern among many of the Anglo-Texian and Tejano settlers.[9]

Other areas in Mexico besides Texas also strongly protested and attempted to resist that loss of a popular Federalist Constitution. The state of Zacatecas sent out a call to arms and paid for its resistance to the central government by a major military defeat. Up to 2,000 civilians were also killed, and they suffered the organized rape and sacking of the capitol by the victorious Mexican Army. Those events were not soon forgotten by the people of Texas. Besides Zacatecas and Texas, the former states of San Luis Potosi, Yucatan, Sinaloa, Durango, Chihuahua, Tamaulipas and California all resisted many central government directives over the next several years in favor of the return to a Federalist government in Mexico.[10]

The Texas Revolution would be largely born out of the frustration felt among most of the now predominant Anglo-Texians and some Tejano settlers in Texas that they had lost equal representation in Mexico. By that time, Texas was not recognized as a separate state and was controlled by the more populous state of Coahuila. Within a short time all of the Mexican States would loose most of their power to the central government. For good reason, many of the citizens of Texas considered that Texas was dominated not only by the policies of the central government, but also by the votes and influence of the other Mexican States.

While sometimes ignored when the causes of the Texas Revolution are discussed, those real concerns were heightened by the fact that many in Texas believed they were about to feel the iron hand of the Mexican military, so familiar in the rest of Mexico. Up to that time, at least, the Anglo-Texian settlers had escaped most of those problems because of their years of isolation in southeast Texas. But this peaceful period appeared to be coming to an end. What made those concerns of great importance to most Texans was that by 1835, an estimated 30,000 Anglo-Texians and their slaves now made up the vast majority of a total of some 35,000 Mexican citizens in Texas. There were actually more slaves in Texas than Tejanos and the Anglo-American citizens of Mexico felt they should have held more of the power in a representative government, but in Mexico, they were ignored.[11]

Almost lost in the emotions whipped up by the belief that a war with the Mexican central government was near at hand, was what is believed to have been the only execution of a murderer during the 15 year history of Stephen F. Austin's colony. In June of 1834, Abner Kuykendall, a member of a prominent family in Austin's colony, was stabbed by a man named Joseph Clayton during an assault at the town of San Felipe. Only recently arrived in Texas, Clayton was arrested and was to be held until the victim recovered. Instead, Kuykendall died almost a month later on July 24, never recovering from the wound. The day after Kuykendall died, Clayton was tried, convicted and quickly executed by public hanging.[12]

By late 1835, a revolution now supported by most Anglo-Texians and some Tejano settlers against Mexican central government rule swept across the State. The Texians lost most of the battles but won the war and captured the President and Commanding General of the Mexican Army, Antonio Lopez de Santa Anna at the battle of San Jacinto on April 21, 1836. Within a short time the Republic of Texas was organized, initially utilizing a series of laws, rules and regulations, plus a newly drafted constitution to govern the Republic, most of which had been written on the eve of the revolution.[13]

The Republic Is Organized

The Constitution of the Republic of Texas was signed at the Constitutional Convention held at Washington on the Brazos, on March 17, 1836. That first constitution included a provision in Article IV, Section 12, calling for the election of several law enforcement officers in each county in Texas. They were, "one sheriff" and a "sufficient number of constables," to be "elected by the qualified voters of the district or county, as congress may direct." Similar provisions, which provide for a sheriff and a sufficient number of constables, are included in each Texas Constitution, except that passed during Reconstruction. This is sometimes overlooked as the guiding legal authority for the establishment of law enforcement in Texas.[14]

Within a few weeks after Santa Anna's defeat at San Jacinto, most of the long time settlers in Texas who had made up the majority of the Texas Army returned home to plant and raise their seasonal crops. But pouring into Texas at that same time were a steady stream of new immigrants, initially said to have been as many as 5,OOO a month crossing into Texas at just one ferry location on the Sabine River, near Nachodoches. Immigration into Texas over the next few years would further increase as a result of wide spread crop failures in much of the Southern United States, the Panic of 1837 and the continuing economic depression in the United States.[15]

So, within a few years, particularly in the larger towns and along the few roads in the Republic, the make-up and the motives of the people of Texas had begun to change. No matter how many came or who they were, most people flocked to Texas to obtain cheap arable land. If they did not expect to live on it for long, they believed they could make money by selling it. As a result the Texas population boomed.

If Stephen F. Austin's Old Three Hundred settlers were known for their history of non-violence before the revolution, the thousands of new settlers swarming into Texas during the late 183Os and 184Os, brought all sorts of men and women into Texas, making it a more violent place and crime did appear to increase in the 184Os. But the increase in crime and criminals in Texas appears to have been at most a small and a gradual increase. In addition to the gradual increase of crime, the more violent times during the Republic appear to have been the result of various Indian raids and two Mexican Army invasions around San Antonio.

Although the Republic was more violent, there was no noticeable outbreak of crime in Texas in the first years after Mexican rule was overthrown. This was true, even as the population of Texas from the birth of the Republic in 1836 until annexation in 1845, would increase to an estimated 150,000 people. In 1850, the first United States census showed Texas with an even larger population, exceeding 212,000, including some 58,000 slaves.[16]

Back in 1836 as the Mexican Army had advanced across Texas, and the Anglo-Texian civilians desperately tried to escape what appeared to be imminent genocide, only the small Anglo-Texian town of Columbia located on the Lower Brazos River, had escaped being burned. As a result, Columbia was selected the first capital of the Republic of Texas. The First Congress, consisting of just 30 representatives and 14 senators assembled at Columbia beginning on October 3, 1836. During that first 81 day session the legislature passed a number of laws, including establishing the original 23 counties in the Republic.[17]

EARLY CRIMES AND THEIR PUNISHMENTS

In the Republic, there were also laws passed designating various criminal offenses. On December 21, 1836, an Act listing Punishing Crimes and Misdemeanors was passed that stipulated that 11 offenses would carry the death penalty. Conviction of treason, murder, rape and burglary of a habitation, were among those offenses that carried the death sentence. Those committing manslaughter, altering a brand or stealing livestock, however, were not hanged but were branded, so that they could be easily recognized. When a fatal shooting or stabbing took place, most killings were claimed to have been in self-defense. Along the western and northern frontiers in Texas and even in the more isolated parts of eastern Texas, who was to say that a stabbing or a shooting was not in self-defense, especially if the only witness was a family member of the killer? As a result, some violent offenders were either never indicted, or they were judged not guilty after trial.[18]

While more murders took place during the days of the Republic than before Independence, most Texans still settled most of their differences by brawling. Bloody brawls, including kicking and stabbing occurred in the back alleys, in the saloons and along the roads of the Republic, wherever there was too hot a temper or too much alcohol had been consumed. As a result, some form of assault, plus illegal gambling were the two most indicted crimes in the 1O years of the Republic. The "Northern Standard," a newspaper published in the early days of the Texas Republic in the northeast Texas town of Clarksville, contains a number of short news stories describing numerous knife fights and killings resulting from stabbing. Duels were also still sometimes fought in the Republic, as they were in the United States and in Europe.[19]

If the first Texans were not hung for their crimes, then the majority paid fines of from 1O cents to 1O dollars each to the courts on conviction of some minor crime. Few were sentenced to spend any time in a jail. Little or no jail time upon conviction was the result of not only a lack of jails in most counties, but also few of the existing jails were either escape proof or guarded 24 hours per day. One example of an early Texas jail was in Colorado County. There in 1838 a jail had been built with private funds by town developers at the county seat of Columbus. All of the bills for construction were not paid and the creditors brought suit against the builders. As a result, the county was never able to use the jail. In addition to a secure jail, someone had to feed prisoners and early Texas county governments had little time or money for such luxuries.[20]

Along with murder, the other heinous offense in Texas continued to be the theft of personal property, because the replacement of most things, including horses and cattle on the frontier, was oftentimes impossible. The theft of a man's few cattle or oxen and particularly his horse, while not a hanging offense was some times the equivalent of a death sentence for the victim. That was because the victim was then unable to plow his fields, or plant his crops; they were unable to get water to their fields or home; unable to feed himself or his family and finally, they were unable to trade or escape out of harm's way. Sentences of whipping and occasional branding for theft were often used in early Texas, as it was in several states in the American south. Sentences of 39 lashes for relatively minor offenses was not unusual. But, if the former owner of a stolen horse or beef, or his friends caught the thief, the punishment was usually much worse.[21]

While verdicts calling for hanging and whipping were in the law books, Texas voters also proved that those they elected to wear a badge and help administer justice was a serious personal decision. This was proved numerous time, as once voters had found someone they trusted, they often reelected them one or more times to continue to be their sheriff for another two-year term. For example, in the 36 Texas counties that were organized by the end of the Republic, 16 of those reelected the same sheriff to at least one more two year term. While professional lawmen did not exist across Texas, they came close to being created in Bastrop, Bexar, Brazoria, Colorado, Liberty, Red River and Victoria Counties, where the same man was elected sheriff for three or more terms. In Nacogdoches County David Rusk was elected to all five, two-year terms as sheriff during the 10 years of the Republic of Texas.[22]

In addition to passing laws, the First Congress of Texas also organized four Judicial Districts in Texas, and appointed a District Judge in each District. Later three additional judicial districts were formed as the population and organized counties increased. The Texas Constitution directed district judges to prosecute in the name of the Republic, for acts "against the peace and dignity of the Republic", and Congress gave them broad powers. District courts in the 1830s and 1840s, were circuit courts, just as many are today. In other words, the district judge and district attorney travelled from county to county in their judicial district to hold hearings and conduct criminal and civil trials.[23]

Although a detailed look at crime and violence in Texas before annexation is not the purpose of this book, everything reviewed indicates that in Texas, while certainly more violent during the Republic than it had been in the 1820s and early 1830s, the act of murder was still a rare crime. When murders did occur, the records of early trials confirm that they were just as likely the result of a disagreement between people who knew each other as between strangers. The relatively low level of crime and violence during the first years of the Republic took place even after the population had quadrupled and some of those arriving obviously took advantage of the weak and isolated, as hostile Indians had done 20 years earlier.[24]

If an independent and more populous Texas was a somewhat more dangerous place, certain roads and frontier areas were much worse. South Texas, including Victoria, Refugio and Goliad counties and the road between Goliad and San Antonio was described as the most dangerous in Texas. During the 10 years of the Republic, with the possible exception of the organized gangs of vigilantes operating in Shelby, Panola and Harrison Counties in East Texas, there were very few outlaws who gained enough notoriety to be long remembered.[25]

Nor were many lawmen shot or killed in the line of duty. But crimes committed in the Republic of Texas was not only of the violent type. Prostitution got a serious start soon after the Revolution. As early as 1844, a madame and three prostitutes arrived in La Grange, Texas from New Orleans and began operating out of a small hotel. In addition, both Galveston and Houston had parlor houses.[26]

One lawman who was killed in the Republic was John V. Morton, who moved to Texas in 1822 and established the Morton ferry on the Brazos River near Fort Bend. Morton had fought at the battle of San Jacinto and in 1837 received 95 votes to win election as the first sheriff of Fort Bend County. Morton was reelected twice and was then killed on Feb. 7, 1843 while sheriff at Richmond, by George W. Pleasants, his former deputy.[27]

One fact seldom mentioned when evaluating the work of law enforcement and incidence of crime in early Texas was the huge size of many of the early Texas counties. With few exceptions, Texas counties did not remain the same size as originally organized in the Republic. They usually shrank in size. One example was Fannin County, which would eventually provide the land for all or part of 29 new Texas counties. Nacogdoches County was originally almost 200 miles long and from 30 to 50 miles wide. Milam County was approximately 16,000 square miles in size, and would later donate enough land to form almost 26 new Texas counties.[28]

As a result, many a county sheriff during the Republic or in the first few years after annexation, were unable to offer much protection to their constituents. At that time the serving of papers, or a violent crime was about all that brought a sheriff away from the county seat. If a lawman located in the county seat could arrive at the crime scene within a few days after an offense was committed, the victim or his family were well served. This was likely the reason why the more heavily populated and large county of Nacogdoches was the first county in the Republic to elect four precinct constables in 1838. Twelve other Texas counties would also elect constables during the Republic. Harrisburg, which later changed its name to Harris County when Houston became the new capital of Texas, elected five constables in Feb. of 1839. In those first Texas counties, there were few roads, only an occasional town, no banks, few mail routes, or doctors or schools. There was also little money to finance the criminal justice system, except for the fees and fines that law enforcement and the courts generated.[29]

Much has changed in Texas during the intervening 160 years, but the low salaries paid to rural law enforcement personnel in many Texas counties proves that few Texans still want to pay for police protection, jails, prosecutors, or the rest of the criminal justice system.

The Courts Begin To Take Shape

As law enforcement in some parts of Texas became better organized, the district court system took on a new meaning. Texas district courts, which initially consisted of just four judicial districts, was organized in 1837, only 12 months after the battle of San Jacinto. By 1840 a total of seven judicial districts were active and this remained unchanged until annexation in 1845, although the number of counties and the individual counties in each district often changed.[30]

In March of 1837, District Judge Robert McAlpin Williamson, a distinguished early Texas Jurist, was holding court in Washington County, one of six counties making up the Third Judicial District of Texas. In what might be called a typical trial from that period, on Wednesday, March 15, Francis Kennedy was indicted by a grand jury for theft of a horse; on Thursday and Friday he was tried, found guilty and sentenced. On Saturday, the judge heard and overruled any defense motions and appeals, then confirmed Kennedy's sentence at 39 lashes and his right hand be branded with the letter "T". The sentence was to be carried out immediately. This court action lasted just four days, from indictment to punishment. Justice in early Texas was swift.[31]

Solving a crime in early Texas usually depended on someone actually observing the offense, or a confession. Without a witness, a criminal could just ride off, or walk away from a crime committed in an isolated area. It was only if the unseen perpetrator later bragged about the crime or sold any goods taken, that they were then suspected or arrested. As a result, crime in Texas was all local crime, and it was not long before constables and justices of the peace, who lived and worked in the small remote districts or precincts across the state and knew the citizens of their area, were the only law and order known to most isolated early settlers in Texas.

Texas Still Had Its Indians

The Texas government faced somewhat different challenges in the Republic than would exist after annexation. During the decade of the Republic, the western frontier of Texas was a land not only still very close at hand to many Texans, it was also a land still completely dominated by various Indian tribes. At that time there was no standing army of any consequence in Texas to protect against continued Indian depredations, so the Republic depended on enlisting for short periods of one to three months, mounted volunteer quasi-military companies, sometimes called mounted riflemen or rangers. Those commands were intended to scout and spy on the frontier and where possible, to interdict and to punish hostile Indians who ventured too close to Texas settlements. They were the only organized armed force standing between hostile Indians and the settler. While they were not involved in law enforcement activities, they were the main protectors of the frontier.[32]

Ranging companies were not, however, the only protection employed by the Republic along the frontier. On June 12, 1837, the Texas Legislature passed an Act, "For the Better Protection of the Northern Frontier," which was signed by President Sam Houston. The act provided for raising some 600 "mounted gun men", for a term of six months service. Officers in that organization were to receive the "same pay as was fixed for corresponding rank in the ranging service," while privates were to receive $25.00 per month. Both officers and men also received a bounty of 640 acres of land. In addition to the mounted gun men, three companies of friendly Indians were also raised to accompany them.[33]

The frontier at the time included all of the land beginning just west of the towns of San Antonio and Austin and then running north along a line near where the towns of Marlin, Dallas and McKinney would later be built. At the time it was not unusual for the Comanche to raid almost into San Antonio. For several years families had been attacked in Central Texas, and numerous men, women and children had been killed or kidnapped. In late 1839, 19 well-mounted and armed men who had attended the court session held in San Antonio rode out of that town one afternoon toward the west to see the countryside before returning home. Just after dark a single rider from the group raced into San Antonio telling of a possible massacre of that party by a large group of Comanche Indians who had gotten behind the horsemen and between them and the town. Next morning a large party of riders left town and found the other 18 Anglo and Tejano Texans, dead, stripped and mutilated. No Indians were sighted by the relief column, but their work was apparent.[34]

The Texas government under President Sam Houston had pursued a policy of friendship to most Indians. Soon after this massacre, the government sought a meeting with the Comanche, hoping to gain the return of all captives taken on the frontier, and to sign a peace treaty to stop such killings. Two commissioners and three companies of the Texas Army were stationed in San Antonio and efforts were made to have the Comanche Indians meet there. On March 19, 1840, some 70 armed Comanche rode into San Antonio, having promised to exchange 15 Anglo and Tejano captives. The Comanches, however, brought only one 15 year old girl with them, Matilda Lockhart. Matilda and her sister had been captured, while her two brothers were killed in a raid on the Texas frontier some 16 months before. The Texans were shocked and outraged, for Matilda was covered with sores and bruises. But worst of all, her nose had been burned off by hot coals dropped on her face most mornings to wake her from an exhausted sleep.[35]

The Indian chiefs and the Texans retired to the nearby Town Council House in San Antonio and the Texans were at first told that Matilda Lockhart was the only captive. The Texans responded by advising the chiefs that they knew better and that they would be held until the other captives were exchanged. The Indians set up a howl and a deadly battle began in the Council House which spread outside and down the streets of San Antonio. Thirty-three Comanche were killed, eight wounded and 32 taken prisoner. Seven Texans had also been killed, one of those was Joseph Hood, the first sheriff of Bexar County. A deputy sheriff named Morgan was also among the 10 Texans wounded during what has been called the Council House Fight.[36]

Five months later, in August of 1840, probably in retribution for the Council House Fight, a large group of hostile Comanche emerged from the Texas Hill Country south of Austin and the Colorado River, killing, looting and burning their way south, through the towns of Victoria and Linnville to the shores of the Gulf of Mexico. The Texans would make them pay when they finally caught up with them. But that was possible only because the Indians returned to the Hill Country along much the same trail, passing just north of the present town of San Marcos. This had made it possible for the Texans to intercept them, killing and wounding many and recovering some captives and loot.[37]

In the early 1840s, when the money could be found, the Republic organized several small Texas Ranger commands, most consisting of 15 men each to range the frontier and provide a warning of approaching hostile Indians. Twice in 1842, Mexican Army commands would also invade Texas and take control of San Antonio for short periods of time. Those small companies of Texas Rangers, various Texas militia commands and armed volunteers provided some protection to the Republic's southern and western frontier, but most of those arriving in Texas initially settled further east, until a line of U. S. Army military forts were established on the frontier after annexation, in 1846.[38]

The threat of hostile Indians sometimes reduced crime locally on the frontier, where everyone depended on his neighbor for support. So it was sometimes in East Texas where elected law enforcement and the judiciary were most often challenged. In the early 1840s, a deadly feud, with strong political, economic and commercial overtones broke out in Shelby, Panola and Harrison Counties between several prominent but unscrupulous families and their allies. Fraudulent land titles, plus missing stock inflamed the desire for violence.[39]

They Were All Part Of Some Mob

The two factions called themselves the Regulators and the Moderators. The Moderators represented the old time residents, who had populated that part of East Texas in the 1820s and 1830s. The Regulators had mostly come later and probably used that name for there had been another group of Regulators, active in the Carolinas before the Revolution. There the name represented a "law and order" movement, but not to those who opposed them.[40]

Initially the Regulators were the most aggressive, and local law enforcement, represented by Harrison County Sheriff Alfred George, supported the group. In Shelby County Sheriff Aaron Llewellen was also initially sympathetic to the Regulators, but excesses by the group caused Llewellen to turn against them and they ran him out of the county. Other lawmen were discouraged from running for office and Sheriff John B. Campbell of Panola County was killed in January of 1841 as a result of this feud.

Then for four years the two sides burned homes and crops, killed cattle and horses, terrorized and oftentimes murdered each other. But while this vigilante justice was rampant, those same families committed other crimes. Smuggling goods from Louisiana into Texas without paying duties went on for many years. The district court, because of intimidation, was occasionally unable to hold court sessions in several of the counties where the involved families lived.[41]

A total of 46 people died as a result of that feud, including 23 who were poisoned at a wedding reception in Shelby County three years after the last shooting. The other 23 killed were either shot or lynched earlier. Sam Houston in 1844, during his second term as President, sent 600 Texas militiamen into Shelby County from Sabine, Nacogdoches, Rusk and San Augustine Counties to arrest the ringleaders of both groups. He then brought them before him, where he forced them to fashion a peace treaty. He then stationed a strong militia command in Shelby County for six months until he was sure the feud was over. In late 1844, after the militia had brought some safety to the local residents, the Seventh Judicial District court returned 22 indictments for murder and some 40 indictments for assault with intent to kill. The many incidents of smuggling and fraud that had taken place were solved in an odd way. When many of those who had bought the smuggled goods failed to make payment to the smugglers, the district judge refused to require payment in a series of civil trials, because he said those claims were no more collectable in court than gambling debts.[42]

"Gone To Texas"

Some of those coming to Texas either before or after the revolution had arrived running from the law. A few would repeat their criminal activity, but many would become useful citizens. It was during that time that the slogan, "Gone To Texas," or just the initials, GTT crudely painted or carved on a cabin door in the southern United States told their neighbors that the family had left for good. The Augustine Hardin family, not to be confused with the family of a famous outlaw later living in Polk County, were one family who had run up against the law in another jurisdiction and believed that Texas might offer them a chance to start over.[43]

Augustine Blackburn Hardin had married Mary Elizabeth Garner in 1819 in Tennessee. He had previously served as a constable, and in 1825 was a deputy sheriff, while his father served as justice of the peace in Maury County, Tennessee. That same year during a confrontation, Augustine and his brother Benjamin Franklin Hardin shot and killed William Williamson and Issac Newton Porter, the latter being a man who had bragged about an affair he had with Augustine Hardin's wife. After the shootings, Augustine and his three brothers, Benjamin Watson, Franklin and William Hardin, along with their families, except for Augustine's wife, fled Tennessee before they were indicted for murder. The Hardin family like thousands of others for whatever reason, had Gone To Texas, arriving in 1827, in what is now Liberty County.[44]

Before the Texas Revolution, Benjamin Watson Hardin served as the sheriff of the Liberty District. Later he was elected sheriff in Liberty County four times, from 1839 to 1845, and on Dec. 2, 1844, he was also elected Liberty County's representative to the Ninth Congress of the Republic of Texas. His brother Augustine had been a delegate during the framing of the Texas Declaration of Independence and then signed the document. Later he served in the Army of the Republic from July 7 to Oct. 7, 1836. Hardin County and the city of Hardin, Texas would be named for the family.

The Hardin family were not the only people to arrive in Texas before and after the Revolution, on the run from debtors, or unpunished acts of violence, or escaping from personal problems. William Barret Travis, the hero of the Alamo, was another. During that period Texas was a place to begin again and while few were as successful as the Augustine Hardin family, many overcame their problems and lived a productive life in the Lone Star State.

Even though slavery was illegal in Mexico, the Mexican government representatives in Texas before the Revolution had allowed slavery to exist in the Anglo-Texian Colonies. Slavery continued in the Republic of Texas, and the Republic's statutes contained a number of laws making it an offense to aid a runaway slave, to hold someone who was not a slave, to permit a slave to break the law and to cruelly treat a slave.[45]

In January of 1844, the Texas Legislature was again able to finance a company of some 40 Rangers led by Captain Jack Hays. Those rangers provided some protection against hostile Indians, along with warning of any possible invasion by a Mexican Army. They were also about the only protection against violence on the Texas frontier, until more counties were organized and local law enforcement was elected.[46]

While in some areas of the Texas frontier there was little or no law and order, in other counties the justice system was active and many felt its bite. Usually because of the lack of funds, neither the legislature nor the courts always functioned effectively during the Republic. Most isolated Texans at that time found their law and order at the justice court and constable level during the Republic of Texas. However, the district court, with its initially appointed but later elected judges, prosecutors and its broad jurisdiction over civil and criminal law, was and still is the primary site for the administration of Texas justice. This is particularly true for violent crimes, other felonies and many civil actions.[47]

An example of the activities of another district court is available in the records of the Republic's Second Judicial District. Augustus M. Tomkins had arrived in Texas in 1836, just five months after the Battle of San Jacinto. On Dec. 19 of that same year, Tomkins was appointed to the office of District Attorney of the prominent Second Judicial District in the Republic of Texas. Benjamin C. Franklin was the first judge in the Second District. Augustus M. Tomkins would hold the job of district attorney for three years, until Sept. 5, 1839.[48]

The Second Judicial District then included six counties of which two, Brazoria and Harrisburg, were among the most important counties in Texas. Brazoria was the most populous county, the site of the first capital of the Republic and it was also the home of Stephen F. Austin at the time of his death there on Dec. 27, 1836. Harrisburg at that time contained the Republic's second capitol city, Houston.[49]

On March 19, 1838, a new session began for the grand jury of the Second Judicial District of the Republic of Texas. According to one observer, it "brought in 120 (total) indictments: 36 for gambling; 27 for vending without a license; 18 for various crimes against property; 14 for assault; 10 for issuing change notes; 5 for fornication; four for murder; one for high treason, and five in which the charge was not clear."[50]

"Of these indictments, the court discharged 37 and changed the venue of one during the term, and the district attorney refused to prosecute five. Twenty-one of the remaining 77 indictments were tried and resulted in conviction. Having no prison to which the convicted could be sent, the court assessed two sentences of hanging, both for murder; 13 fines, totaling $1,040, in nine cases of gambling and four of assault; and 139 lashes in six cases of crimes against property, which were mostly for theft.

The comment made previously that District Attorney Tomkins in Harrisburg was "a terror to evil-doers," appears to have been only part of the story, especially when examining one of his cases against Mrs. Pamelia Mann. Although defended by a former Texas attorney general, District Attorney Tomkins convinced a jury to find Mrs. Mann guilty of forgery, although she could neither read nor even write her own name. Tomkins was also not without his critics and in addition to being called, "a man destitute of all moral principal," was twice indicted in his own court and apparently convicted once, for assault and battery. After expiration of his term of office, he was fined in Harris County for carving on the courtroom furniture and later indicted in Galveston as an accessory to murder, when his brother John was charged with murder. In Travis County he was later charged with assault and battery.[51]

In late 1845, the long hoped for annexation of Texas by the United States took shape and on Dec. 29 of that year, as the flag of the Republic of Texas was lowered and the flag of the United States was raised in its place (the new flag of the Lone Star State was the old Republic's ensign), Texans collectively breathed a sigh of relief.

Somehow, their 10 year experiment as a Republic had been largely successful in overcoming many of the problems Texas faced in 1836, as a weak, divided, financially insecure and runaway province of Mexico. Whatever the future, Texas was now safe and secure from the threat of invasion and genocide. That would not stop those in power in Mexico from declaring war on the United States for annexing Texas, nor would it stop them from pursuing the war and losing more of that nation's territory.

CHAPTER II
THE LONE STAR STATE
1846-1855

ANNEXATION AND THE WAR WITH MEXICO

By New Year's Day of 1846, just three days after annexation, it had dawned on most Texans that they had somehow survived 10 uncertain years of independence, and their future was much more secure. The Republic's worst fear, an invasion by a large and determined Mexican Army, had not occurred. Annexation brought with it the expectation of better security and less strife along the Rio Grande and eventually on the western frontier. Only four months after annexation, however, Mexico chose to invade the 28th State, and a state of war then existed between the United States and Mexico for almost two years.[1]

Texans fought valiantly in the Mexican War under Zachary Taylor from the Rio Grande to Monterrey and with Winfield Scott from Vera Cruz to Mexico City. Most Texans fighting in Mexico were there in volunteer commands, raised in Texas following the battles of Palo Alto and Resaca de la Palma. They were attached to and under command of the U. S. Army. There were three mounted regiments and one infantry regiment composed of Texas volunteers. The mounted regiments, in addition to serving in the regular campaigns, were also used as scouts or spies, escorts and couriers. Few in the U. S. Army command seemed to have really liked the Texas volunteer regiments, but the Army also recognized that without them, winning the war against Mexico would be much more difficult and costly.[2]

It has been alleged that what made Texas volunteer commands so undisciplined was that they were made up mostly of former Texas Rangers. This claim, however, does not appear to be a reasonable conclusion, based on conditions and events.

That is because the first three mounted Texas volunteer regiments serving in the Mexican War at the same time consisted of more than 2,000 officers and men. That was well over a thousand more men than all of the rangers who had served during the entire 10 years of the Texas Republic, even ignoring those who had been killed, moved on, failed to volunteer, or died of natural causes in the meantime. As a result, the three mounted volunteer regiments raised in Texas just could not have been made up primarily of former Texas Rangers. Many of their officers, however, certainly were. There were well-known former rangers like John Ford, R. A. Gillespie, Jack Hays, Ben McCulloch, Samuel Walker, William A. Wallace and George T. Wood, who all served. [3]

In February of 1848, the two sides signed the Treaty of Guadalupe Hidalgo and the war was over. That treaty was doubly important to Texas, for not only did a peace treaty defining Texas boundaries finally exist with Mexico, the government of the United States would garrison the entire Texas frontier, thereby providing the state with continued protection from their most dreaded enemy, the hostile Indian.[4]

Setting The Rules

The first Texas State Constitution adopted in 1845 just before annexation, contained a number of provisions that were carried over from the Republic. The sheriff and the constables were again the only peace officers identified in the Texas constitution. The laws of the Lone Star State would still include the concepts of both separate and community property along with a homestead law. Statute law in Texas in 1846, however, brought jury trials far beyond that existing in many of the other states. Juries in early Texas were given the ability to pass sentences in criminal convictions in all cases except in those few where the penalty was fixed by law, or in capital cases.[5]

Beginning soon after annexation, the Texas legislature began to pass a number of laws that affected law enforcement and the courts. One of those laws is of particular interest to modern Texas. As early as May of 1846, the legislature passed the first Act Requiring the Translation of the Texas Constitution and certain other laws into the German and the Spanish languages. That same month 120 German immigrants would establish the town of Fredericksburg, as they pushed the western frontier further into Central Texas. In addition, other laws were passed which included an Act Allowing the Governor to Offer Rewards for Fugitives; an Act to Authorize the Settlement of Disputes by Conciliation or Arbitration; an Act Defining the Office and Duties of Constables and Sheriffs, and laws organizing the Justice, County and District Courts in the state.[6]

The 1845 Constitution retained the basic structure of the Republic's judicial system, which consisted of the Texas Supreme Court, with jurisdiction over appeals only and also such inferior courts as the state legislature might establish. Justice, county and district courts were already established. Seven Judicial District Courts, each containing from three to seven Texas counties in their district were among those courts carried over from the Republic. The Texas Supreme Court in the first dozen years after annexation, almost to the time of secession, was composed of three competent jurists who laid a firm foundation in the common law of Texas for decades to come.[7]

The all important district court was still a circuit court. This meant that the judge and the district attorney and their staffs moved regularly from county to county within the district, handling both civil and felony criminal cases. There are still circuit courts in Texas today, as many districts contain more than one county, and the officers of those courts travel to each county in the district to pursue the business of the court. In addition to those who represented the government, there were also private attorneys who traveled with the court, representing or prepared to represent those charged with crimes.[8]

With the promise of government stability and more security, a period of immigration and rapid growth began. The population steadily increased and during the first year of statehood, 31 new counties were organized. Those counties were, with few exceptions, carved from most of the very large counties previously created during the Republic. One exception was the creation of a single county, Nueces, which would initially occupy all of the area south of a line running from the town of Corpus Christi, up the Nueces River some 70 miles and then follow another line southwest to Laredo, Texas. Nueces County would initially be over 20,000 square miles in size and include all the land south of that line to the Rio Grande. Several other large counties, some now designated as Land Districts, still dominated the western and northern frontier. Two exceptions were Gillespie and Medina counties, which were rapidly increasing in population on the western frontier. Both counties were organized in 1848, after a large number of German and Alsatian settlers had immigrated into the area during the 184Os.[9]

In the first local elections in 1846 and 1847, law enforcement and the criminal justice system attracted candidates in most Texas counties. All 67 counties now organized in Texas elected from one to 11 justices of the peace, depending on the number of precincts and where candidates stood for election. Thirty five counties elected one or more constables and all but two counties swore in a sheriff. One exception was Washington County, where the commissioning of the elected sheriff was delayed for over a year. In Robertson County, the winners of the first two elections for sheriff failed to qualify, usually a sign that they could not be bonded and no elected sheriff held office there until November of 1847. In addition, the chief justice, later to be named the county judge, along with the district and county clerks in Robertson County also failed to qualify.[10]

On March 2O, 1848, the Texas Legislature passed an Act Concerning Crimes and Punishment, which defined a number of felony offenses and the punishments stipulated in the State of Texas. Conviction of murder in the first degree was punished by hanging; murder in the second degree brought a life sentence. Those assaulting or obstructing an officer serving criminal process would be hanged or spend life in prison. Other punishments included incarceration of not less than one year, or more than 1O years in the penitentiary for conviction of manslaughter, rape, assault, attempted murder, and the maiming or disfiguring of a person. Conviction of burglary of a home with intent to commit any crime, counterfeiting a false-coin of gold or silver, the release of any person lawfully arrested, or perjury in court were punished by not less than five years or more than 1O years in the penitentiary. Public gambling or the branding of another's horse both were punished by fines.[11]

To a defense attorney, any killing-whether by knifing, shooting, or beating, was made out to be in self-defense. It did not matter whether it was the result of an insult, a threat, an attack in the dark, or shooting from behind a door, self-defense would be claimed. After that many a lawyer would make numerous requests for prosecution records and continuances, delaying any trial. In a very mobile society like Texas, the witnesses, as well as the victims would often move out of the court's jurisdiction. If all else failed the accused, it was common knowledge that a jury would seldom convict one of their neighbors of a crime, if they considered him a better citizen than the victim.[12]

The Old Army Arrives In Texas

While Texas was suddenly prosperous and reaping the benefits of statehood, the Texas frontier was still wild and wooly. Much of Texas was unsettled and lawmen were scarce in the wilderness, so parts of South Texas were dominated by bandits, while the most conspicuous public enemy in all of Texas was still the hostile Indian. Much of the population in the new State of Texas would probably have liked to have handled the hostile Indian and Mexican bandit problem like they had sometimes tried during the Republic. More than once they had tried to kill them all. But Texas was no longer an independent nation and the policies of the federal government in Washington would now guide how Indian policy was carried out in Texas.

The government's policy was to extend a line of forts from the mouth of the Rio Grande up the river some 250 miles, and then along a line north to the Red River, each fort located just west of the last scattering of farms, ranches and small towns in several areas. Those forts were to be built in order to separate and protect the settlers and Indians from each other and in the case of the Indians, sometimes to protect one tribe from another. Those forts also acted as logistical bases in actions taken against hostile Indians.[13]

To implement this policy, beginning in 1848, almost a dozen army posts were established along the Rio Grande and the western frontier. They began at Brownsville with Fort Brown and followed the Rio Grande to Fort Duncan, near today's town of Eagle Pass. The line of forts then turned north and consisted of several more army posts including Fort Inge, Fort Martin Scott, Fort Gates and Fort Graham, the last two located just west of today's towns of Gatesville and Hillsboro, then north to Fort Worth on the Trinity River. Regardless of the sometimes accurate criticism leveled at the military during that period, the protection offered by the U. S. Army gave Texas ranchers and settlers their first real protection against the hostile Indian. Over the next few years for the first time in over a decade, the Texas frontier again began to slowly move westward.[14]

California, Precursor To Texas Violence

Soon after the end of the Mexican War, many of those looking for cheap land and opportunity had occasion to look even further west than Texas, toward California. For it was there that the discovery of gold now brought larger dreams of new riches. The rush to the West Coast of all sorts of characters, good and bad, catapulted that part of the new American nation almost two decades ahead of Texas, and elsewhere in the Old West, in the birth of ruthless outlaw gangs and the lawmen to pursue them. Part of the reason that outlawry developed so rapidly in California was that a rough and rowdy group of violent young men were already in California at the end of the Mexican War. Many of those first toughs were among former saloon and street gang members who had come to California in a New York Volunteer Army Regiment, that had actually arrived after hostilities had ceased. Many of those men then took their army discharge in California. Other violent men and outlaws would also soon emerge largely from the underclass of native-born Californians.[15]

What California lawmen and the courts would experience in the next few years, as the Forty Niners transformed the West Coast into a state full of drifters and violence, would be a sign of things to come for much of the West, including Texas following the Civil War. The tiny village of San Francisco with a population of only about 800 in 1849, in only two years grew into a boom town of some 25,000 people. Jack Hays, maybe the best of the old Texas Rangers, had gone to California in 1850 and was elected sheriff of San Francisco County. Later he would be among the founders of Oakland. San Francisco also had an efficient chief of police and because it was a relatively well policed town, it was less violent than many of the mining towns in the Sierra Madre, or in the new town of Los Angeles located several hundred miles to the south.[16]

There were initially few formal courts of law in California to which the first Anglo-American immigrants would submit. When crime became rampant, vigilante justice prevailed as it also sometimes would in Texas and elsewhere on the rough frontier. People were then hanged, whereas if they had been tried before elected judges and selected juries, they likely would have received a lesser punishment. As in Texas, there were also few early jails in California that were stout enough to hold a prisoner for long, so violent criminals when punished usually received a violent sentence-a series of lashes or hanging, but little jail time.[17]

California lawmen, because of the large number of those arriving on the West Coast in the late 1840s and early 1850s, were among the first peace officers in the United States to experience the effect on public safety of large numbers of armed and largely irresponsible young men who were away from the control of home and family. That same type of drifter would appear on the frontier, from Nebraska to Texas, occasionally during, but usually after, the Civil War.[18]

The Settlement Of Early Texas

In Texas, a constitutional amendment was passed in 1850 to allow for the election of district judges, rather than appointment by the governor and legislature. The first United States census carried out in Texas was taken four years after annexation, in 1850. That census confirmed an increase in population in Texas to over 200,000 people including slaves. At that time there were only 7,747 slave owners in Texas and the majority of those lived and worked along the Colorado, Brazos, Trinity and other large river bottoms, or in the rich blackland areas in plantation settlements where cotton was the main cash crop. Without the use of slave labor, commercial agriculture would have been impractical, if not impossible in antebellum Texas. This was because there was always a shortage of free men willing to work on someone's farm in a state where land was for sale-cheap. Decades later, this same problem would, in part, contribute to the growing presence of white and black tenant farmers in many parts of rural Texas.[19]

In the 1850s, the majority of Anglo-Texans farmed their land, without slaves, or they were in the fields working beside one or two slaves. But in those several counties where commercial farming took place, over 50 percent of all households in 1850 owned at least one bondsman and the average age of the head of households was just 38. By 1860, slaveholding had increased to almost 61 percent of landowners and their average had increased to 41 years old. In the 1850 Texas census, some 90 percent of the heads of household had been born in the Southern United States and 72 percent called themselves farmers.[20]

At the time, the bulk of the Anglo population of Texas covered an area east of a line from about Sherman, in North Texas, then south to Waxahachie, Austin, New Braunfels, Victoria and Corpus Christi. A new influx of German and East European immigrants would by the 1850s make people of German birth or parentage more numerous in Texas than the Tejanos and they would be the dominant settlers in the new settlements growing up around the towns of Fredericksburg and New Braunfels. By 1855, Texas would be home to 35,000 Germans, who had immigrated to Texas primarily for religious freedom and not for cheap land.[21]

The dominant Anglo settler of the day in all of Texas was, however, not unlike those in the early days of Austin's colony in the 1820s. They were usually coming from, or had passed through, Louisiana, Tennessee or Missouri. They were also predominantly of Celtic ancestry. In the 1850s, it made little difference whether they were in Scotland, Ireland, the Southern United States, or in Texas, their life was much the same. It was a hard life, full of adversity, lonely, mostly dreary and seldom gregarious, while all too often fraught with danger. Drinking and gambling were the main recreation. Their first houses were crudely built and they lived largely on a diet of fried salt pork, sweet potatoes, cornbread and molasses. They also killed surprisingly little wild game for food, except what they could catch in snares or dead-falls. White bread and milk were virtually unknown in Texas at that time, except in or near a few of the towns where dairy cattle were kept.[22]

What made Texas the destination for so many of the same type of people was the ever present dream of a better life, cheap fertile land and the freedom that life on the frontier offered. Many had come out of the 13 original states surprisingly soon after the Revolution, and had crossed the Appalachians, stayed a while in Kentucky or Tennessee, then crossed the Ohio River into the Northwest Territories. Now many of their sons and daughters were arriving in Texas. To some extent this feeling of finding freedom on the frontier has hardly changed, even in the twentieth century, although the definition of frontier may be different. Its manifestation is still seen in the numerous small frame homes and trailers on many small, isolated pieces of rural property along country roads from Texas to Idaho.[23]

In 1850, there were still few towns in Texas, and the state would be dominated by its rural population for another 100 years, until after the Second World War. Of those towns in Texas in 1850, Galveston was the largest and a major seaport, but with a population of only some 5,000 people. The next largest were San Antonio, Houston, New Braunfels and Marshall. All had populations of just over 1,000 and Austin, the capital, counted no more than 600. Ten years later, the influx of European immigrants, mostly Germanic, had raised San Antonio's population to almost 8,000 and it was again the largest town in Texas. Since there were few towns in Texas over 1,000 in population, there were also few roads and even fewer places to stay along the way.[24]

Clearing The Frontier Of Indians

Keeping up with the westward movement, from 1851 to 1856, a line of new United States Army posts were established along the frontier. That line of forts now ran from Fort Belknap in Young County, south to Fort Chadbourne, then further south to Fort McKavett in Menard County and finally to Fort Clark in what is now Kinney County, near the Mexican border. The army commands stationed in Texas for that 55 year period from 1846 to 1861, and then after the Civil War to 1900, accounted for expenditures in Texas of some 70 million dollars. That was no small sum and amounted to almost one-third of the entire regular U. S. Army budget during that period. As a result, in 1856, for the first time in nearly a decade, a relatively large number of new Texas counties were organized along that frontier.[25]

The extent of the Indian problem in Texas and the importance of the U. S. Army in Texas from 1849 to 1861 is told in just a few statistics. During the pre-Civil War or antebellum period, the U. S. Army fought in 84 different engagements with hostile Indians in Texas, which amounted to just over 38 percent of all army engagements fought in the entire West. During that same period, the War Department assigned to Texas two companies of artillery, four regiments of infantry and two of the five existing mounted regiments in the U. S. Army. Those mounted regiments were labeled at different times dragoons, mounted rifles and after 1855, cavalry. In antebellum Texas, the largest number of engagements against Indians was fought by the U. S. Army during 1850 and again in 1857. This was the result of aggressive actions undertaken during 1850 by the Second Dragoon, Eighth Infantry (mounted) and the First Infantry Regiment, in conjunction with federally funded state troops from the Texas Mounted Volunteers. The large number of engagements in 1857 occurred during the first full year of frontier operations of the aggressive Second Cavalry Regiment, initially commanded by Colonel Albert Sidney Johnston and later by Lt. Colonel Robert E. Lee.[26]

The effect of those aggressive actions against hostile Indians is possible to measure. Following the increased number of engagements in 1850, hostile Indian engagements in Texas almost ceased from 1851 through 1856, and then decreased again in 1858 after the aggressive campaigns in 1857 by the Second Cavalry. But Mexico would pay for the money and effort spent on a better defense against hostile Indians in Texas by the U. S. Army. In the Mexican state of Nuevo Leon, located on the Rio Grande opposite Laredo, Texas, they suffered 809 Indian raids from 1848 to 1870, claiming over 1,000 casualties and four million pesos of lost property. That compares with just 134 Indian raids in all of Texas during that same period.[27]

In order to further reduce the threat of Indian depredations, for at that time Texans saw Indians as the greatest threat, whenever a Texas Governor could convince the state legislature to vote sufficient funds for the purpose, he raised one or more companies of Texas Rangers to take the field against hostile Indians. In 1849, Major General George M. Brooke, commanding the Department of Texas, strongly urged the state to call out five companies of volunteers to assist the army in clearing out the area south of the Nueces River. As a result, in 1850, one of the largest commands ever mustered of state troops, almost 400 men, were initially sworn in for from 30 to 90 day individual enlistments for service in five companies of Texas Mounted Volunteers. Those companies were commanded by Captains John S. "RIP" Ford, William A. "Big Foot" Wallace, J. B. McGown, Henry McCulloch and R. E. Sutton. Several of those companies were then assigned to the U. S. Army and were federally funded.[28]

The first skirmish utilizing Texas troops assigned to the U. S. Army occurred on Jan. 11, 1850, when a mixed command of Second Dragoons and Texas Mounted Volunteers from Fort Lincoln and Fort Martin Scott pursued a group of Indians that had raided around Refugio and Castroville and ran off a large herd of horses. West of Castroville the Indians set fire to the prairie and escaped into Mexico with an estimated 400 horses.[29]

During May and June, the Texas troops assigned to the army at Fort McIntosh, Laredo and San Antonio Viejo took part in eight separate skirmishes with hostile Indians. Usually those Indians were on a raid stealing horses. One Texas Mounted Volunteer was killed and two wounded during those skirmishes. From June 23 to Aug. 27, 1850, Army Captain William Hardee led a large punitive expedition out of Fort Inge into the Rio Grande-Nueces River area consisting of the companies of the Second Dragoons, two companies of Texas Mounted Volunteers and the First Infantry. During that two month period, four skirmishes occurred in which Texas troops took part in two actions. Nine Indians were killed, nine others wounded and three rangers were wounded. The year continued with Captain Ford working independent of the U. S. Army. In 1851 the Texas Mounted Volunteers were discharged.[30]

If the U. S. Army could not stop every determined band of hostile Indians from raiding into Texas, neither could the combination of Army troopers and Texas Rangers. Between 1849 and 1860, mixed army and ranger commands worked intermittently together from the lower Rio Grande to the Indian Territory. During that period, the Texas frontier was too large to always be able to thwart the hostiles. Some Indians always managed to get through any number or combination of ranger and/or army patrols.

From the time of their first organization in 1835, the Texas Rangers had never really been peace officers. As a result, they were not involved like the sheriff, constable, marshal or municipal policeman with law enforcement. They were still protectors of the frontier against bandit and Indian, but they would not be involved in uniformly enforcing the criminal laws of the State of Texas until several years after their reorganization in 1874. From the official organization of the Texas Rangers in 1835 until Secession in 1861, they were a sometime part of the armed forces of the Republic, or they later acted as state troops and helped defend the frontier in the early years of the State of Texas. They had also been a part of the Texas Army during the Revolution, but played little part in that conflict.

During the Republic and at various times before Reconstruction, they were sometimes called Texas Rangers. But early Texas was less enamored with the ranger name than today's Texans, and as a result they were often given other names. They were, however, always state troops and organized as an independent military command reporting to the Republic's presidents and later to the state governor's office. At times, such as in 1850, they were attached to and paid by the U. S. Army.[31]

The rangers played a vital role in the defense of the exposed Texas frontier. Often during that period, however, individual Texas Ranger commands survived no longer than a few months, some never receiving full pay. Some of the men commanding the Texas Rangers during this period were very able. Although Captains Hays, Gillespie and Burleson were no longer associated with Ranger companies, men like Henry McCulloch, William "Big

Foot" Wallace and John S."RIP" Ford would become the next generation of outstanding Texas Ranger leaders. But other leaders would sometimes fall short of shouldering the responsibilities of command during that period.[32]

Establishing An Indian Home Land

Besides the U. S. Army and good work performed by a relatively small number of Texas Ranger commands in the first years of statehood, another method was employed to help reduce the dominance of the hostile Indian on the Texas frontier. Jefferson Davis who was appointed Secretary of War in 1853 promoted the establishment of Indian reservations in Texas to reduce the problems of regulating Indians with no "home land" on which to restrict them. This would be the first time since Sam Houston's efforts 16 years before at establishing a lasting peaceful relationship with the Indians in Texas.

On Feb. 6, 1854, the Texas legislature passed a bill setting aside some 12 leagues (over 53,000 acres) of land to be selected in north central Texas, equally divided into three separate but closely located Indian reservations. Two months later the U. S. War Department ordered that land of good soil, adjacent to navigable water be selected, surveyed and prepared to receive those Indians living in Texas. The first reservation consisted of four leagues of land, or some 17,700 acres, and was located on the Brazos River south of Fort Belknap, near present day Graham, Texas. This was set aside for the Tonkawa, Waco, Tawakoni, Anadarko, Caddo and the smaller Indian tribes in Texas.[33]

The second reservation site of similar size was 40 miles to the west, on the Clear Fork of the Brazos and it was set aside for those Comanche Indians living in Texas. The third site of another 17,700 acres was dedicated for those Indians living west of the Pecos River, primarily the Mescalero and Lipan Apaches. It was located next to the other reservation on the Brazos River. Because Texas public lands belonged to the state, those reservation lands would revert to the State of Texas, not the federal government, if ever abandoned by the Indians.[34]

CHAPTER III
THE FRONTIER MOVES EVER WESTWARD
1855-1861

ONE TRAVELERS TALE

In 1855, in another area of Texas, Ophia D. Smith told of two travelers who had earlier visited Texas and been told a story by the foreman of a hastily assembled criminal jury, describing the capture, trial and execution of a murderer. It is repeated here as it so well demonstrates the ability to adapt to the trials of the frontier, caused by the isolation of most Texas settlers outside of a few of the towns that had been established during the early days of the state.[1]

Smith wrote that after the travelers left La Grange, on the way to Austin, a man named Hamilton or Ham White (who was traveling with them) pointed out a grave at the foot of a tree. He told them that a man had been hanged there. Farther on, he pointed out the place where the ill-fated fellow had committed a murder. Here, Ham said, the criminal was captured just after he had taken his victim's gun and was ready for flight. They bound him and put him in a little house near by until they could organize a court. Lawyers were brought from the nearest county seat, witnesses were heard and the case was argued by lawyers, one acting as counsel for the accused.

When the verdict of "guilty" was brought in, all the men present drew up in line to hear the reading. "All who are in favor of carrying this verdict into effect will move forward one step," charged the judge. Every man moved forward. Ham White, who had been the foreman of the jury, told the prisoner that he was to hang in one hour. "The hell I am," was the murderer's response.

Ham confirmed that, "He would not believe that he was to be hanged, until he was placed on a horse and taken to that tree with that long branch protruding over (what was) an open grave."

"This was the way Texas got rid of her rowdies and villains," White said. "If a murder had been overlooked, what would newcomers have thought of Texans," Ham wanted to know. "Texas had no jails capable of restraining a prisoner. Justice had to be swift."[2]

The First Of The Outlaws

About that same time a very rowdy citizen of Texas came to the attention of law enforcement and the criminal justice system in northeast Texas. Cullen Montgomery Baker, who was born in Tennessee about 1835, was the son of John Baker, a small farmer, and his wife Elizabeth. His mother died when Cullen was about 10 years old, after they had moved to Texas. The family lived near a small community named Forest Home in Cass County. At about 18 years of age, Baker, a hard drinker and trouble maker, was nearly killed in a saloon brawl in the town, when he pulled a knife on another man. As a result, he was then beaten unconscious when the man struck him with a tomahawk. It took several months for Baker to physically recover from the blow; some speculate that he never recovered from the damage to his brain.[3]

After Baker physically recovered from the attack, he appeared to have settled down and on Jan. 11, 1854, at 19 years of age he married Mary Jane Petty. Harmony in Baker's life never did last very long. For some unexplained reason, Cullen Baker a few months later accused a young orphan boy named Stallcup of planning to kill him. Although the boy denied that accusation, Baker nearly whipped him to death with a black-snake whip. He beat him so badly that Baker was then indicted, tried and convicted of assault on Oct. 8, 1854. Only a few hours after the trial came to an end, Baker rode out to the home of the 52-year old chief witness against him, Wesley Bailey, and mortally wounded him with a blast from a double barrel shotgun. Bailey died two days later and Baker and his wife fled into Arkansas.[4]

Cullen Montgomery Baker would remain in Arkansas for several years. While there he is reported to have killed another man, John F. Warthem. Baker stabbed the older farmer in a fight, as Barker was attempting to beat Warthem's wife. He then returned to northeast Texas, this time escaping from the law in Arkansas. Cullen Baker by the eve of the Civil War had murdered two men and brutally attacked another. By that time, he was running from the law in two states, but for several years the law failed to locate and apprehend him. With Cullen Baker on the run, we will return to the story of one of Texas first armed and dangerous outlaws, when he again attracts the attention of the law during the Civil War.[5]

In 1856, William R. Henry was elected sheriff of Bexar County. Almost a year after that, another lawman in Bexar County, San Antonio Assistant City Marshal Frederick W. Fieldstrup was shot and killed by a well-known gambler operating in San Antonio. On May 29, 1857, Marshal Fieldstrup was involved in a gunfight with three men near the corner of Market and Alamo Streets. Three of those involved died that afternoon, including Fieldstrup. In January of 1858, Samuel Lockhart, the first sheriff of Llano County, who had served since August 1856, was stabbed and killed by another professional gambler in Llano.[6]

"THEY MUST BE PURSUED, HUNTED, RUNDOWN, AND KILLED"

These remarks by noted Texan George W. Kendall, summarized the attitude of the majority of people in the Lone Star State at the time concerning most Indians. On the Texas frontier, 1857 had been one of the most active years for the U. S. Army in their campaign against hostile Indians. In January of 1858, Texas Governor Hardin R. Runnels, took office determined to provide more protection to the Texas frontier. To encourage settlement there, over a two month period the Texas Legislature established 32 new Texas counties, all but two along the western frontier. Only seven of those 32 counties would be organized in 1858. Most of the rest would wait the better part of a decade to be organized, due to the Indian menace on the frontier during and just after the Civil War.[7]

Governor Runnels' second effort to better protect the frontier was when a new appropriations bill passed the Texas Legislature in January of 1858. He then appointed John S. Ford to command all state forces, with the title of Senior Captain. Ford would quickly mobilize his command and proceed toward north central Texas where he planned to attack and punish the Comanche Indians to the fullest extent. Captain Ford had been a Texas Ranger for several years after annexation, but had resigned to pursue other interests. Ford was different from most of those ranger commanders who went before him. He believed in discipline and drill, something that was shunned by most Texas Ranger commands, but Ford insisted on discipline within his troops.[8]

Captain Ford's pursuit of the hostile Comanche consisted of four columns of rangers spread across the frontier north of Austin, all moving northwest and led by several ranger officers including Edward Burleson and Allison Nelson. Captains Tankersly and Pitts' commands were also there and rode with Ford. In March of 1858 they arrived at the Texas Indian Reservations on the Brazos River. There, Ford was successful in recruiting about 100 Anadarko, Shawnee, Cherokee, Waco, Tonkawa and Keechi Indians led by Shapley P. Ross, son of the Indian Agent, to accompany his expedition. The large command moved out almost a month later and consisted of some 300 rangers and Indians.[9]

On April 29 they crossed the Red River, followed it for several days and then turned north toward the Canadian River. After crossing into Indian Territory they met the Comanche, fought a day long battle, killed two Comanche Chiefs including Iron Jacket, and swept the Comanche from the field. Ford estimated that he had met up to 300 hostile Comanche and killed 76, some one-quarter of the hostile force. They also captured over 300 horses and took 18 prisoners, mostly women and children. The Texas Ranger campaign commanded by Captain Ford, was quickly followed by another, but less aggressive pursuit of the Comanche in Texas by U. S. Army Colonel Van Dorn's separate command.

In Nov. of 1858, new appropriations made it possible to raise a new ranger command for another incursion against the Comanche. Ford again commanded the troops as they rode into northern Comanche County and established a stockade and camp, called Camp Leon. During this campaign Captain Ford became involved in an incident where a band of seven Indians from the Brazos Agency, and with permission of the Indian Agent, were traveling outside of the agency boundary when attacked by a group of men led by a Peter Garland of Palo Pinto County. All seven of the Indians were murdered on Dec. 27, 1859, and Ford was ordered by the 19th Judicial District Judge to arrest the murderers. Ford refused to arrest Garland and his original mission to attack the Comanche was then embroiled in controversy.

Although Ford's Ranger command, again in conjunction with a group of friendly Indians from the Brazos Agency, probed north attempting to contact the Comanche, no important fight with hostiles resulted and Ford's command eventually was mustered out of service.[10]

THE CORTINA WAR

What is referred to as the Cortina War took place in 1859, when Juan Nepomuceno Cortina led a large gang of cattle thieves that terrorized a thinly populated area in South Texas along the Rio Grande between Brownsville and Rio Grande City. During the Mexican War Cortina had abandoned Texas and fought in the Mexican Army in several battles. Returning to Texas after that war, he claimed to have been one of the heirs of a large land grant near Brownsville that had allegedly been stolen from him by several Anglo-Americans.[11]

In the almost 12 years between the Mexican War and the Cortina War, Juan Cortina lived much of the time at his ranch near Santa Rita in Cameron County and was in almost constant conflict with the Texas state government, in particular the judges and law enforcement in and around Brownsville, Texas. He was twice indicted for cattle theft by a Cameron County Grand Jury. On July 13, 1859, Robert Shears, City Marshal in Brownsville, arrested a Mexican-American who had once worked for Cortina. Marshal Shears was accused of acting "brutal and violent" during the arrest. Cortina, in Brownsville at the time, confronted Shears and shot and killed him, and rode away with the prisoner. On Sept. 28, Cortina rode back into Brownsville at the head of a gang of some 50 men, who took over the town, killing five men, including the City Jailer Robert J. Johnston and Victor Garcia, a merchant who attempted to protect Johnston. This incident began a period of violence, murder and theft that dominated the South Texas landscape and its politics for years. In 1859, at least five Texas Rangers were killed and another four seriously wounded during this fighting.[12]

Two groups of Texas Rangers, the first commanded by Captain William G. Tobin, were unsuccessful in battling Cortina. The second group of Rangers commanded by Captain John S. Ford and a command of 165 U. S. Army troopers commanded by Major Samuel Heintzelman then went after Cortina and his 400 men. Heintzelman attacked Cortina at Rio Grande City, killing

60 of his men and capturing all of his equipment while defeating him decisively. Cortina would reappear again two years later when he attacked the Zapata County seat at Carrizo, where he was again soundly defeated.[13]

On The Eve Of A Civil War

In 1859 Sam Houston ran for governor of Texas on a Unionist platform against Hardin Runnels, a strong states-rights Democrat. Runnels appears to have lost primarily because of his statements concerning reopening of the slave trade, as well as because of the Houston name and the lack at that time of much passion for secession. In addition, two other Unionists, A. J. Hamilton and John Reagan both won the two congressional seats and Texas appeared to have largely repudiated any early efforts at secession.[14]

In 1860 the population had grown to some 600,000 from only 200,000 just 10 years before. Of that number, just over 180,000, or 30 percent were slaves. But the vast majority of Texans still owned no slaves and over 50 percent of those who did owned less than five. By 1860, 95 percent of the white population could read and write and the average Texas household owned over $6,400 worth of property, making Texans rather well off for the time. The average age of the population was still in its twenties, but there was now a slightly larger percentage of people above 50 years of age. There were also 71 newspapers printed in Texas with approximately 100,000 circulation. The year before, Baylor University had awarded 22 bachelor degrees. The largest seaports on the Gulf were now Galveston, Matagorda and Indianola.[15]

Out on the frontier, however, life was just as hard and maybe more dangerous than before. Thomas Milligan had been elected the first sheriff of newly organized Mason County in 1858. A stagecoach line went through the county seat and another of Milligan's jobs was to care for the spare team of mules at the Crosley way station near his home on the outskirts of the town of Mason. On Feb. 19, 1860, while waiting for the incoming stage, Thomas Milligan went to collect the mules, but found himself suddenly surrounded by Indians. He was armed with only a pistol and was later found dead, killed by an Indian arrow that passed through his body, exiting from his chest.[16]

Texas in 1860 was a land of rapidly changing conditions and

contrasts and the federal government had again come under strong criticism for failing to control further Indian depredations and the lack of aggressive military campaigning on the Texas frontier after 1857. But more important, more than a year before Abraham Lincoln's election and not long after John Brown's 1859 raid on Harpers Ferry, a feeling of frustration, fear and distrust swept through the Southern slave states, Texas included. Brown's raid and promise to lead a slave rebellion was exactly what the South had feared and had expected for several years. It set off a commitment of vigilance and practice of stern vigilante measures against those abolitionists who might incite slaves to revolt, and against those slaves who might agree to such actions. During 1860, not only did violence against slaves and abolitionists in Texas increase, the diversity in crimes committed in much of Texas also increased.[17]

Beginning in early 1860, there were almost daily reports in the press of murders, a rash of fires, and talk of a general slave uprising. By the summer of 1860, various newspaper reports had large sections of Bastrop, Jefferson, Waxahachie, Dallas, Belknap, Gainesville, Denton and most of Kaufman and Navarro Counties destroyed by arson. It seemed that almost every day, the papers also carried reports of slave conspiracies and arson in such East Texas towns as Marshall, Sulphur Springs, Rusk and Paris. Although almost all of those newspaper reports were later proved to be false, the fires that were known to have occurred made all of those rumors of other fires and an impending slave rebellion credible to many in Texas.[18]

On July 8, most of the downtown district of Dallas was destroyed by fire of unconfirmed origin. The fire caused an estimated $400,000 in damage, a huge sum for that time. That same day, half the town square in Denton also burned and several stores in other North Texas communities went up in flames. Initially the people in those towns blamed the record North Texas temperatures and the only recently invented phosphorous matches for those fires. But then four days after the fire, Charles R. Pryor, the editor of the "Dallas Herald" wrote letters to a half-dozen other newspapers in Texas telling them that "certain negroes" had been interrogated and revealed an abolitionist plot, "to devastate with fire and assassination, the whole of Northern Texas." Without proof, which never came, but demonstrating the power of the press, Editor Prior set off the most devastating period of "vigilante justice" recorded in Texas. Organized law enforcement in most places simply stepped back and the mob ruled.[19]

On Aug. 5 of 1860, the day before the general slave uprising had been predicted by some, Henderson, Texas, was severely damaged by a large downtown fire. Officials estimated the value of the damage to be more than $200,000. One white man and one black woman were hanged as arsonists. The next day, just west of Tyler, an arsonist rolled a cotton bale under a home and attempted to set it on fire, and many knew that this was a fact and not rumor. On the night of Sept.13, 1860, a Fort Worth vigilance committee hanged a white Methodist minister named Anthony Bewley for plotting to incite an insurrection among Texas slaves.[20]

During the so-called Texas Troubles, which began after the Dallas fire in July and ran until mid-September 1860, it is estimated that in the North Texas region some 80 slaves and as many as 37 whites, including a number of abolitionist ministers, were executed by vigilante mobs for allegedly plotting slave rebellions and committing arson. Scores of other slaves and abolitionists were whipped, or if lucky, the abolitionists were only banished from Texas.

In November of 1860, although he had won but 39 percent of the popular vote and neither his nor any Republican Party candidate's name appeared on the Texas ballot, Abraham Lincoln was elected the 16th president of the United States. Lincoln's election was the last brick in the wall built by both abolitionists and secessionists to divide the nation and to begin a Civil War. Just over a month later South Carolina was the first state to secede from the Union. A dozen more, including Texas, would soon follow.[21]

CHAPTER IV

CIVIL WAR & RECONSTRUCTION 1861-1870

A NATION DIVIDED

In 1859, Sam Houston had again been elected Governor of Texas running on a Unionist platform, that strongly opposed secession. Then during the summer of 1860, there were repeated rumors of imminent slave rebellions and a number of cases of arson and large unexplained fires blamed on abolitionists and slaves. Those fires and the fear of an imminent slave rebellion tilted the sentiment for many and in late Jan. of 1861, a Secessionist Convention was convened in Austin.

By that time, Texans voted slightly more than three to one for separation from the Union. Sam Houston was replaced as Governor of Texas by Lieutenant Governor Edward Clark, after Houston refused to take the oath to the Confederate States. Over the next few months it became apparent that a civil war was imminent and U. S. Army commands in Texas packed-up, closed the doors of their mostly frontier army posts and returned north, primarily through Galveston. On April 12, the war began with the shelling of Ft. Sumter in South Carolina.[1]

Little of the war would be fought in Texas. But, over the next four years there was great concern over several actual and impending invasions of Texas by the Union Army. There was also an increase in Indian depredations occurring along the frontier. Texas had to look at these very different efforts to overrun the state as a single campaign to invade and kill its citizens. Although the Confederate States claimed that they accepted the responsibility for frontier defense against hostile Indians, the violence on the frontier from late 1862 to 1865 tells a very different story. Over the course of the war, the State of Texas did, however, try to fulfill that responsibility, but within a year after the war began its efforts began to falter.[2]

In 1861, the war-time government of Texas opted against forming a ranger organization like that which existed in Texas before secession. Without the back-up of regular army troops that type of organization was perceived as more than likely being ineffective. What then happened was in the Spring of 1861, Henry E. McCulloch took command of the First Regiment Texas Mounted Riflemen, a Texas state military command consisting of some 400 men mainly recruited from the Texas counties along the frontier. They quickly occupied many of the former Union military posts from near the Red River at Fort Belknap, and in several other forts down to the Rio Grande. The occupation of those posts and the patrols they sent out played a major role in decreasing the number of Indian forays into populated areas of Texas in that first war year. In fact, 1861 and much of 1862 were a period along the frontier that was generally more peaceful than some of the last years before the Civil War when the U. S. Army command had been distracted by an impending Civil War.[3]

The Texas Mounted Riflemen were mustered out of service a year later in the spring of 1862. Following the deactivation of that command, the most effective defense against hostile Indians fell to a series of Texas defense forces, which were militia-like organizations that were active in a number of the counties along the western frontier. Those forces were formed under several different names, including Minutemen, Frontier Regiment, Border Regiment and Frontier Organization.

Beginning with the first elections held in 1861, after Texas joined the Confederate States, a number of elective offices in Texas county and state government were seldom filled. Those who held those positions previously had either joined the Confederate military, followed the Union Army out of Texas, or had found a better way to make a living. Law enforcement suffered as older office holders and fewer deputies became common in many Texas counties. From 1858 until after the Civil War, however, no basic changes were made to the existing Judicial Districts in Texas.[4]

The Frontier Is Devastated

Beginning in 1863, the half-hearted attempts of the state and lack of an adequate Confederate military presence defending the frontier, began to be felt. By the end of the year, increased Indian raids which stole large amounts of cattle and murdered anyone they came across, became common along much of the Texas frontier. It is estimated that during that period, hostile Indians succeeded in driving off more than 10,000 head of cattle from just five frontier counties in Northwest Texas. In December of 1863, a war party of an estimated 300 Comanche warriors killed 12 Texans, wounded seven, drove off most of the horses and cattle and burned down 10 homes in rural Montague and Cooke Counties. That would not be the last raid in the area.[5]

In nearby Cooke County and its county seat, Gainesville, the year before had been the site of the so-called Great Hanging at Gainesville, one of the most heinous examples of the lack of the rule of law and rule by mob in Texas during the Civil War. It was there that 40 white men, suspected of being Unionists and abolitionists were hanged and two more were shot attempting to escape. While they were never convicted in court of treason, insurrection or any other crime, a kangaroo "citizens court" had sat in judgment before they were hanged.[6]

The Salt Lake Prairie, located in that same general area and near the Young-Jack County lines northwest of Fort Worth, began to earn a reputation for the number and ferociousness of Indian depredations. One of the victims in the area was newly elected Young County Sheriff Harvey S. Cox. Cox was killed by hostile Indians when a group of riders he was with were attacked on Aug. 16, 1864.[7]

The effects of increased Indian raids along much of the Texas frontier resulted in more death and desolation, as women, children and the few men left were repeatedly attacked. Those not killed along the 175 mile frontier, from Young south to Mason County, either forted-up at strong points for several years for protection against Indians, or they moved eastward and away from the frontier. By 1864, the typical Texas frontier, usually taken as one or two counties deep before the Civil War, was largely burned out and empty. By that time the frontier had retreated as far as 150 miles or more east of where it had been just four years earlier.[8]

It was not only the frontier that was dangerous ground for lawmen and citizens alike in Texas. On the night of Dec. 22, 1864, Sheriff Mat Nolan, twice elected sheriff of Nueces County and a Lieutenant Colonel in the Confederate Army, was on the streets of the county seat, Corpus Christi, talking with J. C.

McDonald. They probably noticed a couple of men approaching, but suddenly one of the men mortally wounded the sheriff with a shotgun he had concealed under a long coat; McDonald was also shot and killed by the other man. Both of the assassins escaped, but before Sheriff Nolan died he named the Gravis brothers as the killers. Neither were ever tried for the murder, but a few years later the Gravis brothers' stepfather, a Union supporter, was appointed sheriff of Nueces County by Union General Canby during the military occupation of Texas.[9]

During the Civil War, Texas acted as a major source of supply to the Confederacy. Men, horses, beef, gunpowder, salt and some manufactured goods, either locally made or imported, all moved east out of Texas and into the other Confederate States. On the Rio Grande a brisk export trade primarily in cotton, bound for Europe or occasionally even the East Coast of the United States to avoid the blockade, crossed the river into Mexico, or was loaded near its mouth. In late 1863, Union forces captured Brownsville and put an end to such trade until July, 1864, when Confederate troops recaptured the city.[10]

In Uvalde County, John Daugherty had been appointed a deputy sheriff in 1856. Following several years of service in the Confederate Army, he returned to Uvalde and was elected Sheriff in 1864. About six months later a gang of men called the Owens gang, rode into Uvalde to challenge the sheriff for arresting a friend. Sheriff Daugherty stepped out of the jail and was shot and killed. The grand jury later indicted six of the gang for that murder, but records are incomplete as to whether any were ever arrested, tried or convicted.[11]

Lee Surrenders and Military Occupation Begins

On April 9, 1865, the Confederate Army of Northern Virginia, led by Robert E. Lee, surrendered to Union forces commanded by Ulysses S. Grant at Appomattox Courthouse. The Confederate Army in Texas held out a little longer, but Texas prepared itself for a military occupation. Lieutenant General Phil Sheridan was appointed Military Governor of Louisiana and Texas. In Texas his army of occupation initially consisted of some 39,000 troops serving in three Army Corps and two cavalry divisions. In addition, two other cavalry regiments, the 4th and 6th were also enroute to Texas. Most of the cavalry crossed Texas overland, while the bulk of the army landed in Texas ports on the Gulf

Coast. On June 19, the Union Army occupied Texas' largest port at Galveston. It was at that time that the news of the Emancipation Proclamation was first broadcast in Texas.[12]

This unusually large number of Union troops was sent to Texas, not so much because of the fear of further insurrection, but more to intimidate Napoleon III of France. The French had already established a puppet empire in Mexico supported by French Army troops, and the U. S. desired to force them to abandon plans to stay in the western hemisphere. Steele's Division of the XIII Corp was stationed in Brownsville, while Weitzel's XXV Corp was moved all the way from the James River in Virginia to Fort Ringgold Barricks and the town of Roma further up the Rio Grande. Part of that command was also kept in support in Corpus Christi. By 1866, 29 infantry companies of the regular army plus volunteers, including the 4th Cavalry, 1st Artillery and units from the 19th, 114th and 117th Infantry Regiments were stationed along the Rio Grande. The United States was clearly prepared to go to war with France over its occupation of Mexico.[13]

Often ignored is the fact that during the last years of the Civil War, 1864 and 1865, thousands of slaves had been sent west from Louisiana, Georgia, Mississippi and Alabama to avoid their liberation by the advancing Union Army. Many ended up in Texas, a state initially with the smallest number of slaves among the Confederate States. When later freed upon publication of Lincoln's Emancipation Proclamation by the Union Army of Occupation, those large numbers added significantly to the instability so prevalent in Texas at that time. Suddenly many of those poor people were without means of support or even a familiar place to look for work. Most would also be made to sooner or later suffer from the resentment and bitterness already felt by much of the white population in Texas, for a freedman was a constant reminder of the lost war. But this came as little surprise to the United States Government, for four months before the Union Army arrived in Texas, Congress had already established a government agency, The Bureau of Refugees, Freedmen and Abandoned Lands to help protect the former slaves in the South.

PRESIDENTIAL RECONSTRUCTION

During August of 1865, Andrew J. Hamilton was appointed provisional governor of Texas by President Andrew Johnson, and a provisional government was established during what has been called Presidential Reconstruction. Hamilton, or his representatives, made hundreds of appointments during 1865 and ordered the registration of voters in preparation for a return to citizen voting after a new state constitution was written. By late in 1865, most former Confederate soldiers returning home from the war and a host of others fleeing the ruin and destruction of a defeated South brought their problems to Texas.

Demobilized Confederate soldiers began their homeward journey usually with no more than a dirty, ragged uniform. Lacking any money or food to sustain them, most faced a journey of several hundred miles, while some walked or rode more than a thousand miles back to Texas. Few had a horse or wagon. If they ate before they began their journey it was usually because Union soldiers shared their rations with them. It was also not unusual for Union soldiers to exchange small amounts of Confederate money or sometimes even give them small amounts of money, along with the loan of a "stray" horse or wagon, especially for groups of ailing and lame Confederate veterans. After that the former Confederate soldiers usually depended completely on the generosity of civilian and Union troops they met on the way home for food. Grant also provided those who surrendered a parole paper to pass Union sentries and a free pass on "all Government transportation and rail roads," to help on the journey home. Even so, some of those travelling to Texas from far away Virginia would require up to three months to complete the journey.[14]

Not all Confederate soldiers surrendered their only firearms to the Union army. Other soldiers avoided any sign of surrender by just walking away from their units. As they returned, the sudden abundance of firearms in a community already tense due to federal occupation, hastened the breakdown of law and order that took place in many areas of Texas beginning during and just after the last days of the Confederacy. The years immediately following the Civil War would oftentimes be violent and contribute greatly to almost three decades of increased crime and violence in a land where previously little crime and few violent criminals had prospered before that war.

On Jan. 8, 1866, delegates to the State Constitutional Convention were chosen and during the winter of 1866 a new Texas Constitution was written. This new Constitution recognized the Thirteenth Amendment, along with the promise of basic rights of person and property to freedmen. At the same time, it denied freedmen the right to vote, hold office, serve on juries and attend public schools. In the general elections that followed, the Conservative Unionists, a coalition of former Confederate officials and many secessionists who had failed to extend equal rights to blacks in the new constitution, elected James W. Throckmorton as governor.[15]

It did not take long for some of those defeated in the war, to become involved in a new war, this time against either those upholding the law, or against those who had opposed secession. Across Texas a series of feuds would be ignited between various extended families and their close friends, who hoped to gain economically during the chaos reigning after of the war. In Karnes County, long time Sheriff John Littleton, who had been reappointed sheriff by Union Army General Canby, was killed on June 25, 1866. Littleton, who had aligned himself with a local Unionist faction in the county run by the Sutton family, was ambushed as he returned from San Antonio with warrants for the arrest of a number of supporters of those fighting the Suttons, the Taylor faction. This would be the beginning of the long lasting Sutton-Taylor Feud, which would pit supporters of the two families against each other for almost two decades to come.[16]

On Aug. 20, 1866, Presidential Reconstruction officially ended as President Andrew Johnson declared the rebellion ended in Texas and returned control to the civil authorities in the state. If the Conservative Unionists thought that laws like many of those recently passed, and an attitude ignoring the loss of the war would stand, they were greatly mistaken. Using those attitudes of non-repentance, and the laws recently passed in southern states, including Texas, which disenfranchised black citizens, along with the increasing attacks on and violence shown against Unionists and freedmen, the U. S. Congress from March through July of 1867, passed three new Reconstruction acts which promised to began the process of Reconstruction anew. As a result, with the passage of the new Reconstruction acts, all of which were passed over the veto of President Andrew Johnson, the Union Army again stepped in and removed hundreds of recently elected officials including Governor Throckmorton. Many of those officials were replaced with Texans who were thought to be more loyal to the Union views. Presidential Reconstruction may have ended, but Congressional Reconstruction had just begun.[17]

Congressional Reconstruction

Government under the 1866 Texas Constitution lasted only 14 months, for the three Reconstruction Acts again imposed military rule on Texas and E. M. Pease was appointed Military Governor. In addition, General Edward Canby, head of the Fifth Military District again made most of the almost 200 appointments to county and state offices in 1867. Later in the military occupation other army generals, including Winfield Hancock and Joseph Reynolds would make additional appointments. During the first four years following the Confederacy's surrender, some one-third of county offices remained vacant. General Canby also appointed just a single constable in Austin, DeWitt, Fayette, McLennan and Navarro counties. By 1866 the concern over a European presence in Mexico had lessened and the Union Army had been reduced to 8,500 men. At that time few had been sent to the Western frontier. Occupation troops were then based in small Union army garrisons of one or two company strength, and spread across Texas at 37 different locations.[18]

As onerous and as hated as the military occupation of Texas was by the people of Texas, the establishment in 1867 and 1868 of 13 army posts along the Rio Grande and the western frontier of Texas brought for the first time in almost five years some real security to the Texas frontier against Indian raids. The signing of the Treaty of Medicine Creek Lodge in Kansas on Oct. 21, 1867, also brought about a promise of more security on the frontier. Kiowa, Cheyenne, Kiowa-Apache, Arapaho and Comanche Indians in that area agreed to move to reservations in Indian Territory. But, that did not put an end to raids by those not signing any treaty, or even some of those who had pledged to cease raiding into Texas.[19]

The U. S. Army posts after the Civil War were either reoccupied antebellum posts or new forts established in areas of greatest danger. In the five years from the first skirmishes in 1866 to 1870, a total of 50 battles took place between Texas based army commands and hostile Indians. The largest number of battles during that period took place in 1870, as more Indians from the reservations in Indian Territory, left and raided into Texas. One of those battles fought was on the Little Wichita River between elements of six companies (60 men) of the Sixth Cavalry led by Captain C. B. McLellan and an estimated 250 Comanche warriors. Two soldiers were killed, 12 wounded and 15 Indians were confirmed killed. Eighteen Congressional Medals of Honor were awarded for that one major battle.[20]

Under the U. S. government's Peace Policy, Quaker agents were put in charge of administering the reservations in Indian Territory. In theory that appeared sound, but in practice the Quakers failed, along with the U. S. Army to control their Indian charges. Numerous Indians left the reservation at Fort Sill, raided into Texas, killing, burning and plundering along the frontier. They then simply returned to the reservation to draw a food ration and rest up for the next raid, with little or no consequences for their actions. This treaty also barred any Texas based army patrols from crossing the Red River in pursuit of hostile Indians, without specific and direct orders from army command.[21]

The three Reconstruction Acts passed by the U. S. Congress in 1867 began to have their effect on the people of Texas. Many believe that prolonged Reconstruction was a major cause of the violence and outlawry in Texas over the next several decades. It is true that as the incidence of crime, even petty crime rose across Texas, it was easy to assign some of the blame to almost anywhere one wanted. Crime and criminality was also rampant in many other areas of America. In 1868, nearly 80,000 crimes were reported in New York City alone.[22]

Above all, however, it was the lack of respect for the law and individual rights which played a major role in the lawlessness in Texas. That lack of respect was derived from a host of causes, of which a lengthy Reconstruction was only one, but a powerful one. County jails around Texas which had been seldom used before the war were suddenly put into service by the military, and the newly appointed lawmen. Most of those jails had been used mainly for the occasional drunk and disorderly. As a result, they were often found lacking and numerous outlaws escaped their walls, causing even less respect for the law.

As the loss of respect and an absence of effective law enforcement in many areas of Texas helped increase the amount of violence and crime, the U. S. Military stepped in and further contributed to that increase in violence by selling thousands of cheap surplus firearms throughout the West, including in Texas. In 1867, J. Miller & Company in Galveston, Texas, obtained a large stock of various types of army surplus rifles, pistols and shotguns. Miller & Company paid the army under $5.00 for each of those weapons, and flooded Texas with firearms cheap enough for any day laborer to own, if all were not in the best working condition. As a result, during the coming years it was not just the gunman and outlaw gangs that spread violence. Shootings and robberies happened everywhere, including those committed by people who could barely load or pull the trigger of the firearms they carried.[23]

While much of Texas grew more violent by 1869, the violence now rampant across North Texas had begun as early as 1863. This was the result of a collection of draft dodgers, deserters from both armies, various outlaws and other riff-raff who used the Indian Territory as a sanctuary. In northern Texas, two violent episodes have already been noted. In each of those incidents well over 100 black and white, men and women, were shot and hanged in anti-Unionist vigilante outbreaks just before and again during the war. This occurred because before the war, parts of North Texas had opposed secession and Unionist sentiment was always very strong in the region. As a result a large amount of violence among North Texas neighbors occurred.[24]

Another Look At An Early Texas Outlaw

One of those already looked at earlier in the book because he had committed several violent crimes before the war, was Cullen Montgomery Baker, who lived in Northeast Texas. In 1854 he had killed an older unarmed white man and escaped into Arkansas. A few years later, after committing another murder in Arkansas, he had returned to Cass County, Texas. Baker had escaped what must have been no more than a half-hearted attempt by the law of two states to arrest him. In 1861 after the war began, he first joined the Confederate Army, but in 1863 he had deserted. By the end of the war in 1865 Baker ran an outlaw gang in northeast Texas that was active during the first years of the military occupation.[25]

Baker had few redeeming features. He was a ruthless bully and killer of the weak. He seemed to concentrate on older unarmed white men and former slaves, but he did not hesitate to attack and batter women. He sometimes shot and killed Reconstruction officials, including members of the U. S. Army, whose command structure during the early military occupation of Texas seemed generally incapable of understanding how to pursue and arrest many of the most wanted criminals of the day. The military even understood just how incompetent they themselves really were at that type of work, and several times requested more funds to pay for special detectives and police service to take them out of law enforcement duties. But Washington continually refused.[26]

Baker was also the very opposite of how the daring highwayman or outlaw is portrayed in the Old West. He typically attacked from ambush, oftentimes suddenly appearing out of the dark and usually when he had the complete advantage of isolation and numbers on his side. He was as likely to abuse women as men. Baker never robbed a bank, a stage coach, or a train, but specialized in robbing army supply wagons. He committed his crimes, all of which were violent and included multiple murders, in a dirt poor region of Northeast Texas and nearby Arkansas where poverty was a familiar part of the life to most of those who lived there.

A serial killer by today's standards, he was very likely brain damaged from a blow to the head he received in a saloon brawl at 18 years of age. He usually attacked and killed his victims with a knife or a shotgun, although he was reported to carry as many as six pistols at a time. Cullen Baker probably killed as many as 15 men and wounded about the same number during the 15 year period that he preyed on the people of Cass, Bowie and Marion Counties in Texas, plus in the nearby areas of Arkansas. Baker as a man was of little value and was certainly someone who needed killing himself, as did the members of his outlaw gang.[27]

When he was killed on Jan. 6, 1869, Cullen Baker was not killed by lawmen or by the army. He was discovered drunk, sleeping on the ground alongside a member of his gang in the backwoods of Northeast Texas. He never awakened before his brother-in-law, a man he had terrorized for years and had attempted to kill, reversed the roles and shot both Baker and the other man in the head. Baker was one of the first of many Texas outlaws to terrorize the people of the Lone Star State beginning about the time of the Civil War, and extending into the military occupation and Reconstruction period. Baker, like many others since, blamed others for his life of crime. In Cullen Montgomery Baker's case it was the Union Army and black men that made him do it.[28]

Two of Baker's prominent gang members and later outlaws on their own, Bob Lee and Benjamin F. Bickerstaff, were chased out of northeast Texas only a few months after Baker was killed when some of the gang was captured near Pilot Grove and then scattered further west. Ben Bickerstaff was killed by elements of the Sixth Cavalry near the town of Alvarado, south of Fort Worth in April of 1869, three months after Cullen Baker was killed. Lee was also shot and killed by troopers of the Sixth Cavalry soon after, while he was resisting arrest near Sherman, Texas.

During 1868, an organization at the time supported by an increasing number of people, the Klu Klux Klan, had also become active in northeast Texas, possibly because of Cullen Baker's success in intimidating black freedmen and easily avoiding capture by the Union Army. General Winfield Hancock, while in command of the Fifth Military District, had assigned only two troops of Union cavalry to the area in early 1868. After Hancock was replaced, General Joseph Reynolds did assign more troops to the region in November of 1868, but he assigned mostly infantry, who were practically worthless chasing mounted outlaws in an area they were well acquainted with.[29]

Two Teenage Killers

About that same time, two other young men in Texas began their outlaw careers. One was 17 when he killed his first man, and he claimed that at one time he rode with Cullen Baker's gang, but that appears unlikely. His name was William Preston Longley born on Oct. 6, 1851, the sixth child of Campbell and Sarah Longley in Austin County, Texas. Bill Longley would go on to become a noted gunman who is credited with killing close to a dozen men from Texas to Wyoming, before being hanged in Giddings, Texas in 1878.[30]

The other young boy, at the time just 15 and two years younger than Bill Longley, was John Wesley Hardin, who was the son of a Methodist minister. He would soon become the most prominent gunman and most successful self-confessed killer in Texas.

The career of both Hardin and Longley as gunmen and outlaws is difficult to analyze, for both were given to bragging and even writing about the men they said they killed. Hardin would eventually write a book about his exploits. Both seemed to have embellished their reputations and adventures many times. When Longley did this, he oftentimes took credit for unlikely events. Hardin was little different.

Bill Longley and Wes Hardin each killed their first man less than a month apart, and separated by only some 100 miles.

Both of these young men each murdered a black freedman in the waning days of 1868, within a few months of the killing of Cullen Baker in North Texas. Hardin, at 15, shot and killed his first man in Nov. 1868, not far from his home near Moscow in Polk County. Within a few days, he also killed several Union soldiers sent to arrest him and went into hiding. Bill Longley, less than a month later, on Dec. 20, 1868, while accompanied by two other white men, shot and killed Green Evans, one of several Black men they had met on a back road in Washington County. When arrested almost a decade later in 1877, Longley bragged to a newspaper reporter that he had already killed another Black freedman the year before he shot Green Evans. Was this type of claim, which was never corroborated, the truth or a lie? Similar stories would be repeated again and again, clouding Bill Longley's reputation and life's experience.[31]

The two Black men who had been with Green Evans returned to Bell County and informed their former slave master, Captain Alfred Evans, of the murder. Captain Evans immediately armed the dead man's brother and stepfather with shotguns and he went with them back to Washington County to pursue those who had killed Evans. Bill Longley, Johnson McKeown and Jim Gilmore were soon identified as those who had attacked Evans and a warrant was sworn out for each of them. They all quickly disappeared from sight. Longley claimed years later that he had also shot and killed a Black trooper in a Sixth Cavalry Regiment patrol in April of 1869.

According to Longley's able biographer, Rick Miller, there is no documentation of this murder either in county records or in the records of the Sixth Cavalry. Longley also claimed that soon after the Green Evans shooting, he had joined Cullen Baker's gang in Northeast Texas. The problem with that claim by Longley is that Baker had been killed only two weeks after Longley had shot Evans, making any contact between the two men separated by several hundred miles, impractical.[32]

Longley probably never left Washington County, but somehow he escaped being arrested on those warrants issued for the murder of Green Evans. It is unknown if there was ever a serious search for him by law enforcement after Captain Alfred Evans returned home to Bell County. It was this cavalier attitude and lack of enforcement of the law by many county lawmen after the Civil War that would lengthen Reconstruction, spawn a hated state police force and end up working to the detriment of the people of Texas. Longley was next heard from in Bastrop County, during early 1870, after he had joined with his sister Francis Caroline's new husband John C. Wilson in first raising hell and then "murdering, robbing and ravishing colored people in that section of the State." Those comments were included in a letter written by Bastrop County Justice of the Peace James E. Brady, to Texas Governor E. M. Pease on Feb. 11, 1870, requesting military assistance capturing Wilson and Longley.[33]

As a result of the request for assistance from Governor Pease, a $1,000 reward was issued by General Joseph Reynolds, Commander of the Fifth Military District on March 1, 1870 for the arrest and delivery, "dead or alive," of John Wilson and Bill Longley, "Murderers and Horse-thieves." Wilson was said to have been killed in Brazos County, soon after the reward was posted in 1870. But, Longley would soon leave Texas on the run and end up in Wyoming, enlisting in the U. S. Second Cavalry Regiment on June 22, 1870. Eventually, however, he would return to Texas.

While Bill Longley ran from the law to Wyoming, John Wesley Hardin appears to have spent the next several years traveling around Texas on the dodge, bouncing from odd job to odd job, or hanging out with relatives along the way. During that time, Hardin's reputation as a gunman grew and he was soon involved in the Sutton-Taylor feud.

Cullen Baker, Bill Longley and John Wesley Hardin were all teenagers when they killed their first man. They were also among the earliest of what would later become prominent Reconstruction outlaws, who first came to the notice of lawmen in Texas during and just after the Civil War. They might even be thought of as homegrown, in contrast to the many outlaws and gunmen who travelled through or ended up in Texas in later years.

Before the war, not all Texans had joined the secessionist movement and some remained loyal to the Union throughout the war. A number of those loyalists left Texas for safer territory, but some, particularly those living within the few larger pro-Union communities stayed on in Texas. However, throughout this period, those supporting the Union were always in jeopardy of suffering from some type of discrimination or violence. As a result, during the Civil War and through the military occupation of Texas, most Texans whether white, Black, Secessionist, Unionist, rich or poor and whether living on the frontier or in deep East Texas, all lived in a more violent time, where murder and assault, lynching, robbery and mayhem occurred on an almost daily basis. Some of those violent acts were also most likely never made a part of any record.

In 1869, another Texas Constitution was signed into law by a legislature controlled by the Radical Republican political machine. That constitution made some significant changes in the organization of government from all of the previous state constitutions. Justices of the peace were moved out of county precincts and into the courthouse, where they formed the county court. Each justice then could appoint a constable to serve papers, but this type of arrangement only further weakened county law enforcement, as it did away with precinct lawmen and magistrates for five years following the Civil War.[34]

Although some constables were appointed by the justices, no constables were elected in Texas counties from 1869 to 1873. In 187O, however, the new Texas Governor, Edmund J. Davis, appointed a number of town constables in Bonham, Bremond, Clarksville, Cleburne, Crockett, Henderson, Kaufman, La Grange, Linden and Mount Pleasant, Texas. On March 3O, 187O, President Grant signed a bill ending Congressional Reconstruction in Texas, and on April 16th, General Reynolds turned over all authority to the civil officials.[35]

In 1869 and 187O, the sheriffs in Harrison, Goliad and Nueces Counties, all of whom had been appointed by Union Army generals during reconstruction, were murdered. Those murders were unlikely to have been any part of a grand conspiracy, but their occurrence certainly showed a continuing disregard and contempt for the law across Texas. That was especially true when that law emanated from an order signed by a Union Army commander. Partially as a result, it would not take long before Texas would became a much more violent land.[36]

John Wesley Hardin in Abilene, Kansas, during June of 1871.
Original is a tintype in Hardin's personal photo album.
(R. G. McCubbin Collection)

CHAPTER V
A TIME OF INCREASED VIOLENCE 1870-1873

THE DUTY OF GOVERNMENT IS TO PROTECT CITIZENS

Five years of military occupation and Reconstruction had finally ended, but life in Texas in 1870 was still played out under the Constitution of 1869. In addition, the Radical Republican political faction still exercised control over the elective offices and the administration of state government. During the Feb. 1870 session of the state legislature, the 1870 elections that were to occur later that year were postponed to 1872. The governor was then given authority to appoint up to 8,500 local officeholders, thereby putting all the power in the hands of the governor and his appointees. The volume of crime and crime rates rose significantly in 1870 and 1871, particularly violent crimes, and an increasing number of lawmen were finding themselves less and less capable of coping with that violence. This was particularly true with regard to racial crimes.[1]

Typical of many crimes involving race was like one incident that occurred on June 13, 1870, when three white men accosted a Black female on the street in Brenham, Texas, and began to verbally abuse her. Another white man interceded on her behalf, but was threatened by the three men when one of them drew a pistol. He went to the sheriff and filed criminal charges against them. Washington County Sheriff W. M. Thompson and a deputy named Crozier approached the three men. A man named Hansboro, who was carrying a pistol was asked to give up his gun. He refused and the sheriff then arrested Hansboro, who drew his pistol and fired a shot at the sheriff that missed.

Deputy Crozier drew his own gun and fired one shot that by mistake mortally wounded his sheriff. As Sheriff Thompson fell, Hansboro then tried to shoot Deputy Crozier, but was subdued and arrested, along with the other two men charged in the incident.[2]

Race was not the only cause contributing to the cycle of increased violence circulating through much of Texas. By the early 1870s a number of men who made their living from crime took up residence in the state. In Dallas County, John Younger, already a wanted man and brother to outlaw Cole Younger, shot and mortally wounded Deputy Charles Nichols and a friend who had both gone to a community near Dallas to arrest John Younger and an unidentified man traveling with him. Deputy Nichols may have already met Younger, for he foolishly did not immediately disarm him. He also let Younger and his companion eat breakfast before taking them to jail. After eating, the two attempted to escape, but their horses were under guard. They then returned to where they took breakfast and shot Nichols and his friend, then chased those away holding their horses and rode off toward Indian Territory.[3]

Governor Davis, for all the partisan political problems existing in state government, clearly recognized the lawlessness then rampant across the state and attempted to do something about bringing law and order back to a turbulent Texas. His first effort was to push for and then sign a law on June 13, 1870 to further protect the Texas frontier. That act called for the raising of 20 companies of Texas Rangers, "for the protection of the northern and western frontier," against hostile Indian raids. Each company was to consist of 62 officers and men. By the end of 1870, fourteen of those companies had been posted on the frontier. There would never be more than those 14 companies raised for the primary purpose of guarding the frontier against hostile Indians; however, they sometimes came across bands of outlaws and were instructed by Adjutant General James Davidson to arrest cattle thieves and turn them over to local law enforcement.[4]

The governor's second effort to reduce violence in Texas was one of the most controversial moves made during his administration, but a logical move considering the alarming increase in violence. A month after the ranger bill was passed, an act establishing the Texas State Police was also passed, with Adjutant General Davidson, to head both the rangers and the State Police.[5]

Texas State Police

During the meetings and deliberations associated with the 1868-1869 Constitutional Convention in Texas, Governor Davis appointed a Special Committee on Lawlessness and Violence. Recommendations were made that Texas needed a statewide police organization that could go into all jurisdictions and chase outlaws across county lines and make arrests anywhere in the state. The committee undertaking those deliberations cited a figure of 1,035 murders that had been committed in the three years between 1865 and 1868, as an indication of the violence then rampant in Texas and the need for a State Police organization. Crime had not decreased in the years since those committees had met, in fact crime had increased.[6]

The Police Act of July, 1870, authorized a police force of 257 officers and men, although the actual force never quite reached 200 total. The State Police were said to have been empowered to arrest those who committed crimes when local law enforcement failed to do so, and the State Police were able to call on local law enforcement for assistance. In fact, the State Police also spent much of their efforts protecting freedmen along with Radical Republican officeholders and their supporters, few of whom appeared to have ever received equal protection under the law from local law enforcement. The Freedmen's Bureau would call upon the State Police many times to assist in their efforts to better protect the former slaves in Texas.[7]

When first organized, the State Police were commanded by James Davidson, serving concurrently as Adjutant General and Chief of Police. Initially four districts were organized on July 7, 1870. Those first captains appointed were M. P. Hunnicut, E. M. Alexander, L. H. McNelly and Jack Helm. Hunnicut and Helm would not last out the year. Soon there were eight State Police districts scattered across Texas. Initially those districts were headquartered in Waco, Clarksville, Brenham, Austin, New Braunfels, Brownsville, Houston and Woodville, Texas, and they would be commanded by either a captain or a lieutenant. The location of the various headquarters, the captains commanding them and the number of districts would change over the almost three years of operations. Only one of the eight district commanders in the State Police was over 40 years of age and two were less than 25 when the police were first organized.[8]

On or about July 13, 1870, the State Police requested that all elected and appointed law enforcement agencies in Texas supply them with a list of those who were locally indicted, or had outstanding warrants, or who were not yet arrested in their jurisdiction. Across Texas, most towns, even the smallest were organizing some type of police force. Usually that meant a town or city marshal or constable, and at least one deputy marshal. Less than two decades later, those town constables would be back in county precincts and the local city marshals would be called chief of police. A description of the police agency or sheriff's department supplying the information was also requested. That information was sent to the Chief of Police, State of Texas, Austin, Texas, and was contained in several different reports. Sometimes those reports were hand written, or the information was contained in a series of printed forms (Report of Persons Evading Arrest, Report of Crimes Committed, or Report of Escapees) for the previous several years. In somewhat of an overkill, some of the reports went as far back to 1857![9]

In an analysis based on those reports of the Texas sheriff's and other law enforcement agencies for the years 1865 to 1870, some 4,425 crimes had been committed across Texas. Only 588 (13 percent) had resulted in arrests made and even fewer in convictions. Many sheriffs appear to have been judicious in answering that request for information. Those reports show that most county sheriffs at the time had one, or at the most only two, deputies. Because constables were not elected at that time in Texas, and their work had come down to little more than running errands for justices of the peace, there were no reports from constables. Some municipal police departments, however, did answer the questionnaire.

Asher R. Hall, the sheriff of Harris County, which contained the increasingly important town of Houston, answered the State Police query for all in the county. Sheriff Hall had three deputies in his department. There was also a town marshal and deputy marshal and five policemen averaging 32-years of age in the city of Houston, the county seat. From almost all locations, the continued lack of secure jails in most Texas counties was also brought to the attention of the State Police through those reports.[10]

The State Police recruited men who had fought in both the Union and Confederate armies and a large number of freedmen. From 40 percent to 60 percent of the State Police were said to have been freedmen, but that is difficult to confirm for the ethnic make-up and birth place of many policemen were not posted in the records. Very few of those recruited seemed to have had any experience in police work and many appear to have been as prejudiced against the ordinary Texas citizen, as most Texans were prejudiced against the State Police. Regardless, there proved to be some very effective lawmen recruited, while some were as corrupt and dangerous as those they chased. The majority fell in between.[11]

The real problem for most Texans with the State Police was attitudinal, in that it was a police force organized by a generally hated Reconstruction government. In addition, the policemen themselves were mostly outsiders to the area they worked in, and there were a large number of Black freedmen employed as policemen. Only five years after the defeat of the Confederacy and emancipation of slaves in Texas, there was little chance that such a police organization could prosper, much less survive for any length of time.

Two early captains of the State Police may have been the best, and the worst examples of the men employed. One of the worst was undeniably Jack Helm, who in 1868 and 1869 had been a member of a special police force led by C. S. Bell, whose group of Regulators were sanctioned by Union General Reynolds. Over several months this police force attacked several families in DeWitt and Goliad counties, including the Taylor Party, which was made up of the Taylor family and friends, supporters of secession and the Confederacy. It was a time in Texas when weak and partisan law enforcement led to the beginning of various family blood feuds across the state and that incident set off a feud that would take the lives of several dozen people. That group of special police played a large part in fueling the feud, as they were said to have killed 21 people in two months and turned over only 10 offenders to local law enforcement.[12]

When employed by the State Police, Captain Jack Helm made his first arrests on that same day, July 18, by arresting both William M. Moore and Jacob Johnson in DeWitt County for attempted murder. Later his company arrested and then murdered two leaders of the Taylor faction. The outcry was so loud that Jack Helm would finally resign from the State Police on Nov. 30, 1870, after less than six months of service. Helm also served as sheriff of DeWitt County, and was later shot and killed by Jim Taylor and John Wesley Hardin on Aug. 1, 1873.[13]

Exemplifying what has been called the best, is probably

Captain Leander H. McNelly, who incidentally made the third arrest in the State Police on that first day, July 18. He arrested Joe Barker, a freedman in Williamson County, for the murder of Don Wallace in Bastrop. McNelly initially commanded District #4 during the first year of the State Police. During his career in the State Police, Captain McNelly then commanded District # 3 for several months in mid-1872, before returning to District # 4. He also led what was called the Rio Grande Expedition, a punitive police expedition and criminal roundup along the Rio Grande, initiated to break-up a number of large cattle theft rings. But that command actually saw little action along the border and McNelly was back in Burton, Texas within a month.[14]

McNelly went on to make the transition from State Policeman to the ranger service in 1874. His unique assignment as a Captain at that later time was, however, not as an integral part of the Frontier Battalion, but in the Washington County Volunteer Militia Company "A". That was a Special Force, organized to guard primarily against Mexican and Anglo bandits and cattle thieves operating between the Nueces River and the Rio Grande. It was an area he knew something about from his days in the State Police. His excellent handling of that assignment, had much to do with sanitizing his reputation for having previously served with the State Police during Reconstruction.[15]

A War Between The Races

Starting in 1865, much of Texas was involved in what can only be candidly identified as a race war. There is little question that many Black freedmen after emancipation committed a disproportional amount of crimes against property; they stole a large number of things, and theft or larceny was against the law. But, those crimes were to a large extent not violent crimes. While that type of crime against property had historically been regarded as a heinous crime on the frontier, few freedmen were on the frontier and their punishment was not always left to the law. Furthermore, most white Texans were not as colorblind as Captain Alfred Evans of Bell County, who had previously armed two of his former slaves to accompany him when he went searching for Bill Longley.[16]

Some white Texans murdered and even more made every effort to mistreat many of the new Black Texans. Some may have believed those measures were needed to get even for, or to stop some suspected theft of their property, but most appeared to have been violent toward Blacks primarily because of the bitterness and hate caused by losing the war. Without the protection provided in some areas by the State Police, many more Black Texans would have been murdered or assaulted for no reason other than that they were Black. Four times Governor Davis declared martial law in different Texas counties and sent in state troops to avert a violent breakdown of law involving rioting white Texans. In the first six months of the State Police organization, from July 18 to Dec. 31, 187O, there were 173 offenses committed that were listed as "disturbing the peace" and "rioting." Many of those would have been offenses committed against Blacks, with the addition of a number of the listed murders and assaults that also took place during that period.[17]

During that period in Texas, numerous men and some women also ran afoul of other law enforcement departments, not just the Texas State Police. Because of the nature of most police work then and now, much of that work is naturally intrusive and resented by many who come in contact with the police, not just the offender. For all of the later criticisms lodged regarding the State Police's intrusion into the life of ordinary citizens in Texas, there were many instances where local law enforcement, the courts, individuals and groups of citizens wrote the Adjutant General requesting the assignment of State Police officers to their county or area. There were also a number of letters written thanking that police organization for their work.[18]

There were 14 confirmed deaths of Texas State Policemen killed in the line of duty during the just over two and one-half years they were active. Two of those policemen were shot and killed by John Wesley Hardin. The first killed was State Police Private Jim Smalley, who with two other men were transporting Hardin to Waco from Longview, following Hardin's earlier arrest. On the evening of Jan. 22, 1871, the party had camped and while the others visited a nearby farm looking for feed for the horses, Hardin produced a small pistol, shot and killed Private Smalley and rode away.

Some nine months later, on Oct. 19, two Black state policemen recognized Wes Hardin in the small town of Nopal, Texas located near the Gonzales-DeWitt County line. Private Green Perrymore ordered Hardin to surrender his weapon and Hardin appeared to be handing his pistol to the state policeman when he rolled the gun into his hand, shot and killed Private Perrymore. The second policeman, John Lackey shot at Hardin, but was himself wounded several times by Hardin and a group of men riding with him. Besides attempting to arrest young John Wesley Hardin, a known killer and outlaw, State Policemen crisscrossed Texas in an effort to reduce other instances of violence and crime.[19]

A Classic Gunfight

There have actually been very few of what might be called classic gunfights recorded in Texas, where two or more men stood and shot at each other at close range, as made famous in the gunfight at the OK Corral. One of those gunfights took place on March 14, 1873 in Lampasas, only a month before the Texas State Police were disbanded.

Captain Thomas Williams, a longtime respected member of the State Police led seven State Policemen out of Austin to enforce the new law against wearing a weapon within a city limits. They chose Lampasas as their first stop, a community that had a history of violence and whose sheriff, Shadrick T. Denson had been shot at just five days before while attempting to make an arrest. As it turned out, they would have been better off had they have gone elsewhere.[20]

As the State Police rode into town, they soon saw a number of people wearing guns and arrested one man, said to have been Bill Bowen. According to one story, Bowen suggested that if they went into Jerry Scott's Saloon they would have no problem finding others wearing a weapon. Captain Williams, along with Privates Wesley Cherry, J. M. Daniels and Andrew Melville entered the saloon, while the other state policeman stayed outside. Inside were maybe a dozen men, including three of the five Horrell brothers, Martin or Mart, Tom and Merritt, who ran cattle on a ranch outside of the town. Mart Horrell had appeared in district court earlier that year and had been fined one cent for unlawfully selling an estray horse. His brother Ben had twice seen the inside of a court room, having been charged on Jan. 17, 1873 with threatening the life of a human being and three days later for the theft of a colt. Captain Williams looked around and told one of several men in the group that he was under arrest for wearing a pistol. No one knows who shot first, but when it was over, Captain Williams and Privates Cherry and Daniels were dead and Melville was mortally wounded. Martin Horrell was wounded in the shoulder and some reports also have Tom Horrell being wounded out in the street by the other policemen.[21]

Several days later a large contingent of State Police arrived in Lampasas and after a coroners inquest, arrested Jerry Scott, Allen Whitecraft and James Grizzell, along with the wounded Mart Horrell. All had been in the saloon at the time of the shooting. Policeman Melville, who had been mortally wounded inside the saloon, died a month later. Mart Horrell, Grizzell, Scott and Whitecraft were taken to Austin and placed in the Travis County jail. They were later moved to the jail in Georgetown, north of Austin. On May 2, however, members of the Horrell family and friends rode into Georgetown and broke all of the men out of jail.[22]

There is some confusion in a number of newspaper reports and in written accounts about where those men were jailed, and how they either walked out of, or were freed from jail. In the Lampasas County District Court records, there is confirmation that Tom Horrell and Jerry Scott were never indicted for murder by the district court before they had been released/broken out of jail in Georgetown in May of 1874. But the point is moot, for by the time the murder indictments were later returned, the Horrell family had packed up, and driving their cattle before them, had moved to the Lincoln County area of New Mexico. No one tried to stop them from leaving Texas. The State Police were already being disbanded, and the sheriff in Lampasas County probably thought it would be good riddance.[23]

While not without some major faults, the State Police organization from its inception on July 18, 1870, until the act was repealed in April of 1873, compiled an impressive list of arrests made. Records show that the State Police in just 33 months of operation were involved in handling some 10,000 criminal arrests; over 3,100 of those resulted in arrests for violent offenses and 696 were for murder. Over 1,200 of those arrests were made of those who stole livestock (horses or cattle) or illegally slaughtered a beef. Almost 1,900 of those arrests were for illegal gambling, while over 1,200 arrests were for robbery, theft and swindling. More than 500 were for carrying a deadly weapon. There are no records except in Texas widely scattered court houses regarding who was ever tried, found guilty or went to prison for committing those alleged offenses. Regardless, that is enough activity to make any other law enforcement agency envious, including the Texas Rangers, especially since most of those in the State Police had no prior experience in law enforcement; in fact many had little experience even living in a free society.[24]

As the State Police closed their offices around the state, Policeman Philip Peter, Badge #178, who had only joined the State Police a month earlier on Feb. 19, 1873, made the last arrest in Gillespie County. He arrested a man named John Thomas on March 31, 1873, for a miscellaneous offense, but before his trial was held, Thomas broke out of jail. Later, he was recaptured, tried and sentenced to two years in prison.[25]

It is noteworthy that a number of letters were written about ongoing cases after the closing of the State Police. One written on May 1, 1873, by Police Lieutenant J. M. Redmon is interesting. Lieutenant Redmon thought enough of a wanted Texas badman to write headquarters in Austin, summarizing the status of the ongoing investigation of a man named (John Wesley) Hardin, who was wanted for the murder of several freedmen and two State Policemen. Some three months later Wes Hardin and Jim Taylor would also shoot and kill former State Police Captain and DeWitt County Sheriff Jack Helm in Albuquerque, Texas. Helm was said to have been armed with no more than a pocket knife when he was shot and killed.

When Bill Longley left Texas with a price on his head in 1871, he had fled as far away as Wyoming, where he enlisted in the U. S. Army. Longley would desert just two weeks after he enlisted, then be captured, court martialed and sentenced to two years of hard labor, some of the time with a 24 pound ball attached by chain to his ankle. Almost two years later, just as his sentence was completed, he again deserted, but this time they did not catch him and he headed home to Texas. By coincidence, Bill Longley would arrive back in Texas in early 1873, following an absence of almost three years. Upon his return, Longley went to his father's farm in Bell County. There were claims that he shot and killed another Black man in Comanche County later that same year, but it has not been verified. What was verified was that Longley was seen in Bell County carrying a pistol on July 1, 1873, and left the area immediately, for there was still a sizable reward for his capture resulting from a past indictment in Bastrop County.[26]

While the State Police were active, other lawmen in Texas also enforced the law and like those in the State Police, some paid a price for it. In Galveston, Texas on April 4, 1873,

Galveston Policeman John Ferguson was walking down Mechanic Street when a mentally deranged man, James B. Helms, went amok. He stabbed three people on the street and when arrested by Officer Ferguson, also stabbed that officer, mortally wounding him and then stabbed a second officer. At Helms' trial for the murder of Galveston Police Officer John Ferguson in Feb. 1874, Officer Ferguson's son walked into the courtroom and shot James Helms in the back of the head, instantly killing him.[27]

Davis Voted Out Of Office

From the time Governor Davis took office in Jan., 187O, until he was voted out of office in 1873, the Texas state government was controlled by what has been called the Radical Republican political faction. That group managed to stay in office for a longer than expected period, to a large extent by delaying some elections, appointing numerous officials friendly to their policies and passing laws that lengthened the term of their own party's influence. Just as Texas prepared to vote for a major change in political administration, on Sept. 8, 1873, Jay Cooke & Company, one of the largest and most respected banking houses in New York, declared bankruptcy. In Texas this event was hardly noticed, but that important banking house had helped the U. S. Government finance the Civil War and the construction of the important Northern Pacific Railroad. That bankruptcy and other similar occurrences would help precipitate the financial Panic of 1873, which would impact Texas and the rest of the nation. For the next several years the U. S. slipped into a major depression as over 1O,OOO businesses failed, the values on the stock market dropped and massive unemployment swept through the nation.[28]

In Jan. of 1874, Edmund J. Davis was defeated and Richard Coke was elected governor of Texas. This was the first election in Texas since 1865, in which all Texans were able to vote and that election brought an end to the carpet bagger government and Radical Republican political dominance of Texas politics. After his defeat, Davis refused to vacate his office and asked President Grant for support. He was, however, ignored by Grant, and finally left office. The Edmund Davis administration was above all a government that had failed miserably to protect its citizens. It was also hated by many, and would deeply influence the type of state government that would be organized in Texas over the next 100 years.

CHAPTER VI
THE TAMING OF THE FRONTIER
1874-1876

THE STATE FIGHTS TO GAIN THE UPPER HAND

In the roughly eight years between the beginning of the military occupation in 1865 and 1873, when the administration of Governor E. J. Davis was turned out by the voters, the incidence of crime had increased significantly. During that same period economic growth in the state of Texas had all but ceased. Davis left the state with high debts and high crime rates, but his actual departure caused many to have higher expectations for the future.

Since secession, only 12 new Texas counties, an average of just one per year, had been organized. All had been carved out of existing counties in the eastern part of the state, except for Pecos County, a large and very sparsely populated area in West Texas, even to this day. The population in Texas had almost tripled between 1850 and 1860, but had only grown by some 35 percent during the next 10 years. Those population increases in Texas were also generally limited to only those counties with a larger town within their boundaries or to those counties containing a large number of newly counted freedmen.[1]

During 1874, there were massive crop failures in Texas. Most were caused by grasshoppers and potato bugs, brought on by the lack of rains. As a result, many were forced to leave the security of the farm to search for other work. Texas was so heavily in debt that Governor Coke found that income to the state would cover only about half of the state's existing programs. By 1874 the national economic Panic of 1873 finally hit hard in Texas. A major reduction in state programs was the only solution. State salaries were cut and school funding almost ceased. The state prison system was directed to become self-supporting by raising their own food and they began leasing out some convicts to work for private employers. State pensions were paid in land, rather than currency. Because of the increases in crime, some had thought about reorganizing the State Police under the new administration, but its unsavory reputation and the lack of funds available for an organization to police the entire state, led the legislature to look for an alternative.[2]

That alternative was shaped by the recognition that future growth in Texas depended to a large part on further westward expansion, and that movement waited only upon driving the last Indians out of Texas. To confirm the importance of the western frontier in Texas, among the first legislative acts of Democratic Governor Richard Coke's administration was the passage on April 1O, 1874 of legislation to provide more protection for those living in the shadow of hostile Indian raids. To do this, the Texas Legislature passed laws establishing and funding several groups of state troops, all under the command of the Adjutant General of Texas, who reported directly to the Governor.

One group was called a "battalion of mounted men" in the controlling legislation, and named the Frontier Battalion. It consisted of six companies of 75 men each and would be under the direct command of Major John B. Jones, a former Confederate Army officer. In addition, in each of those Texas counties along the frontier, a company of Minute Men was organized to guard against "hostile Indians, Mexicans, or other marauding or thieving parties." The various commands of that group were to be called out when the Frontier Battalion was unavailable or insufficient to protect the frontier. Another command of State Troops formed a few months later and also headed by Jones was a Special Force, somewhat strangely named the Washington County Volunteer Militia Company "A." That company was first assigned to DeWitt County, the site of the troubles between the Sutton and Taylor factions. Later it would be sent to pacify the region between the Rio Grande and the Nueces River.[3]

The Frontier Battalion was intended to act primarily as an Indian-fighting command and was by design paramilitary in nature. Not entirely by coincidence, that force was also not issued uniforms, which made it even less a burden on Texas taxpayers. The Frontier Battalion would consist of six companies, each commanded by a captain, with occasional lieutenants, sergeants and corporals included, in addition to the private soldiers. Almost as an afterthought, but to satisfy those who desired some type of state police organization, the law establishing the Frontier Battalion, gave each officer in both the Frontier Battalion and in the Minute Men commands, "the powers of a peace officer." This clause would come back to haunt the state in years to come. That law was, of course, the formal organization of what would fortify the legend and eventually be called the Texas Rangers, although the word "ranger" was not used anywhere in that legislative act. [4]

On June 27, 1874, some 700 Comanche and Cheyenne warriors attacked a buffalo hunters camp named Adobe Walls in the Texas Panhandle. Not entirely caught by surprise and secure behind thick adobe walled buildings, 27 well-armed and accurate shooting buffalo hunters held off those hundreds of Indians. When they saw that they could not massacre those at Adobe Walls, the Indians broke off the fight, taking it north into Kansas and into other parts of Texas where unsuspecting travelers and settlers were attacked and killed, or taken captive.[5]

Partially as a result of the fight at Adobe Walls, it would be the U. S. Army, rather than the rangers in the summer of 1874, that began the most ambitious and successful campaign ever undertaken to rid the Southern Plains and the Texas Panhandle of the Comanche, Kiowa, Cheyenne and Arapaho Indians. It would be called the Red River War and it would last some nine months and extend into 1875. Five separate army punitive expeditions, all moving toward the Palo Duro Canyon area in Texas and consisting of elements of the 4th, 5th, 6th, 8th, and 9th Cavalry, along with strong infantry and artillery units, plus scouts, took part in this campaign. At no time during the first 35 years after annexation were more engagements, 24 in number, fought with hostile Indians in Texas than in 1874. The Red River War would drive the majority of those Indians not killed from northwest Texas. They moved, either out of the area entirely, or onto the reservations already existing in the Indian Territory around Ft. Sill.[6]

With hostile Indians mostly swept from the Staked Plains and the Panhandle of Texas, buffalo hunting on the Southern Plains was suddenly a serious commercial enterprise. A very dangerous game of chance as practiced before the Red River War, hunters got serious in their slaughter of buffalo by the spring of 1875. Many groups set out from Fort Griffin and Rath City to hunt the region from where Midland is today, up and onto the Staked Plains near Lubbock. Other hunters came down from Kansas and hunted into the Texas Panhandle. There was little Indian trouble in those first years following the Red River War. During 1875 and 1876, a permanent army post, Fort Elliott, would be established in the Texas Panhandle at Sweetwater, later renamed Mobeetie, Texas. As a result, more hunters would begin to use that area as a base for slaughtering the buffalo.[7]

In 1876, the Texas legislature would create the boundaries and give names to 54 new counties that would cover the South Plains and the Panhandle of Texas. It would be two decades before some of those counties were actually settled enough to be officially organized. But with the promised building some years later of several railroads from Ft. Worth and Kansas toward the Panhandle, this served as a way to allow for the rapid organization of various county governments, after the anticipated arrival of new settlers sometime in the future. Before those settlers arrived in the Panhandle of Texas, however, cattlemen would drive large herds of cattle to the area, and stake out huge ranches on private and public lands. A cattle industry would soon flourish in the Texas Panhandle, and the cowboys who worked for those large ranchers would be numbered among those officials elected in the first counties organized.[8]

An Unprecedented Crime Wave

As the government in Texas and the U. S. Army concentrated on making the frontier a safer place, crime and violence throughout much of the state was rampant. The activities of outlaws, the numerous acts of lawlessness by everyday citizens, and the number of murders in Texas by the mid-187Os was unprecedented. As a result many parts of the Lone Star State had been transformed into a very violent land. Some were driven to move toward the frontier, for there an enemy was at least easier to identify. But crime did not exist only in Texas and the Old West. In New York the Democratic Party political leader "Boss Tweed," was convicted of over one-hundred counts of fraud. The Grant administration was also mired in charges of graft and corruption.[9]

Following the Civil War, law enforcement in some Texas counties had occasionally failed to enforce all of the laws because they had attempted to support a group of friends and allies. This began to change as the lawmakers in Austin passed a number of necessary and sometimes unpopular laws, which lawmen and citizens alike eventually had to begin paying attention to. Even if some of those new laws were unpopular with many Texans, their

Major John B. Jones, Frontier Battalion commander. (Author's Collection)

enforcement appears to have been largely responsible for the eventual reduction of violence and crime in many communities. Gambling in a public place and the consumption of alcoholic beverages at certain times and in some communities was suddenly against the law. The sale of intoxicating and spirituous liquor was prohibited within two miles of a number of schools, churches and academies. Earlier, the carrying of a firearm in most areas of the state, except in the frontier counties, plus indiscriminately shooting that weapon, had been made a crime.[10]

Regardless of how effective those and other laws were to be in reducing violence in many areas of Texas, some lawmen, particularly in the rural areas of Texas, were less than rigorous in enforcing such laws among their constituents than they were enforcing the law among those drifters who passed through their county. Selective law enforcement in some Texas communities would unfortunately be the rule, rather than the exception, for the better part of the next hundred years.

The year 1874 appears to have been something of a turning point for lawmen in Texas. While crime was on the increase, the presence and activities of a number of noteworthy outlaws in Texas were suddenly coming under scrutiny of both a new political administration and sometimes more dedicated lawmen, who generally made it clear that rampant crime would no longer be permitted. As a result, the legislature not only made new laws, it organized and supported groups of lawmen to enforce those laws. But the genie was already out of the bottle and it would take the better part of two decades to bring law and order to some areas in Texas.

Blood Feuds And Violent Families

One problem peculiar to the state were the activities of a number of what can only be characterized as, violent families, who were supported by their in-laws and friends, and then set out to kill off another local clan. If not tolerated by local law enforcement during and immediately after Reconstruction, many of those outlaw families were at least less than aggressively pursued. In addition, some well-known individual outlaws like Wes Hardin and Bill Longley were pretty much left alone as long as they were killing mostly Black freedmen, or just passing through to another jurisdiction.

Longley and Hardin were not the only gunmen in Texas who murdered Black citizens. In the town of Jacksboro in North Texas in 1874, a cowboy named Joe Horner shot and killed one Black army trooper and wounded another after a quarrel in a saloon. The two appear to have been stationed at Fort Richardson in the 10th Cavalry. Horner, like some others who committed similar crimes, would never be arrested for that crime. This would not be particularly noteworthy except that Horner would, some 17 years later end up in Wyoming. He had adopted the name Frank Canton and as a law officer played a major role in the infamous Johnson County War. Canton would then move to Indian Territory where he would be a deputy U. S. marshal under Judge

Issac Parker and then finish his days out as Adjutant General of the Oklahoma National Guard.[11]

One of the most violent families in Texas at that time was the Samuel Horrell family of Lampasas County, whose five sons over the next several years were usually in trouble with the law or with some of their neighbors. After being deeply involved in the murder of four State Policemen in early 1873, they had then packed-up and quickly moved to New Mexico. But the people of New Mexico and the Horrells did not take to each other, and just 12 months later in late February of 1874, the family, including their sons Merritt, Tom, Mart and Sam Horrell, would return to Lampasas. They left another son, Ben Horrell, and a brother-in-law buried in New Mexico, as both had been shot and killed there during the past year.[12]

They were barely back in Lampasas before they were attacked by a sheriff's posse coming to arrest them for their part in the earlier State Police murders. When they were unable to capture the family, the sheriff and his posse rode away. In September of 1874, Merritt Horrell and Bill Bowen, who were charged with the murder of those Texas State Police in early 1873, surrendered to the law. They were acquitted at trial and the family settled down to reestablish their new cattle ranch, a few miles south of Lampasas, just into Burnet County. It would be but a short time, however, before they were again accused of the theft of range cattle by nearby ranchers including the most vocal, John Pinkney "Pink" Higgins. Several years would pass, however, before the Horrell-Higgins feud would escalate and lead to the death and wounding of a number of the participants.[13]

In South Central Texas, two other extended families were at that same time involved in the Sutton-Taylor feud. That blood feud had been going on since the end of the Civil War and again burst out into the open when the Taylors saw an opportunity to eliminate their main rival, Bill Sutton. On March 11, 1874, Bill Sutton, his pregnant wife, Laura, and a friend, Gabe Slaughter, arrived in the port city of Indianola to travel by steamboat to New Orleans. As they walked toward the ticket booth on the lower deck, Jim and Bill Taylor stepped out of hiding and shot down both Sutton and Slaughter. In the confusion, the two Taylors escaped. They had planned to leave South Central Texas by hiding themselves with the drovers taking a herd of cattle to Kansas. As part of the plan, they immediately rode to Cuero, Texas, where their friend John Wesley Hardin was involved in rounding up the cattle and readying them for a drive up to Comanche County. When he arrived in Cuero, Bill Taylor lost interest in the cattle drive, and stayed around the area celebrating the murders. As a result he was arrested for Bill Sutton's murder and placed in the Indianola jail. He later escaped and quickly left the area.[14]

Texas Gets Rid Of The Hardins

Wes Hardin and Jim Taylor had left Cuero even before the cattle herd departed. They rode to Comanche County, where they planned to pick up another herd of cattle being gathered in the area by Joe Hardin, Wes Hardin's brother. That cattle herd was largely the result of using false bills of sale to cover up the theft of range cattle. It was planned to drive all of those cattle to Kansas when the first herd arrived from Cuero. Wes Hardin, though a well known pistoleer with more than one outstanding warrant out on him by that time, had been ignored by the law in De Witt and also when he arrived in Comanche County. Thirty years later former Comanche County Sheriff Carnes, when asked why Hardin was not arrested on an outstanding warrant, said that there was no jail in Comanche County, so he had no place to keep him. This, of course did not explain why that same sheriff sent two Comanche County deputies into Brown County with Joe and Wes Hardin and some of their band to pick up cattle whose ownership was in question.[15]

John Wesley Hardin and the activities of his brother, Joe and friends, would not be ignored in neighboring Brown County. Wes Hardin waited for the first cattle herd's arrival from Cuero and passed his time acquiring a fast horse and becoming involved in racing that horse on the edge of town. He may have had luck at racing, but delaying his departure from Comanche was a decision he would live to regret, for it would be events in Comanche County that would finally put him in prison a few years later.

Brown County was another predominately ranching county adjacent to and west of Comanche County. In March of 1874, in an effort to return the rule of law to that part of Texas, Brown County Deputy Sheriff Charles Webb, a former Texas Ranger, was assigned by Brown County Sheriff J. H. Gideon to break-up a suspected cattle rustling gang led by Joe Hardin, who was operating in Brown and Comanche Counties. A big horse race took place on May 26, 1874, outside of Comanche, but later that day John Wesley Hardin, Bud Dixson and Jim Taylor shot and killed

Deputy Charles Webb outside of Jack Wright's saloon in Comanche. Hardin was wounded by Deputy Webb. Even though Comanche County Sheriff Carnes now arrived to disarm and seemingly protect Hardin's group, it was only moments before a mob gathered and in turn disarmed the sheriff and threatened the killers. Deputy Webb had been a popular lawman in Comanche, as well as Brown County. Wes Hardin and Jim Taylor ran toward several horses that were tied nearby, quickly mounted and rode out of the square. After the sheriff said he could not guarantee any of the group's safety, Joe Hardin and the rest of the gang spent the night camped on the prairie outside of town.[16]

The next day a large crowd gathered in town, watching the two houses where the Hardins had previously stayed. There were many threats of lynching the Hardin family and friends. Some of the gang slipped back into town while Wes Hardin stayed away and tended his wound and cautioned those with him to avoid showing themselves. Soon Joe Hardin, Bud and Tom Dixson were arrested. During the next week things continued to go downhill fast. A group of rangers from Company A, in what may have been one of the Frontier Battalions earliest efforts at law enforcement, and as many as 500 local men joined in the man-hunt for the remaining Hardin gang. The posse also seized the cattle that had been assembled for the cattle drive to Kansas, and the other cattle herd as it arrived from Cuero.[17]

On the afternoon of May 31, two of Hardin's gang hiding in the vicinity of Comanche, Alexander Hamilton "Ham" Anderson and Alec Barekman, were spotted and killed by the posse of local law enforcement and a few rangers. After midnight on June 1, some 30 heavily armed ranchers, believed to be mostly from Brown County disarmed the guards in the Comanche jail, took the three prisoners out of jail and lynched Joe Hardin, Tom and Bud Dixson at the edge of town. John Wesley Hardin had already left Comanche, heading toward Gonzales and DeWitt Counties. He would spend the next three years constantly on the run, leaving Texas a few weeks after killing Deputy Webb and fleeing first to Louisiana, then to Alabama and Florida. In January 1875, the Texas legislature offered a reward of four thousand dollars "for the apprehension and delivery of the body of the notorious murderer John Wesley Hardin." That was a lot of money and it was a blow to Hardin, who would not return to Texas until three years later under arrest and in chains.[18]

The increased level of violence and killings that had swept

across much of Texas beginning in 1869 had continued at about the same level until 1878. There were few corners of the state that did not feel the effects of that period of violence in the 1870s. At the same time a new group of elected officials and better local law enforcement, along with the filling of many court positions, some of which had been vacant for almost a decade, had their effect on crime. But true reform in Texas would have to await the adoption of a new state constitution. That was necessary in order to overcome many of the problems brought about at the state and local level, contained within provisions of the 1869 Constitution.[19]

Outside of Texas, in addition to the continued effects of the nation's deep depression, the discovery of gold in the Black Hills in 1875 caused a massive migration of those out of work toward the West. On the Northern Plains various Indian tribes were still belligerent and a year later in 1876, George Armstrong Custer and 264 officers and men of the Seventh Cavalry Regiment would be killed on the Little Big Horn.[20]

In Texas 14 lawmen are known to have been killed during 1875 and 1876. During those two years, policemen in Austin, Cuero, Decatur, and Denison, two constables, one each in Hill and Houston Counties, one ranger with Captain McNelly's command in South Texas, two sheriffs and five deputies from different sheriff's departments from around the state were killed in line of duty.[21]

Of those lawmen, Ranger L. B. "Sonny" Smith was the only man serving under Leander McNelly who was killed in the line of duty when McNelly was in either the State Police or the rangers. His time of death on June 12, 1875, makes Ranger Smith probably the first ranger in the Frontier Battalion to have been killed in the line of duty while acting as a peace officer. Prior to that time any rangers that had been killed were fighting Indians. On Dec. 29, 1876, the last Texas Sheriff killed by hostile Indians, Sheriff Jack Phillips of Bandera County, was murdered while riding alone toward the west end of his county. In Mason County, on Aug. 10, 1875 Deputy Sheriff John Wohrle was murdered and then scalped by Scott Cooley, in a savage act of revenge.[22]

While violence played a major part in the life of those in many Texas counties, a somewhat different view of crime is worth examining by looking at Fort Worth, a boom town in North Texas where gambling, drinking and whoring formed the basis for the popularity of that part of town that was just beginning to be called

Hell's Half Acre. Fort Worth's location on the banks of the Trinity River, and on a direct line between the vast ranch land of South Texas and the railroads in Kansas, made it a natural cow town. The first trail drive of Texas cattle passed through Fort Worth in 1866, and at its height in 1871, some 600,000 cattle passed through the town in that one year. In 1876, the first railroad station was built in Fort Worth and the train arrived soon after. As a result, Fort Worth would replace much of Kansas as a major stock yard from which cattle was shipped East to market. In addition, before the railroads built West, three stagecoaches a week left Fort Worth to begin their 17-day journey to Yuma, Arizona, before going on to California.[23]

In 1876, Fort Worth City Marshal John Stocker was appointed to replace Marshal Tom Redding, who had pretty well been made the laughing stock of the town and was discharged. Before Redding left his job, however, he had hired 27-year-old Timothy Isaiah Courtright, a former Union Army soldier and scout as city jailer. Courtright had ambition and in April of 1876, he ran for and was elected to the first of three, one-year terms as city marshal in Fort Worth. Courtright, called "Long haired Jim," would never kill a man while he was city marshal, but he was very active in his peace keeping efforts. He would be involved in numerous fights and would shoot at and wound more than one man to keep the lid on violence. Jim Courtright would gain a solid reputation as a lawman, and would effectively keep the peace in a violent Fort Worth, until he lost the 1879 election.[24]

After losing that election, Courtright hung around Fort Worth and then moved to New Mexico and worked as a range detective, where he was involved in two gunfights in which four men were shot and killed. Within a few years, however, Courtright would move back to Fort Worth and open a private detective agency, but he would be pursued by those trying to extradite him back to New Mexico. Although he initially ran from the law, he eventually returned to New Mexico and won acquittal. "Long haired Jim" Courtright would then be killed by Luke Short, a gambler, when he again returned to Fort Worth years later in 1887.[25]

A New Constitution To Fit The Times

In many parts of the state, 1876 represented a time when the Reconstruction constitution of 1869, which established a government organized under federal military rule was finally swept

Timothy "Jim" Courtwright, City Marshal in Fort Worth,
circa 1876-1877.
(Western History Collections, University of Oklahoma Libraries)

away. To do this, constitutional convention delegates had initially met in 1875, a year after Governor Edmund Davis was defeated. Ninety delegates attended the beginning of the convention. They were predominantly white, with only six Blacks present, all from among the 15 Republican delegates. The group would draft a fiscally and politically conservative document that can only be called antigovernment in its content.[26]

For example, the power of the Texas governor was severely curbed and most prominent state and county officials including the county sheriff and constables, plus district, county and other judges were to be elected, making them subject to public review, not government control. Of much importance to most Texans and based upon the shared experience of the Civil War and Reconstruction, there was an absolute ban on the suspension of the writ of habeas corpus.

The largest number of delegates to the State Constitutional Convention were farmers. The Grange, to which most belonged, was the foremost interest group in the state at that time. The delegates passed along numerous mostly conservative provisions for the new constitution. One of those was a provision that real property could only be taxed on its appraised value, thereby limiting property tax rates in an effort to avoid loss of property for nonpayment of increased taxes as had often occurred during Reconstruction. A local-option provision was also included which allowed counties or precincts to prohibit the sale of alcoholic beverages within their jurisdiction. The state school system was abandoned and replaced by local control of schools through an elected board. Because of the need for more farm labor during certain times of the year, school attendance was not initially made compulsory. At the same time, the new land-grant university system was generously endowed with income to be derived from 42-million acres of public land. Most provisions for the construction of state highways were for a time also abolished, in favor of a system where local citizens were called to work on local roads by the county, and fined if they did not appear.[27]

It was the State Constitution of 1876 which set forth the judicial system in Texas as it basically exists today and is one of the most complex systems in the United States. The constitution of 1876 established two appellate courts; all of its judges, except in some municipal courts, were chosen in partisan elections, and its trial courts did not have uniform jurisdiction of subject matter. Little has changed today. There are still three levels of trial courts in Texas, the district, county and inferior (justice and municipal) courts. For the criminal and civil defendant, the district courts in Texas are the courts of record in law and equity.[28]

It was in the state constitution of 1876, that another appellate court, the court of appeals, was given jurisdiction of appeals in criminal, probate and county court cases. This left the supreme court in Texas free to hear appeals coming from district courts in the increasing case load of civil cases after the Civil War. It did not really relieve the Texas supreme court from a gridlock caused by the number of cases it still had to hear. It would take a later amendment to the constitution in 1891, to help straighten out that problem.

In 1876, Texans would vote overwhelmingly in favor of the new constitution. That same constitution is still in effect today, and for almost three decades after its passage, there were but few amendments. Armed with a new constitution, a better organized judiciary and law enforcement officers most of whom were newly elected and divorced from the patterns of the past, a new attitude was taking hold in the state that said that violent crime would no longer be condoned in Texas. Over the next few years, the law set out to bring to justice a number of famous and not so famous outlaws. It would be a long, difficult and never ending effort.

CHAPTER VII
END OF THE ROAD FOR MANY TEXAS OUTLAWS
1877-1879

HARDIN GOES TO PRISON

John Wesley Hardin had often relied on his extended family to hide him, to ride with him and support him in his troubles with the law. He was seldom disappointed. By 1877, Texas' best known killer of men had fled the state some two years earlier, but with a reward on him of $4,OOO dead or alive, he was not forgotten. Nor would Texas Governor Richard Hubbard let him be forgotten and he called upon the only group with authority to chase Hardin outside of Texas, the Frontier Battalion. It was suspected that Hardin had his wife and children with him, and that he still maintained contact with his family in Texas.

So the State of Texas, recognizing that the rangers had little experience at detective work, wisely hired John R. Duncan to be their detective in the Hardin case. "Jack" Duncan was a Dallas city detective, who was appointed a special ranger and assigned to track down and capture or kill Wes Hardin. Duncan began that work by going to Gonzales County. When he arrived there he made efforts to get close to the father of Hardin's brother-in-law, Neill Bowen, whose son Brown Bowen was also a fugitive and was said to be living in the same area as Hardin. When Duncan learned that Neill Bowen's son Brown was living in Alabama, he returned to Austin. There he and Lieutenant John Barclay Armstrong from the Frontier Battalion, who would represent the State of Texas in any arrest or extradition, obtained train tickets and proceeded to Alabama in search of Bowen and Wes Hardin, who was by now using the name John Swain.[1]

John Wesley Hardin (alias John Swain). Photo taken in Florida or Alabama in 1875. Original is a photo in Hardin's personal photo album. (R.G. McCubbin Collection)

Upon reaching Montgomery, Alabama, more of Duncan's detective work finally located Hardin's residence only a mile north of the Florida state line in the small town of Whiting, Alabama. There was no sign of Brown Bowen. On a visit to Whiting on Aug. 23, 1877, Duncan found out that Hardin had left with several men that same day to gamble in Pensacola, Florida, but was returning by train later that afternoon. They contacted William Chipley, Superintendent of the Pensacola Railroad for assistance. By chance Superintendent Chipley had been in a violent fight with Brown Bowen sometime earlier and hated the man, and immediately contacted Escambia County Sheriff William Hutchinson. Sheriff Hutchinson joined them with several deputies and an arrest was planned to take place in Florida, on the train arriving from Pensacola. The group boarded the train before Whiting, and found John Wesley Hardin seated, smoking his pipe. Hardin was actually leaning back in his seat when Florida Sheriff Hutchinson and his Deputy A. J. Perdue entered the car from behind him and pulled him to the floor. While they were struggling, Lt. Armstrong walked up and slapped Hardin on the head with his pistol, knocking him out and ending any resistance.[2]

A gambling friend of Hardin's named Jim Mann, believing that they were set upon by a band of robbers, pulled his own pistol and attempted to shoot those attacking his friend. He was shot and killed by another Florida deputy, Martin Sullivan. Jim Mann was not wanted for any crime, but if anyone had identified themselves as "the law," Mann had paid no attention. Brown Bowen was not in the crowd with Hardin. His earlier vicious attack on William Chipley was the worst mistake Bowen had committed since coming to Florida, for it made Chipley an enemy who ran him to ground even after the two rangers hurried back to Texas with Hardin. Their haste was understandable; however, they had not really attempted to find Brown Bowen, who was charged with the murder of Thomas J. Haldeman in Texas, a close friend of the Suttons. But through his contacts just a week later, Superintendent Chipley quickly found Bowen in Pensacola. Bowen was then arrested on Sept. 17 and extradition was arranged back to Texas, without the services of any Texas lawmen. He would be tried and convicted of the murder of Haldeman in Gonzales, during October of 1877 and hanged there on May 17, 1878.[3]

Wes Hardin had been arrested and returned to Texas to stand trial for the murder of Comanche County Deputy Sheriff Charles Webb. He was found guilty of murder in the second degree and sentenced at the end of Sept. 1877, to 25 years imprisonment at Huntsville State Penitentiary. He would, however, wait almost another year in the Travis County Jail for a ruling on his appeal. When his sentence was affirmed, he was transferred to the State Penitentiary at Huntsville.[4]

A record of Hardin's conduct in the Texas State Penitentiary confirms that harsh disciplinary punishment began soon after his delivery to the prison. On Jan. 18, 1879, he received 39 lashes for "mutinous conduct", and about a year later on Jan. 9, 188O he received another 2O lashes as punishment for "trying to escape from prison under conspiracy with other convicts." These two examples of harsh disciplinary treatment early in his incarceration apparently led to a change of attitude, for over the next five years he was only written up seven times for "laziness" and "throwing food on the floor." In 1893, he again drew attention to himself when he was punished for "gambling" and "trying to incite convicts to riot and impudence."[5]

Hardin, while confined under sentence for 2nd degree murder, was taken to DeWitt County in 1891, tried and convicted of manslaughter (Cause # 7712) in the killing of James Morgan in 1873. He was sentenced to a two year term, which ran concurrently with the unexpired time of his 25-year sentence for murder. These would be the only two trials and convictions for violent crimes that John Wesley Hardin would be called to account for in his life. The second trial and conviction for manslaughter, actually aided Hardin in his later efforts when requesting a pardon, for it proved that no other jurisdiction in the state planned to indict him for any crime.[6]

After serving 16 years of a 25 year sentence, on Feb. 17, 1894, Hardin would receive a "full pardon" and restoration of citizenship and rights of suffrage, from Jim Hogg, the governor of Texas. John Wesley Hardin, who most agree was the killer of more men than any other in Texas, walked out of prison and into a somewhat appropriate new profession, that of an attorney-at-law.

Several things had become clear in Texas since 1876 when the new state constitution was approved. The first was a new attitude toward law and order in the state government and in many of the counties. More zealous county law enforcement and district criminal courts, along with state governors who believed in using the Frontier Battalion more and more in law enforcement situations would shorten the careers of numerous outlaws. But the state also understood that the rangers oftentimes lacked the ability to do effective detective work and were not above hiring the best from other agencies when needed to assist them. John Wesley Hardin and Brown Bowen were the first of the really bad outlaws in Texas to feel the strong arm of the law, but in rapid succession, they were not the last. The Sutton-Taylor feud had for all practical purposes ended during the waning days of 1875. First, there was the killing of Cuero City Marshal Ruben Brown who was heir-apparent of the Sutton faction, and then a month later the gunning down of Jim Taylor and two friends in Clinton, Texas. An uneasy truce followed.[7]

Bill Longley Brought Back To Hang

Bill Longley had been a wanted man for almost a decade and after his return to Texas, he killed another man, a minister named Roland Lay with a shotgun in 1876. Like Hardin, he soon rode out of Texas as the law got too close. Using the name of Bill Jackson, Longley avoided towns but passed through Nacogdoches and Shelby Counties in East Texas during the Spring of 1877, before crossing the Sabine River into Louisiana. On the way to Shreveport, his destination, he came upon the small town of Keatchie, Louisiana, and there decided to hide out by going to work on W. T. Gamble's farm. Longley must have thought he would never be found in this out of the way place in Louisiana,

William P. (Bill) Longley, photo taken in Galveston jail in 1877, while awaiting appeal in Lee County murder trial. (R.G. McCubbin Collection)

but he could not have been more mistaken, as a newly elected Louisiana constable and a Texas sheriff working together would soon prove him wrong.[8]

June Courtney was a 38 year old native of Alabama, who had been elected constable in a precinct containing the town of Keatchie, Louisiana. Constable Courtney met newcomer Bill Jackson and the two, along with several other men, began hunting foxes together. The longer Courtney talked with Jackson, the more suspicious he became of the man. After he received a wanted poster on Longley, he was convinced that Bill Jackson was actually Bill Longley. Courtney contacted Nacogdoches County Sheriff Milton Mast in nearby Texas, and the two decided to capture Longley for the reward. Mast wrote to Lee County, Texas where an arrest warrant was outstanding and he soon received a capias warrant for the arrest of "William Longley, alias Bill Black, alias Chadwick" and to deliver him to Lee County.

Sheriff Mast and a deputy traveled to Louisiana and arranged for Constable Courtney to talk Longley into helping him "arrest a bad Negro", something they thought Longley would relish and show up for. Constable Courtney was then simply to walk Longley toward the two Texas lawmen so he could be arrested without suspicion. As Courtney and Longley left his house, Courtney drew his pistol as Sheriff Mast and his deputy came forward and arrested Bill Longley. They put leg irons, chains and handcuffs on Longley, practically threw him in a wagon and took him back to Texas. "Bloody Bill" Longley was in the Lee County jail on June 9, 1877.[9]

On a murky Friday morning on Oct. 11, 1878, some 16 months after he was jailed and 13 months after being found guilty of the murder of Wilson Anderson, William Preston Longley's appeal had been denied and he was hanged by the neck in Giddings, Texas. An estimated 2,000 people came to watch the hanging. When the trap door opened, Longley's feet hit the ground before his neck snapped. The sheriff and his deputy quickly drew him up until his feet cleared the ground and he then took nearly seven minutes to strangle to death.[10]

Kill Them All

The last of the so-called Reconstruction outlaws were rapidly being killed off by the end of the 1870s. It was soon the turn of the Horrell Brothers in Lampasas County. Samuel Horrell survived his last gunfight in 1877 and lived to die in bed in Eureka, California on Aug. 3, 1936, but a number of his friends did not. Brother Merritt Horrell was killed by John "Pink" Higgins in a Lampasas saloon in January of 1877. About that same time more family and friends of both sides were involved in gun battles. As a result, Lampasas in 1877, was one of the most deadly places in Texas, when 19 murder indictments were returned by the grand jury in just that one year, in that one county. Then brothers Tom and Mart were shot and killed by a vigilante mob in the jail in Meridian, Texas the next year, where they were being held on suspicion of the murder and robbery of a popular Bosque County merchant, J. F Vaughan.[11]

When that vigilante mob killed Tom and Mart Horrell in Meridian, they were not the only vigilante group active in Texas at that time. Earlier, the Sutton and Taylor families had fought for years taking vigilante justice when possible. West of Fort Worth in Shackelford County another group of vigilantes, in an effort to silence a former sheriff who had ridden with that mob for over a year, had him arrested and brought to the jail in Albany, Texas. On the night of June 22, 1878, the mob entered the Shackelford County jail and shot former Sheriff John Larn, allegedly for cattle theft, but more likely to keep him quiet. It was no different in Mason County, where a lawman had also been a part of that mob.[12]

In Central Texas east of the state capital at Austin, the small railroad depot town of McDade, had a mighty reputation for vigilante activity. It began just after the Civil War when lawlessness and violence became a serious concern in the area. Between 1875 and 1883, some 26 men were killed and several others beaten in different shooting or lynching incidents that occurred in 1875, 1876, 1877 and twice in 1883. That violence was the result of vigilante groups in and around McDade, which lasted until 1912, in a town with so few people that it did not show up in most census lists.[13]

It was a somewhat different breed of outlaw that Texas would experience in the last two decades of the nineteenth century. Some of those new outlaws during the 188Os and 189Os, would sometimes even wear a badge. That is because, some of those handy with a gun when down on their luck, did not hesitate to hold up a bank or a stagecoach. They would also kill others or occasionally each other, or sometimes have a number of cattle in their herds that carried different brands. As accomplished gunmen, they also took up work that allowed them to intimidate those not so expert in handling a six-gun.

In addition to former sheriff John Larn in Shackelford County, who was murdered by a vigilante mob, his deputy John Selman was also accused of stealing cattle from their neighbors. "Long Haired Jim" Courtright, several years after he lost the job of marshal, ran a protection racket in Fort Worth's Hell's Half Acre, until killed by gambler Luke Short. Outside of Texas, the Earp Brothers and Henry Newton Brown would also be accused of crimes while wearing a badge. Brown, a former deputy constable in Tascosa, Texas and before that a Lincoln County New Mexico outlaw, was lynched along with three others, including his deputy, after a failed bank robbery in a nearby county, while he was city marshal in Caldwell, Kansas.[14]

The Frontier Battalion was not immune from the same type of occurrence. That organization also had their share of men using two or three different names during that period, who were always wary of the approaching stranger in the event he might be carrying an arrest warrant with their name on it.

Out on the Texas plains the hostile Indian still made life difficult for the hunter, traveler and the settler. In March of 1877, a group of Comanche Indians had come out of the Indian Territory with a permit from Fort Sill to hunt in Texas. The game they wanted to hunt, however, was the buffalo hunter, or anyone else travelling across Texas, and the livestock from any ranch. Fort Griffin and Rath City, located in northwest Texas near where Abilene is today, were the center of the buffalo hunting trade. When one hunter was killed and scalped and others were attacked, a group of some 40 buffalo hunters left Rath City and tracked the Indians to White Horse Canyon, on the Staked Plains, and a battle began. Neither side won, but a cavalry detachment from Fort Griffin later took up the chase, killed two Indians, captured several more and forced them back to the reservation.[15]

Trouble In Far West Texas

In 1877, El Paso del Norte was a large Mexican town located on the west side of the Rio Grande, or Rio Bravo, only a few miles south of the New Mexico border. The much smaller town of Franklin, Texas, with no more than about 500 population, sat where the Texas town of El Paso would be located in a few years. The years immediately before, during and after the Civil War, saw some very bitter times in that vicinity for both Union and Confederate sympathizers. There was great animosity among some of those in the Anglo-American community over how some had handled themselves during the war and Reconstruction. There was also some animosity between the Anglos and the Mexican-Americans, plus within the Mexican population itself, but cross border marriages and trade were everyday occurrences, and traffic went both ways at the time, which only required a horse or a shallow river crossing site.

In the late 187Os, a stagecoach arriving from San Antonio or Fort Worth three times a week, was one way to visit the area, and it was a journey almost 7OO miles long and fraught with danger. Except for several army posts in between, various Indian tribes ruled the land between those locations and the safe arrival of supplies, mail and travelers was always something to celebrate. In just four years the first railroad would reach El Paso, built from the West coast, and about that same time, the last of the hostile Indians would quit Texas. In 1877 the land and the people along the Rio Grande were little changed from when it was all a part of Mexico. True, there was an elected slate of El Paso County officials holding office including a sheriff, but outside of the influence those officials had around the courthouse, the population and territory in Texas along the upper Rio Grande was largely outside of the influence of elected Anglo lawmen and the courts.

The army saw fit to close Fort Bliss in late 1876, and Fort Quitman was then closed in January of 1877. During that period there was only an occasional U. S. Army command moving through the area that provided any security against hostile Indians. Bliss would be reopened in 1878, when it would first be relocated to some empty buildings in the town of Franklin. Sadly, its reopening would be partially the result of the murder of five American citizens in 1877, by a number of Mexican citizens along with the rioting of hundreds of Mexican-Americans and the looting of the county seat at San Elizario. Those troubles have been called, The Salt War of San Elizario.[16]

THE SALT WAR OF SAN ELIZARIO

The Salt War had its origins almost a decade before the violence occurred in October of 1877. In 1867, Samuel A. Maverick, probably because of a continuing interest in the area which started when he made a trip to El Paso in 1848, and as a holder of a certificate that could be used on any public land, suddenly laid claim to much of the land thought to contain numerous salt deposits. Those salt deposits were located some 1OO miles east of El Paso in an inhospitable part of the Great American Desert. For almost a century they had occasionally been tapped as a source of salt for the people living in the area. Then the shipment of salt from the salt lakes by the people of San Elizario stopped in 1867. Several months later it became known that Maverick's land claim did not cover all of the available salt, and the wagons from San

Elizario began to roll again. More recently several groups in San Elizario had been commercially mining the salt deposits on a small scale.[17]

It is important to understand that the so-called salt war, although at times very violent, was a long struggle between changing groups of equally greedy Mexican-Americans and greedy Anglo-Americans for political and economic power. The struggle centered over the control and ability to take away and sell large amounts of salt from a number of natural salt deposits out in the desert of West Texas. Throughout the length of the violence, it was complicated by repeated examples of trickery, greed and chicanery, and only during the siege in San Elizario did it develop into an armed invasion and murder of United States citizens by foreign nationals.[18]

Charles Howard was an elected district judge in El Paso County and in 1872, he set out to gain control of the salt deposits. Years later, in Sept. of 1877, when several men prepared to travel to the deposits and bring back salt, they were arrested upon order of Howard. This caused a riot in the town of San Elizario and Howard was seized and held for several days. To gain his freedom, he agreed to relinquish control of the salt deposits and four friends, John Atkinson, Jesus Cobos, Charles E. Ellis and Tomas Garcia, signed a $12,000 bond guaranteeing he would keep his word. Howard was released, but a month later and in full view of all present, he murdered Louis Cardis in El Paso, a man whom he blamed for his seizure by the mob and who had been involved in some of the shadier aspects of the salt war for over 10 years. The people in San Elizario then demanded Howard's arrest and forfeiture of his bond, for Louis Cardis had also been their patron. Howard was arrested and placed in jail, and the El Paso area was in turmoil.[19]

As a result, the commander of the Frontier Battalion, Major John B. Jones was sent to that still remote town of El Paso, by railway to Topeka, Kansas and Santa Fe, New Mexico and finally by stage to El Paso. At the time, there was no ranger command in far West Texas and Jones had been told to ready an existing company for service there. Jones, in a decision he surely would regret, decided that El Paso was too remote to move an existing company there. Instead, in a matter of just a few days he organized a new 24 man command of the Frontier Battalion, called a "Detachment of Company C," under a newly commissioned Captain John B. Tays. That decision would turn out to be one of his worst mistakes made by Jones while in charge of the Frontier Battalion. It was a major miscalculation of how deeply held the feelings of hatred and greed were by both groups of antagonists involved in the salt war. Major Jones newly formed ranger company would be caught in between. After the organization of the ranger command, Howard was taken before a magistrate and arraigned for murder and allowed bail, another mistake. Major Jones then rode away from the area too soon, leaving his hastily recruited and inexperienced detachment involved in a very volatile situation.[20]

In December of 1877, 16 wagons left San Elizario to collect salt from the salt deposits. Judge Howard, now out on bail, foolishly traveled to San Elizario to file suit to gain control of the salt when it arrived back from the desert. His arrival was noted and when an armed mob of some 350 people rioted, he took refuge in the local government quarters. But no violence had yet happened. The group trapped were all Anglo-Americans and included a county judge, a justice of the peace, two other respected local citizens and the newly organized Frontier Battalion command. The mob was made up of local Mexican-Americans and it is believed up to some 150 people who had crossed the river from nearby Mexico.[21]

When called on to come to the aid of the American citizens and to help prevent any violence, the sheriff of El Paso County found it initially impossible to raise a local posse because of the fear caused by the reported size of the mob. On two occasions, elements of the United States 9th Cavalry and the 15th Infantry Regiments, which were on detached duty in the El Paso area and commanded by Captain Thomas Blair came near San Elizario. In a display of cowardice and bad judgment, Blair refused to go to the aid of those trapped American officials and rangers, although the military were obviously better organized and armed than the mob. In effect, the army's refusal to provide relief to those in San Elizario assured the violent death of some or all trapped there.[22]

The violence associated with the siege of the Anglo-Americans already in San Elizario began on Dec. 13, 1877, with the sudden killing of one of Charles Howard's friends and bondsmen, Charles Ellis. Ellis was seized, hacked to death and then mutilated. The ranger command next came under fire and about mid-day, 4th Sergeant Conrad E. Mortimer of the Frontier Battalion was killed by rifle fire. Four days later during a cease-fire, Charles Howard proposed that he would surrender, "as it is the only chance to save our lives, but they will kill me." When the group surrendered, all were told there would be no more violence, but that Howard would have to give up his claim to the salt.

Although promised that he would not be molested, Howard knew the kind of men who fought against him and as he had predicted, he was executed by a firing squad. Whatever one might think about Charles Howard, he and the other men executed would die bravely. John Atkinson, another of Howard's bondmen, was the next to be executed by the mob, but he was shot eight times before finally killed. John E. McBride, who had previously acted as an agent of Howard', and was now a member of Tay's ranger command, was also executed. Although Captain Tays later claimed he had not surrendered his command, the rest of the rangers surrendered their weapons and all were allowed to ride away. The mob remained to plunder and destroy the town of San Elizario.[23]

After the mob looted San Elizario and the rangers returned to the scene with a sheriff's posse, they recovered the bodies of those killed. In the aftermath, few felt the wrath of the state and federal government over the riot and murder of five American citizens. The Salt War of San Elizario was a sorry spectacle by most participants. Few of those who played a part could have been very proud of their actions. But it was those elements of the 9th Cavalry and 15th Infantry Regiments commanded by Captain Thomas Blair of the U. S. Army who failed to answer a call for help from Texas state troops and American civilians, who emerge from this debacle as the most tarnished.[24]

Another Outlaw Bites The Dust

One Texas outlaw whose reputation far exceeds his criminal accomplishments is Sam Bass, who was born in 1851 on a farm in Indiana. Orphaned before he was 13, he lived five years with an uncle before escaping and working his way to Texas. He arrived in Denton during the summer of 1870, when he was 19 years old. Bass seems to have perfected few skills, after a fast horse that he had acquired and raced, called the Denton Mare, played out. He and several others then agreed to drive a small heard of cattle to Dodge City, but then pushed the cattle further north to South Dakota where they finally sold the cattle. Instead of returning home, they took the owner's money and gambled it away in Deadwood. By 1877, he and the men with whom he now surrounded himself began to rob stagecoaches and then a Union Pacific passenger train which gained them some recognition in their new calling. That recognition then caused some to be killed by lawmen chasing them. The gang then broke up and Bass managed to make his way back to Texas.[25]

Sam Bass. Only authentic image of Bass, believed to have been taken in the summer of 1876 in Dallas, Texas. (R.G. McCubbin Collection)

During late 1877 and the spring of 1878, Sam Bass and the new gang he formed stopped two stagecoaches and held up four trains in North Texas, all near Dallas. The gang, reportedly, had little success at finding much loot during their robberies, but were very successful in attracting most of the lawmen in North Texas to their trail. A number of county sheriffs formed posses and the Frontier Battalion formed a special command, all chasing after Bass and his gang. The gang rode south headed for the small town of Round Rock, some 25 miles north of Austin, planning to rob the bank. During that time, however, an informer wrote Major John B. Jones divulging the gang's plans.[26]

On July 19, Bass and the men who rode with him were caught up in a deadly gun battle at Round Rock. Williamson County Deputy Sheriff A. W. Grimes, who first approached the gang members was quickly killed and Travis County Deputy Maurice B. Moore, who Major Jones had brought with him from Austin, was wounded. The few rangers in town then took up the battle, killing one gang member, while two others rode out of Round Rock. One of those was Sam Bass, who was badly wounded. The day after the battle, Bass was found mortally wounded in a pasture north of town and died the next day.[27]

Sam Bass was not very good in his only profession, that of train, stagecoach and bank robber. He saw little money and did not last long on the job. Yet, he is one of the most recognizable outlaws in the history of the state.

THE VIOLENCE SLOWS

Sam Bass should have looked around a little harder for a profession that he might excel in, for some other would-be outlaws were apparently doing just that. As the year 1878 came to a close, almost a decade of unbridled outlawry in the Lone Star State began to slow. In just two years, 1877 and 1878, John Wesley Hardin was arrested, convicted and placed in prison for 25 years, while Bill Longley was finally hanged in Giddings. Hardin's brother-in-Law, Bowen Brown was also brought back from Florida and hanged in Gonzales, Texas, for a murder he committed nearby. Sam Bass and his gang had a very short outlaw career in Texas, and were shot to pieces in Round Rock.

A close look at the troubles in Mason County in the 187Os are covered in some detail in Appendix A. So it enough to say that, out in Mason County all of the steam had gone out of the so-called Mason County War, as new lawmen were elected who refused to ride with and support the mob; on the other side of that war, George Gladden was in Huntsville for life, Scott Cooley was dead and John Ringo was in jail indicted for murder.

In South Texas, another important gunman named King Fisher had been arrested for murder and livestock theft and stood trial in 1877. When he was released after avoiding conviction, he would reform and a few years later be appointed a deputy sheriff, then became the acting sheriff of Uvalde County. In Lampasas, three of the four Horrell brothers lay dead from gunfire and the Higgins-Horrell feud was over. So were the feuds in Shackelford and DeWitt Counties.

Of great importance to the future well being of the State of Texas was that the most violent of outlaws, the Reconstruction outlaws, were almost all dead, in jail, or had fled the state. By almost any measurement, acts of indiscriminate violence and wanton killings across Texas following the Civil War declined between 1879 and 1881. In some areas acts of violence would abate only briefly for by the mid-188Os, crime across much of Texas would again increase. But, much of the violence that would take place in the last two decades of the nineteenth century would be committed by men who were individually less prominent, and had not gained much of their reputation as standing in defiance of the military occupation. As a result, few outlaws in the 188Os and 189Os would attract the following earlier gunmen did. In other states, gangs headed by Reconstruction outlaws and outlaw families would also fall on hard times.[28]

Sam Bass may have actually been the first of that new breed of outlaw, instead of the last of the old breed as he is often portrayed. For those victims of violence that would take place in the future, however, that violence was just as unwanted and just as fatal as that committed by the more vicious outlaws just after the Civil War. But, by the end of the 187Os, law enforcement and the courts were obviously winning their initial battles against outlaws in many areas of Texas; it would take much more effort and many more years to even begin to bring the rule of law to most of the Lone Star State. There were, of course, exceptions as to the reduction of violence and crime on the Texas frontier after 1878, and one of those exceptions would be in the isolation of West Texas.

In August of 1879, with a wife, two daughters and six rangers from the Frontier Battalion as escorts, Lieutenant George Baylor left San Antonio and set out on the long and lonely trip to El Paso. They spent 42 days on the road, arriving in and making the town of Ysleta their headquarters. Baylor would take over the remnants of Lieutenant Tays' company that had been treated so badly during the salt war and continue to chase Indians in Far West Texas. The U. S. Army was also still stationed in a number of garrisons and they were on patrol across the western frontier of Texas. They would cross into Mexico several times in 1877 to chase cattle rustlers. But the final slaughter of the buffalo, the coming of the railroads, the building of more towns and increased settlement, particularly around existing military posts, along with better policing around the reservations in Indian Territory, meant that the Indian's reign of terror was almost over in Texas.

In the Texas Panhandle, Captain G. W. Arrington of the Frontier Battalion was also still chasing hostile Indians, and in September of 1879, he moved his command in Company C to a new camp site on the White River in Crosby County. From that base, Arrington and a ranger command would for the first time chase hostile Indians out across the arid Staked Plains and into New Mexico, and return without losing a man. The result of that chase was significant in that they would find the route and the water holes that hostile Indians had used to reach Northwest Texas from New Mexico, and then return without fear of being run down. Captain Arrington's exploration into New Mexico during a 30 day journey in December of 1879 and January of 1880 put an effective end to the Indian's use of that war trail.[29]

The next few years would see many changes occurring across the state. One significant change that would occur was in the Texas Panhandle, where the first county, Wheeler County, had been organized in 1878. That would signal the opening of a large and important region of Texas to cattle ranching and settlement of an increasing number of towns, particularly along the long ribbons of steel being laid on the different railroad right-of-ways.

CHAPTER VIII
THE VIOLENCE RETURNS
THE 1880s

TEXAS BEGINS TO SORT ITSELF OUT

Thirty-five years after annexation, the census of 1880 confirms that Texas had a population of just over one and one-half million people, and was the eleventh most populous state. But, Texas was still a rural state and less than 10 percent of its population lived in an urban setting. During the decade of the 1880s, however, the number of Texas towns would double in number. Though most were small towns they were conveniently located and most supported several hotels, shops, a doctor or two, schools, a bank and many provided comfort to any traveler. As one might expect, Texas had drawn most of its population since the Civil War from the defeated South. Both families and individuals from Alabama, Mississippi and Louisiana made up most of the immigrants moving to the already settled parts of the state, while those arriving from Tennessee and further north seem to have favored the less settled areas in west and north Texas. Between 1880 and 1882, more German, Austrian and Czech immigrants also arrived in Texas. There were so many that by 1887, there would be over 129,000 Germans in Texas, a larger number of foreign born immigrants than from nearby Mexico.[1]

Although most of the trade with Texas had historically entered the state through its Gulf of Mexico ports, railroads entering Texas from Kansas now made Grayson County in North Texas, the most populous county in the state in 1880, with just over 38,000 people. There, a higher percentage, some 30 percent lived in the towns of Sherman and Denison than in the countryside. Grayson County with four railways crossing the county had developed into a major gateway to Texas for those arriving from the north, and for trade with St. Louis and the East. There had been settlements in the area since 1833. While this area was booming, it also had more than its share of problems with crime and criminals beginning in the late 1870s and extending into the 1880s, when it lost an unusually large number of its lawmen, eight, to foul play.[2]

In other parts of Texas, Fayette and Washington Counties both had over 27,000 population each, but neither had a town of any consequence within their county at that time. The largest town in Texas in 1880 was Galveston, with a population of just over 22,000. San Antonio, headquarters for all federal military forces in Texas, was the second largest city with 20,550 people. As if to confirm its rural heritage, there were only six other towns throughout the rest of the state that had populations of over 6,000 people.[3]

By the 1880s, churches were an important part of the ideological and social life in Texas. They preached the Old Testament which was appropriate, for much of Texas saw itself as still truly beset by heathen enemies. There were already laws on the book that forbad the interruption of church services. Those laws were enforced in the rough frontier towns as well as in the more established communities in East and Central Texas. While some communities in the late 1870s had passed laws meant to reduce gambling, the carrying of firearms, playing cards in a public place and keeping a disorderly house, the Texas Blue Laws only became widespread after 1881.[4]

Blue laws were those laws passed at the state level, making many previously inappropriate and immoral acts, now criminal offenses. Those included arrest for using abusive language, working at certain retail trades on Sunday, seduction and selling intoxicating or spirituous liquor on Sundays, to minors, or on voting day. There were also the county-option laws, which when passed made the sale of any alcoholic beverage in some county precincts illegal. The enforcement of a few of those laws by a number of sheriffs and constables only became popular just before election time, otherwise some lawmen largely ignored their enforcement, while others never failed to uphold all laws.[5]

Because many of the gambling and alcoholic beverage indictments were misdemeanor offenses, it became common practice to present all of those indictments at just one, or at the most during two, settings of the grand jury each year. Most were then transferred to a lesser court for pleading, trial and sentencing. The number of repeat offenders in that type of crime was overwhelming, for bad habits, even if suddenly against the law, would die slowly, if at all. It was not unusual even in some sparsely settled counties to return as many as 40 indictments each year for gambling and another 25 or more for different liquor offenses. The record may go to Burnet County, where with a population of barely 7,000 persons, 87 separate indictments for gambling offenses were issued in 1881. In addition, between six and 15 persons were typically indicted for unlawful carrying of a pistol in those counties where this was a violation of the law during the 1880s.[6]

A Dangerous Place In Which To Live

A rare opportunity to examine the number and disposition of criminal cases tried in courts of record across Texas is provided by a little known compilation by the Attorney-General's office for the five years ending Dec. 31, 1887. While there are some problems with using some of that information without a detailed explanation of the data, an analysis of the murder cases in that compilation is rather straight forward. In the State of Texas during that five years (1883-1887) there were 2,101 murder indictments (averaging 420 murders per year). Of those 2,101 people indicted for murder, 1,282, or 60 percent of those were then tried for murder. Then, 558, or 43 percent of those who were tried, were convicted of murder. Based upon the above information, the Crime Rate calculated for murder ("rate" refers to the number of crimes per 100,000 population) for each of those five years averaged 24.7 murders per 100,000 population, which for comparison purposes is a rate approximately four times higher than the Texas murder rate in the year 2000. It is also 1.4 times higher than Texas murder rates in 1980, when murder rates were at an all time high of 16.9 murders per 100,000 population, the highest year since records have been kept. Texas in the 1880s was indeed a dangerous place in which to live.[7]

Looking back at the total number of murder indictments during the mid-1880s, only some 27 percent of those 2,101 indicted were tried and convicted of murder. Of those 558 who were indicted and then convicted of murder, 56 were given the death penalty (40 later affirmed after appeal) and 135 were sentenced to life imprisonment. Those whose sentences were not affirmed, along with the remaining 367 convicted of murder, would have served some number of years of imprisonment or had their cases successfully appealed and then either dismissed or remanded.[8]

When the railroads began to cross Texas in the late 1870s and early 1880s, they did much to bring civilization to the frontier by way of the towns that grew up along their right of ways. Between 1870 and 1880, railroad mileage in Texas increased from 591 miles to over three thousand miles. This is important, for no matter how often a stage coach, wagon train or group of riders crossed the arid wastes of West Texas, there were few safe places to stop and build a future without a permanent town and place to acquire water and supplies in the vicinity. The railroads made that possible. Settlement of many areas on the frontier still went slowly, for no one still had figured out how to make it rain in West Texas. Some seemed to almost forget that fact, because the early 1880s were wet years in much of Texas. But the dry years that soon began, plus the Great Blizzard of 1886 and the deep drought that followed during 1886 and 1887 would remind all of the need for rain, for many Texans still made and lost much of their money off the land.[9]

In contrast to much of Texas that showed significant population growth in the 1880 census, in the Texas Panhandle and on the Staked Plains, there were still less than 2,000 people counted in some 20 organized and unorganized counties. At that same time, however, there were already more than 100,000 sheep and an estimated 97,236 head of cattle grazing in the Texas Panhandle. Six years later there would be an estimated 300,000 head of cattle scattered across that same area. Wheeler County, the first county in the Texas Panhandle to be organized in 1879, by the next year had a population of 512. Oldham County, which would not be organized until Jan. 12, 1881, already had 387 people in 1880. Nearby Floyd and Randall Counties with an official population of just three people each in 1880, were almost a decade away from their official organization.[10]

Cattle ranching was beginning to be such an important industry in the Texas Panhandle that the Canadian River Cattlemen's Association, later named the Panhandle Stock Association of Texas, was formed. Fearing the expansion of a range war and level of cattle theft similar to that in Lincoln County, New Mexico, the Canadian River Cattlemen's Association already had a representative in Lincoln County to watch events. On Nov. 22, 1880 they sent just over a dozen men from Texas to help Lincoln

County Sheriff Pat Garrett chase and capture or kill stock thief Billy the Kid and those who rode with him.[11]

THE LAST INDIAN RAIDS

Around El Paso in far West Texas, during the month of January, 1881, newly promoted Captain Baylor of Company A of the Frontier Battalion set out to investigate what appeared to have been an Indian raid that killed several people on the stagecoach in Quitman Canyon, 1OO miles southeast of El Paso. Baylor took 15 men from his own company, received help from Lieutenant Charles Nevill's command from Fort Davis along with Pueblo Indian scouts. After a long chase, they caught up with the Apache raiders in the Diablo Mountains. On the morning of Jan. 29, 1881, Baylor's command killed four warriors, two women and two children. Several escaped, but all appeared to have been wounded and were given little chance to survive in the middle of winter without food or water.[12]

That action in the Diablo Mountains has long been reputed to have been the last Indian fight in Texas, but that appears to be less than an accurate assessment of events going on in the state. A little over three months later on April 24, Lipan Apaches raided along the Rio Frio, above Uvalde, Texas. A number of horses were stolen and a Mrs. McLauren was killed during the fight with the Indians. On May 3, 1881, Lieutenant John L. Bullis and 36 Seminole-Negro scouts from Fort Clark, having crossed into Mexico after those same Indians, attacked their camp. They killed four men, and captured one woman and a child and recovered 21 stolen horses.[13]

Many of the books written about rangers in Texas in the early 188Os and 189Os, talk somewhat wistfully about the vanishing frontier and the changing role of the Frontier Battalion in the last two decades of the nineteenth century. Walter Prescott Webb suggested that the "Frontier Battalion should have been disbanded-because the frontier was gone." If the frontier was only judged by the presence of hostile Indians, he was accurate. But, hostile Indians in Texas had actually been few and far between since the U. S. Army's punitive campaigns in the Texas Panhandle in 1874. This did not make the rangers and the U. S. Army's efforts at protecting Texans against the relatively few but still deadly raiders that came out of Indian Territory Reservations or from Mexico any less important or vital to those without any other protection. To protect the frontier in the mid-1880s, the U. S. Army still maintained 13 forts and some 2,600 troops along the Rio Grande and in West Texas.[14]

A Close Look At Crime In The Lone Star State

At the end of 1888, Adjutant General King compiled information regarding the "Operations of Frontier Battalion from May, 1874, to Nov. 30, 1888." This extremely valuable and little known compilation, provides us with a rare statistical look at the operations of the Frontier Battalion from its formation for the first 14 years and six months of its life. The Frontier Battalion's own records claim that they had participated in 56 engagements with outlaws and Indians and that fourteen rangers were killed, averaging slightly less than one per year and another 17 were wounded. During that same period they killed 69 outlaws and 35 Indians, plus wounded 27 more outlaws and 12 Indians. They also captured 77 outlaws and four Indians. Their own records further explain that during that period, they tracked down 72 escaped convicts, appeared in court 240 times and caught 75 fence cutters. Also among those they hunted during those 14 plus years, were 512 murderers and 463 other violent criminals. They also went after 1,669 cattle, horse and other thieves and recovered 11,580 cattle and horses.[15]

It was recognized in the Texas Penal Code during the 1880s, that certain criminal acts were more serious than others, and not only the more violent crimes. The punishment for conviction of the theft of a horse, calf, mule, hog or coil of rope, were now different. The revised laws said that the type of punishment for theft depended not only on what was stolen but on the value of what was stolen. The theft of a horse, because they were normally more valuable, carried the greatest penalty of from five to 15 years in the State Penitentiary when convicted. It was still not a hanging offense. The records of many indictments filed across Texas also tried to establish those guidelines by descriptions of what had been stolen: "a mare," "a colt," "a pig," so much lumber, or an amount of money was now used to establish the value of what was stolen, often right in the indictment.[16]

The fight against crime and a new breed of criminal in Texas in the 1880s was not just centered on the frontier, for many areas in East and North Texas were now more dangerous than the frontier. In many counties and towns across Texas, local lawmen and prosecutors again saw an increase in the number of crimes committed. One of those areas where violence had not decreased for long was in Grayson County, now the most populous county in Texas. Over a 17 year period from 1873 to 1889, eight local lawmen and were murdered in that area.[17]

The first lawman killed during that period was Grayson County Deputy Constable, John Stark, on March 1, 1873. On July 4, 1879, Constable James C. Nelms was murdered in Precinct #2. On May 5, 1881, Dallas Hodges, constable in Precinct #7, approached two men as they rode through the small community of Gordonville in northeast Grayson County. When Hodges identified himself, both men drew pistols, shot and killed the constable and escaped across the Red River into Indian Territory. Two months later on July 8, the two murderers were tracked down to a house in Indian Territory almost 100 miles north of Sherman, Texas. The posse consisted of three deputies and five other men, including two of Dallas Hodges' brothers. They traded shots with the two murderers and four other men they had surrounded. One of the Hodges brothers was wounded and Grayson County Deputy Sheriff R. D. Coleman was killed when the desperados shot their way out of the house and through the posse to make their escape.[18]

During that same period it was no safer for lawmen in the two larger towns of Grayson County. Denison Police Officer Charles Patman was killed in a saloon during an attempt to disarm a local man on May 5, 1875. On Oct. 30, 1879, another Denison policeman, Joseph E. Johnson, and Constable Spence went to a home to arrest Frank Porter for theft. Before Porter could be searched he doused the lights and fired shots at the officers. Constable Spence returned fire, but Porter shot and killed Officer Johnson and escaped in the darkness. Three months later in the neighboring town of Sherman, City Marshal Samuel Ball was escorting a young man named Alf Johnson out of a local saloon where he and others had been causing a disturbance. As they stepped outside Johnson pulled a pistol and shot Marshal Ball at close range in the right side of his chest. Ball, who was a hard man and had been involved in previous shootings, jerked the pistol from the man's hand and shot Johnson three times with his own weapon, killing him on the spot. As this happened, Alf Johnson's brother fired a wild shot in Marshal Ball's face, which missed but blinded him with the powder from his bullet, allowing his assailant to escape. Ball would die six days later, on Feb. 2,

1880, as a result of the wound to the chest.[19]

Finally, two-time elected Grayson County Sheriff Robert L. May, was shot and killed on May 26, 1889 in the small town of Howe, some 12 miles south of Sherman. Sheriff May was killed by shots fired by Benjamin Isom, who had been disarmed earlier by a local man. Benjamin apparently was given another weapon by his cousin, Mandrew Isom, and he shot and killed Sheriff May when he arrived at the scene. Benjamin Isom received a life sentence and Mandrew was sentenced to 40 years in the State Penitentiary as an accessory.[20]

If the death of those eight lawmen in a relatively short period of time in just one Texas county had anything in common, it was that none of the killers, with the possible exception of those who fled into Indian Territory, were noted gunmen or wanted outlaws. Unless they were already running from the law, three of the eight killers would have been released after payment of a small fine for the problems they were involved in before they shot a lawman. The fourth, if found guilty of theft, would likely have spent only a short time in jail or paid a fine. The way those offenders had been handled by the lawmen they killed also indicated that the officers did not consider the men dangerous. But shots fired from their weapons killed the officer just as dead as if Bloody Bill Longley or John Wesley Hardin had pulled the trigger. The type of murderer seen in this examination of eight murders in Grayson County in the 1870s and 1880s would be very similar to most violent crimes committed in Texas over the last two decades in the nineteenth century. It might be said that the profile of the typical killer over that 20 years was that they resembled someone thought to be no more dangerous than your next door neighbor.

Some Also Killed For Money A Century Ago

One Texas gunman who would first come to the notice of Texas lawmen in the 1880s, was not like your next door neighbor, unless your next door neighbor killed a dozen men and during much of his life worked as a killer for hire. That man was James B. Miller, sometimes known as Deacon, or Killing Jim. Like Bill Longley and Wes Hardin almost two decades earlier, Jim Miller killed his first man in Coryell County while he was still 17 years old. As a harbinger of evil deeds to come, Miller's first victim was his brother-in-law, John Coop, who was sleeping outside his home on the porch when Miller walked up and shot him in the head following an earlier disagreement. He was arrested, tried for murder and convicted, but after winning an appeal was released and never retried.[21]

Miller left the area and three years later, was working on the Emmanuel "Mannen" Clements ranch in Runnels County, just south of Abilene. Clements was a cousin of John Wesley Hardin and also related by marriage to the Taylor family, of the Sutton-Taylor feud. Both Clements and Hardin rode with the Taylors more than once. Mannen Clements was never directly implicated in rounding up the stolen cattle that Joe Hardin and his gang were involved in before they were lynched in 1874 in Comanche County. But that was less than 75 miles away, so he most likely played some part. He had already taken several cattle herds to Kansas. Wes Hardin went along on one of them and was said to have murdered more than one man while on the trail. When Runnels County was organized in 1887, Mannen Clements ran for sheriff, but was shot and killed in the Senate Saloon by a political rival, Ballinger City Marshal Joe Townsend.[22]

A short time later, Townsend was riding home one night when he was shot out of the saddle by a shotgun blast. Townsend did not die, but his left arm was so badly mangled that it had to be amputated. Although suspected, Jim Miller was not arrested, but soon left the area and moved to Pecos, Texas. He would continue to visit the Clements ranch often, for he married Mannen Clements daughter, Sallie, in 1888. That made him related by marriage to John Wesley Hardin. Miller lived a peaceful life after his marriage, but he would again attract the attention of lawmen in the 189Os.[23]

Out in New Mexico one killer (who like Jim Miller more resembled those in Texas a decade earlier), had been captured and put in jail with the assistance of a number of Texas gunmen, who had been sent into Lincoln County by the Panhandle Stock Association of Texas. Billy the Kid then shot his way out of jail and went into hiding. Then on July 14, 1881, largely as a result of a tip received by John W. Poe, a stock detective for the Stock Association, Sheriff Pat Garrett shot and killed Billy in Fort Sumner, New Mexico.[24]

On July 19, 1881, John B. Jones died. After leading the Frontier Battalion since its formation in 1874, he had been appointed Adjutant General two years before his death. During the time Jones served as Adjutant General he was involved with supervising not only the Frontier Battalion but other state troops, including organizing various regiments and brigades that would be the forerunner to the final organization of the Texas National Guard. John B. Jones was the most important lawman in Texas during those critical years in the 1870s, despite the fact that he has been criticized for sometimes committing critical errors while leading the Frontier Battalion. Regardless, he still gave vital direction to, and instilled the necessary discipline in that unit, especially as they made the transition from Indian fighter to peace officer. About the time Jones died, several of the better known ranger captains resigned and also left state service. Within a short time, former ranger captains G. W. Arrington, Charles L. Nevill and T. L. Oglesby all resigned and would be elected sheriffs, respectively of Wheeler, Presidio and Maverick Counties.[25]

Texas had long suffered from a lack of secure county jails. By the mid-1880s, however, that problem had been largely overcome and many sheriffs now maintained a secure county jail. Another indication as to the incidence of crime is that during 1887, a total of 13,153 people were incarcerated in Texas county jails. Most of those locked up (3,650 or 28 percent) were held on a charge of some type of theft. There were also 734 people held on murder charges and when taken with another 1,872 incarcerated for robbery, assault and rape, a total of 20 percent or 2,606 of those incarcerated in 1887 were charged with some violent crime. Five counties would lead the list of those holding the most men in their county jails during 1887: Dallas (863), Harris (763), Bexar (431), Fannin (416) and McLennan (402). All counties containing large cities, except Fannin County. Those charged with murder during 1887, were concentrated in Bexar with 25, Robertson with 21 and then 18 prisoners each in Cherokee, Lamar and Trinity County jails. The large number of those charged with murder and held in Trinity County, a small rural East Texas county with only some 7,000 population is the most surprising. But all Texas counties did not have a full jail, for in reply to questions asked concerning those incarcerated in their county jails during 1887, some replied as follows: Kendall County advised that "crime was almost unknown;" Newton County wrote that "the sheriffs office do not contain the name of a single person as being incarcerated in the jail in 1887," and San Patricio County advised that "only one person was incarcerated in the county jail," that year.[26]

Bringing Law And Order To Far West Texas

In El Paso, if the hostile Indian was no longer a major threat to most Texans, a host of men handy with the six-shooter would prove to be. Captain George Baylor was one ranger captain who usually avoided confrontation with outlaws. Upon arrival in El Paso County in 1879 he had chosen the smaller town of Ysleta, at that time the county seat, as his headquarters. It was quieter than El Paso, but by doing so he had also appeared to have left a greater number of Texas citizens unprotected. When he had first arrived on the Rio Grande he had also chosen not to punish anyone for the riots and the murder of several citizens and two rangers during the salt war. As a result, there were a number of people in El Paso and Austin, plus serving rangers who severely criticized Baylor for that lack of action, and later for the lack of discipline shown by many of those in his command.[27]

The citizens of El Paso would, however, not let George Baylor ignore them. As the first railroad to reach El Paso slowly approached, the people there had such poor local law enforcement that they called upon the governor for help. Baylor was directed in January of 1881 to send several rangers to El Paso to help keep the peace. On April 11 of that same year, Dallas Stoudenmier was sworn in as the new City Marshal of El Paso. The city fathers had every reason to expect their 6' 4" marshal would tame the town, for Stoudenmier arrived in El Paso having already fought in the Civil War and he had also served briefly under Captain Waller in Old Company A of the Frontier Battalion for about seven months.[28]

On April 12, 1881, Baylor was approached by the Jefe politico from across the river in Paso del Norte to help his men search for 3O head of cattle stolen from his ranch in nearby Mexico and driven across the river near El Paso. Baylor refused to go himself and sent just one ranger to accompany those searching for the missing cattle. Two days later, more Mexican cowboys returned to El Paso, only this time they were also looking for two of their friends who had originally come looking for the stolen cattle and stayed behind to continue searching. This time Constable Gus Krempkau, who had come to El Paso as a member of the Frontier Battalion with Baylor from San Antonio two years before, and ranger Fitch accompanied the group in their search. When they reached John Hale's ranch, the two men they were looking for were found murdered, probably as they ate what was to be their

Dallas Stoudenmier, El Paso Town Marshal standing. Those sitting are unidentified. (Author's Collection)

last meal two days before.[29]

Ranger Fitch went to find John Hale and two of his cowboys who had been heard bragging about the killings the day before. Constable Krempkau brought the bodies back to El Paso for a coroners inquest. When the inquest recessed for lunch, City Marshal Dallas Stoudenmier who had attended, wandered away to eat his noon meal. Suddenly Hale and former City Marshal George W. Campbell, began complaining about Krempkau's testimony which they said would lead to the indictment of Hale's self-confessed cowboys for murder. Gus Krempkau was in hearing distance and challenged Campbell to explain himself. Campbell told Krempkau that he had no problem with his conduct and moved to mount his horse and ride away. As he started to mount, Hale, who had been drinking and was somewhat hidden by the horse, pulled his pistol and shot Constable Krempkau in the chest. Krempkau pulled his own gun from its holster and shot Hale.[30]

A few moments later the door of the Globe Restaurant flew open and Marshal Dallas Stoudenmier came running out. He pulled his revolver from its holster and fired a quick shot at John Hale who was already mortally wounded, but his bullet missed Hale and hit a man further down the street who died the next day. About that time, the dying Gus Krempkau shot again, this time hitting George Campbell in the foot. Almost immediately Stoudenmier shot him in the right arm and Campbell dropped his pistol. As he attempted to pick it up, Dallas Stoudenmier shot him through the body wounding him fatally. Hale and Krempkau had both died after each shot the other in the opening moments of the gun battle. So in less time than it takes to tell this story, four men were left dead or mortally wounded in the streets of El Paso.[31]

On May 28, 1881, the Southern Pacific's first train arrived in El Paso on rails that had been built from the West Coast to Yuma and across the Arizona and New Mexico desert. This line would then continue to be built east out of El Paso to Sierra Blanca, where in December of 1881, it would connect with the Texas & Pacific railroad that had begun laying tracks out of Ft. Worth in April of 1880. A second railroad line would soon be built from El Paso through the desert to Alpine, Marathon, Del Rio, and finally connecting with another line being built out of San Antonio.[32]

Just a few days after those four men died on El Paso Street, Marshal Stoudenmier was involved in a second gunfight when he shot and killed the man he replaced as city marshal, William Johnson. Johnson had attempted to assassinate Stoudenmier on a dark street, but his shotgun blast missed and he died instead, shot almost a dozen times. Stoudenmier's easy use of firearms had one quick effect, it sent much of the underworld riding out of El Paso and north into New Mexico. He also did a credible job in managing the jail and the various paper work required. About a year later Dallas Stoudenmier was fired as El Paso's marshal, largely due to his drinking and abrasive personality. Although then appointed a Deputy U. S. Marshal, the Manning brothers killed him in El Paso on Sept. 18, 1882.[33]

The Fight Against Crime Goes On

As so often happened in the past, the capture of criminals was not always left only to the uniformed police officer. Some communities ably assisted their lawmen in the capture of outlaws, while some took revenge when the wrong man won the gun battle. Less than two weeks before Christmas of 1882, Waxahachie Deputy Marshal L. K. Allen broke up a confrontation between two men on the courthouse square. One of them, Charles Smith, appeared drunk and Deputy Marshal Allen attempted to arrest him. Instead of going quietly, Smith broke away and ran down College Street toward the railroad. Allen chased him as Smith pulled a pistol and they began a running gun battle. When Deputy Allen ran out of bullets he took cover, but about that time the two men were overtaken by City Marshal John H. Spalding who was mounted on a horse and he attempted to arrest Smith. As Spalding dismounted, he was shot and killed by Charles Smith. Smith then turned and attempted to escape, but the gun fight and killing of Marshal Spalding had been witnessed by hundreds of people who then chased Smith and cornered him in an outdoor privy. Smith refused to surrender and was shot a number of times by several men in the crowd who carried shotguns. He died on the spot.[34]

In Karnes County on the day after Christmas in 1884, Sheriff Edgar Leary was alone when he arrested the first of two men in a disturbance taking place in a saloon in the town of Helena, about eight miles northeast of the county seat. After jailing a man named McDonald, Sheriff Leary went back to Helena to arrest the second man, Emmet Butler. Butler stayed in the saloon drinking until the sheriff returned and then ran out through the back door,

Austin City Marshal Ben Thompson in uniform with other officials, circa 1881. (Texas State Library & Archives Commission)

shooting the sheriff as they both got outside. The shooting was seen by several and one man shot and wounded Butler, who was still able to mount his horse and begin to ride away. Emmet Butler rode no more than 50 yards, when another bystander shot him through the head and killed him.[35]

Back in 1851, Ben Thompson's family had left England and immigrated to Austin, Texas. He lived there almost 10 years before beginning a vagabond life moving around the West over the next two decades. Thompson was well known as a gambler, saloon keeper, Texas Ranger and gunman. During those years he returned often to Austin and in 1881 ran for Austin city marshal and won. Ben Thompson was no stranger to violence and is credited with having been in, and survived 14 gunfights and killing several men. Thompson was said to have been an excellent peace officer, but resigned in 1882 after killing Jack Harris in Harris's theatre and club in San Antonio. After he resigned as Austin city marshal he began drinking heavily and on March 22, 1884, met King Fisher, who was now a deputy sheriff in Uvalde County and in Austin on business. Both men took the train to San Antonio that day and attended a play. They later visited the Theatre where Thompson had killed Jack Harris two years before and after a fight in a back room with several employees, Thompson and Fisher were shot and killed.[36]

By 1884, just over a decade after barbed wire was invented, many were stringing the wire around both small and large pastures, as much to keep things in as keep them out. Almost as soon as it began to go up in many areas, however, a group of dedicated fence-cutters sprung up, who would cut the fence time and time again and defend their deeds with talk of free range. Those men usually stole no large number of horses or cattle, but those who cut fences regularly also owned little property and were among that group of petty thieves, drunkards and men usually down on their luck, who did not object to a night in the local jail.

Fence cutting was almost impossible to prove, for unlike cattle theft, once the fence was cut, there was no evidence of who did it. In 1884, to reduce the cutting of fences, the Texas State Legislature passed a law making fence-cutting a felony. A pair of cutting pliers in the saddlebags was enough to warrant an arrest in most jurisdictions. The law also made the big ranchers provide a gate every three miles and made it illegal to fence out small land owners. Because few elected lawmen or their deputies had time to watch for evidence of fence cutting, much of the job of catching the fence-cutters after 1884 fell to the Frontier Battalion.[37]

The amount of violence in the state had dropped for several years after 1878. By 1885, however, that year turned out to be another banner year for killing peace officers in the State of Texas. At least 13 lawmen died in the line of duty that year and most were killed in seemingly innocent situations that suddenly turned violent. One of those killed that year included, Constable J. D. L. Johnson in Cooke County. Johnson had served a writ of attachment for $56.OO to be secured by attaching a wagon and two horses on J. H. Rainey. He also served an arrest warrant on Rainey's son, Elmer, for carrying a weapon.[38]

As was the custom at the time in rural areas, the elder Rainey asked if his son could be bonded out by a neighbor and avoid a night in jail. Constable Johnson agreed, and on the way to the neighbor's residence the father attempted to remove the wagon and team of horses which had been attached by driving across the Red River into Indian Territory. Constable Johnson stopped the effort and J. H. Rainey threatened the constable with a shotgun.

He and the constable then fought over possession of the shotgun until Rainey told his son to kill the constable. Elmer drew his weapon and shot and killed the constable, and then wounded a special deputy. Both were arrested and J. H. Rainey received a 13 year sentence, while Elmer Rainey received a 20 year sentence in the State Penitentiary for killing a lawman over a $56.00 debt. Both convictions were appealed and both were affirmed.

In Fannin County during 1887, an unusually large number of men, 416, would be jailed. During that same year, Sheriff Thomas A. Ragsdale and his Deputy Joseph Buchanan, were both shot and killed while serving arrest warrants on Sam and Eli Dyer. The two killers were captured and a week later taken out of the jail by a mob estimated at 100 men, and hanged from a nearby tree. In another incident, South of Bryan, Texas, 40 convicts leased from the Texas State Penitentiary, who were working at Clay's farm, overpowered their guards and armed themselves. The next day they fought with a posse near Bryan and killed Brazos County Deputy Robert Smith, and Bryan Police Officer Levi P. Smith (no relation). All of the escaped convicts were captured and nine were then charged with the murder of the two officers.[39]

The leasing of convicts from the Texas State Penitentiary had been going on for some time. By the 1880s, convicts were regularly employed on railroads, in rock quarries, on contract farms as in Bryan, and on the prison's own farms. There were now two state penitentiaries, one outside of Huntsville and the other near Rusk. By 1887, the total prison population had increased to just over 3,700 convicts, with some 1,200 newly received and about half that many discharged each year. Others left as a result of receiving a pardon, while some died each year, plus almost 800 had escaped in the first eight years of the decade. That many escapes highlights one of the continuing problems existing at the state penitentiaries.[40]

Near the Mexican border in Webb County, Private Frank Sieker, a new recruit and younger brother of Captain Ed Sieker of the Frontier Battalion, was killed during a gun battle between seven rangers and two Mexicans believed to be escaping convicts. Another ranger, William H. Bohannon died of typhoid fever after a scout in the Hill Country during the summer of 1885. Two days after Christmas in 1885, Lamar County Deputy Sheriff Henry Clay Davis was murdered by a man named Garrett that he had arrested on a minor offense in the Springhill community. Garrett shot and killed the deputy after he had been allowed to go home and get some clothes before going off to jail. A posse led by Sheriff W. T. Gunn caught up with and wounded Garrett who was later lynched by a group of citizens from Springhill.[41]

The Great Blizzard Of 1886

During the winter of 1885-1886, a natural disaster hit the cattle business from Montana to the Staked Plains of Texas in the form of the Great Blizzard of 1886. This was followed by an equally devastating drought during the rest of 1886 and 1887. Those cattle that survived and made it to market were in such bad shape that beef prices crashed. Cattle which had brought $9.35 a hundred pounds in Chicago in 1882 brought only $1.9O in 1887. This wiped out both the smaller as well as some large ranchers in Texas, and the cowboys that had worked the range were turned out to find other work. Many of the ranches effected in Texas had been purchased by Eastern and European interests just two or three years before the crash in stock prices. Not only had many overstocked the range, they then lost most of their stock as a result of the blizzard and drought. Many Texas cattlemen bought back their land at pennies on the dollar, but neither farming nor the cattle business would ever be as profitable as it had been before the 188Os.[42]

During 1886 a second sheriff in Karnes County was killed in just a little more than 18 months. On Sept. 6, Karnes County Sheriff Lafayette Elder and his brother, Deputy James Elder, were standing outside a polling place in the town of Daileyville, when up rode two men. One of the men was recognized as a murder suspect. When the lawmen approached the suspect, he and the other man with him shot and killed both Elders and a bystander named Pullian. As the shooting continued another bystander was killed and three wounded, including another deputy sheriff, Jack Bailey. In the confusion, the two killers escaped.[43]

Back in July of 1878 when John B. Jones was frantically searching Austin for lawmen to accompany him to Round Rock for an expected confrontation with the Sam Bass gang, he had asked Travis County Deputy Sheriff Maurice B. Moore to go with him. Moore was wounded in the gunfight that developed in Round Rock when the bank robbery that Sam Bass attempted to pull off went awry. After he recovered, Moore stayed in law enforcement and nine years later in the summer of 1887, while he and another deputy, Sam Platt, were serving an arrest warrant on Wilson McNeil in Travis County, Deputy Moore was shot and killed by an unknown person from inside the McNeil residence. No arrest was made for the murder, for Wilson McNeil was himself outside the residence in plain sight talking with Deputy Platt when Moore was shot. Only McNeil's wife and children were in the house and they denied the shooting. In 1905, Wilson McNeil would again be arrested. At that time he was tried and convicted of a murder and hanged in Georgtown, only a few miles north of Austin.[44]

In 1888, the five Marlow brothers, who for several years had lived in Indian Territory came to the attention of a deputy U. S. marshal living in Young County, when he received a telegram advising that the Marlow's were suspected of stealing horses in Colorado. In addition Boone Marlow was wanted in another Texas county for murder. A posse arrested all five Marlow brothers for suspected theft of horses and took them to Young County for arraignment. After several months in jail they were released on bond and awaited trial. Then an arrest warrant arrived for Boone Marlow from Wilbarger County for murder and during his arrest popular Sheriff Marion D. Wallace was mortally wounded and died later on the day before Christmas in 1888. All but Boone Marlow were arrested that day and held in jail pending a meeting of the grand jury. Charles Marlow (Cause # 386) was finally charged with that murder in 1889.[45]

After a foiled jail break, all the brothers except Boone who was still free, were put in a wagon on Jan. 19, 1889 and moved to the Weatherford County jail for safekeeping. But they never made it, for they were ambushed on the way. Alf and Epp. Marlow were killed along with a guard and two of the mob that came to lynch them. A deputy U. S. marshal and a constable from the Belknap Precinct were wounded. Charlie and George Marlow, along with two other prisoners were also wounded, but in the confusion they escaped and survived their wounds. They were then recaptured later that day when they went directly to their home in Young County. Nine days later, on Jan. 28, three men from Indian Territory brought in the body of Boone Marlow for the reward.[46]

Of those who had attacked the Marlows and the men who had supposedly acted as guards, five local lawmen from Young County were later charged with obstructing a deputy U. S. marshal in the performance of his duty in a federal grand jury in Dallas. One of those, Constable Eugene Logan was also indicted for the murder

(Cause #385) of Epp. and Alf Marlow in Young County.[47]

Out in the Texas Panhandle the Ft. Worth & Denver City Railroad arrived in Amarillo during the fall of 1887, and by the next year work on the line began to move it toward its eventual destination in Colorado. The railroads brought with them more settlers and tradesmen and hurried the organization of more local counties. Then on Jan. 10, 1889, the sheriff of Potter County, James Gober, shot and mortally wounded a constable while he was on duty serving warrants in an Amarillo saloon on several men previously indicted for illegal gambling. Constable M. M. Givins had been elected constable in Precinct #1, just two months earlier in Nov. of 1888. Givins would die from the wound two days later.[48]

At his murder trial Sheriff Gober claimed his gun went off accidentally and since no eyewitness had seen Gober pull the trigger, he created enough reasonable doubt to win an acquittal. He was, however, never able to serve again as sheriff, as his bondsmen withdrew their support and the county commissioners pushed for his dismissal. Gober was unable to find anyone in Potter County to act as a surety, despite the fact that the county judge was his father-in-law. On Oct. 14, 1889 the office of sheriff was declared vacant and A. F. Criswell was appointed sheriff to fulfill Gobers unexpired term, just two months away. Jim Gober soon left the state.[49]

Jay Birds And Woodpeckers

In Fort Bend County, as the 1880s came to a close, one of the last of the great Texas feuds was brewing. Once again, the bitterness left over from the late war and Reconstruction would play a large part in the initial violence, but greed and the desire for power were just as critical. Those who fought, proudly labeled themselves as either Woodpeckers or Jay Birds, local names given their political affiliations. The problems initially grew out of the animosity caused because freedmen made up almost 75 percent of the voters in that county just after the Civil War. During the first two decades after the war, freedmen or those who worked with them held most of the county and some state political offices in Fort Bend County. They called themselves Woodpeckers. The district clerk, treasurer, tax assessor and three commissioners were all freedmen, as were most justices and constables, in addition to Walter Burton the respected state senator. In 1885, Tom J.

Garvey, a white man was appointed sheriff by the Woodpecker county commissioners to serve out the unexpired term of the former sheriff they had previously supported, Garvey's uncle, Tom Blakely. Garvey was among those who would later use the votes of the Woodpecker supporters to be reelected to office.[50]

After 1888, race played less and less of a direct role in the feud, as more and more white men ran for political office in both of the local parties, and the racial mix in the county turned almost equal. Both of those groups thought of themselves as Democrats, so except for a few Republicans, including a not yet famous Carry Nation who was married and working in Fort Bend County, the fate of Fort Bend County in the late nineteenth century was in the hands of the Democrats. As violent as the rivalry would become, many in both groups were related to each other. By August 1888, Sheriff Garvey, who was at onetime a Jay Bird, had switched alliance to the Woodpeckers when that group promised to support his run for sheriff. They swept the elections that October.[51]

During 1889, the feud turned violent. Kyle Terry, a Woodpecker and the youngest son of a very prominent family in Fort Bend, walked up to the brother of a political rival on the street of Richmond, the Fort Bend's county seat, aimed his shotgun at Ned Gibson and shot him dead. From that time the Jay Birds looked for an opportunity to get even with Terry, Sheriff Garvey and Judge Parker. They especially wanted Parker for he had been heard to tell Terry just before he murdered Ned Gibson that "venison is better than no meat." All interpreted the comment as meaning that it was better to kill any Gibson family member, than none at all. Governor Sul Ross sent Frontier Battalion Sergeant Ira Aten and seven rangers to Fort Bend county to stop further violence. However, after Aten and his rangers arrived, four more men would be killed and a number wounded within sight of the courthouse.[52]

Sergeant Aten, soon after his arrival had made the mistake of sending half of his already small command out of the area on other peace keeping duties, leaving him with only three men. On the night of Aug. 16, 1889, a group of Jay Birds led by Volney Gibson went after Judge Parker as he left the courthouse, in an effort to even the score for Parker's part in the murder of his brother Ned. As Parker saw the men coming for him he fired two shoots and ran for the courthouse, but was wounded twice as he pushed through the front door. Sheriff Garvey and Deputies

Smith and Mason heard the shots as did many others in Richmond, including Ira Aten. Aten and Garvey met each other a block away but Aten was ordered away by Sheriff Garvey who told him, "I am sheriff of this county and I am going to handle this situation myself. You keep out of this." Aten stepped back and went toward the Jay Birds down the street, but could not take a gun away from Volney Gibson, who threatened the ranger. Sergeant Aten then walked away from the trouble, for with most of his men gone, he had too few to keep the peace in that volatile situation.[53]

Within a few minutes Sheriff Garvey's uncle Tom Blakely, who was the former sheriff, and was said to have also been one of his deputies and lived nearby, walked up to the courthouse. He was shot and killed by Henry H. Frost, a leader of the Jay Birds. About that time, Judge Parker also stepped out of the courthouse and was wounded again by rifle fire, as the Jay Birds approached the courthouse and began to fire at him and Garvey. Sheriff Garvey was then badly wounded, but not before he shot at Frost and mortally wounded him. Although wounded, Garvey supported himself on a hitching post for a time and then dropped to the ground where he would die from the shots of Frost and the other Jay Birds. Frost also lay wounded in the street. Both of Garvey's deputies had taken cover behind an iron fence and helped run off the Jay Birds as more people came toward the courthouse. With the fight over, Frost was taken to his home where he would die the next day.

After he had failed to stop the violence, Ira Aten wisely went to the telegraph office, where he wired the governor to send the militia to Richmond. At 7 P. M. the next evening, Governor Lawrence Ross himself stepped off the train with two militia companies and additional rangers from the Frontier Battalion. It would take several days of negotiations between the governor and both groups, plus arrests of the leaders on both sides before they arrived at an acceptable truce. The sheriff was dead and both groups would accept no one locally to replace him. The Woodpeckers claimed the right to name Garvey's successor. Largely because the supporters of the dead sheriff could not raise sufficient money for a bond to be made for their man to take Garvey's place as sheriff, it was agreed that Ranger Ira Aten would serve out the unexpired term of Sheriff Garvey.[54]

In the weeks and months following, a number of prominent Woodpeckers would move out of Fort Bend County, including the recovering Judge Parker. Fifteen Jay Birds were indicted in the gunfight at the courthouse, but Henry Frost was known to have shot Sheriff Garvey and had paid for his efforts. What was left was the trial of Kyle Terry for the earlier shotgun murder of Ned Gibson, which was held in Galveston. On Jan. 21, 1890 as the Galveston trial was about to start and all parties were arriving at the criminal courtroom, Volney Gibson pulled out a pistol and shot Kyle Terry through the heart, instantly killing him. Terry was also armed and had attempted to defend himself by drawing his own weapon. The hammer of Terry's pistol, however, had caught on his drawers as he pulled it out of his waistband as he was shot. Gibson was arrested and released on $10,000 bond, but would die in bed of tuberculosis on April 9, 1891, almost a year to the day after he was released on bond and before any trial.[55]

Jim Miller, a killer for hire, circa 1905.
(R.G. McCubbin Collection)

CHAPTER IX

THE END OF AN ERA

THE 189Os

A CONFUSED AND TROUBLING FUTURE

From its beginning, Texas had looked for its future in its frontier, its abundance of cheap land, the railroads and its freehold farmers. But that frontier was now rapidly disappearing and the great mass of poor farmers who had arrived in Texas both before and after the Civil War had remained predominately poor. By 189O, some 25 years after the end of the war their most marketable commercial crop was still cotton, but prices had fallen from 31 cents per pound in 1865, to 11 cents in 1875 and would fall even further to about 5 cents a pound just before the turn of the century. Regardless, they had little choice but to plant more cotton each year, along with some wheat and corn, the latter an important feeder crop for farm animals. The lack of adequate rain in many of the years following the drought of 1887 only added to the frustration. As a result, in 189O most Texas farmers and much of the south were still trapped in an early nineteenth century economy, with little hope of escaping within their lifetimes. As a result, Texas would remain very much an agrarian state throughout the first half of the twentieth century.[1]

At the time of the writing of the last State Constitution in 1876, the majority of rural Texans had pinned their hopes on the Grange as their political savior. A decade later it was the Farmer's Alliance, which by the end of the 188Os had a membership of just over 3 million farmers nationwide. Those two organizations were powerful enough in Texas that their platforms in the elections of 1887 had supported a state constitutional amendment for statewide prohibition of sales of alcoholic beverages.

Local option and other prohibition laws were already on the books in many communities across Texas. Regardless, the belief was widespread that alcohol and drunkenness were at the heart of most criminality, as well as child and spousal abuse, and that taking alcohol away would eliminate much of the violence and bring peace and prosperity to Texas. That major effort to establish statewide prohibition was narrowly defeated in 1887.[2]

Nothing stopped the erosion of prices paid for most farm crops. This resulted in the inability of many farmers to borrow money with which to pay taxes on farm property, to buy seed to plant the next year's crops, plus surviving until the next harvest. By the early 189Os more and more Black and white farmers in Texas were becoming tenants on land that they had once owned. This trend would continue into the twentieth century and begin a slow but sure movement of the next several generations of Texans away from the land and into the newly building towns and cities.

As a part of the new Populist Party's message, the people of Texas were told that their problems were not their fault, but the fault of the railroads, the bankers, Wall Street capitalists in general, and intellectuals. During the 189Os parts of Texas suffered through a number of violent labor strikes and riots, some of which would rival the period of Reconstruction for their violence. Overall, Texas in the 189Os saw fewer murders and less violence than in the previous two decades. But there was a new round of vigilante activity that began anew in the 189Os and carried into the next century. As a result, the Blacks and many in the white underclass, who were certainly neither bankers nor capitalists, were largely the victims of renewed vigilante justice.[3]

Another outcome of this distrust of capitalism was a Texas constitutional amendment establishing a railroad regulatory agency headed by a Railroad Commissioner, which was a major issue in the gubernatorial election of 189O. Even more critical to many was that during the 188Os, the appellate courts in Texas had also gained a reputation for overturning a number of criminal convictions for what was called "hypertechnicalities." In 1887, the Court of Appeals was said by its critics to have been "only organized to overrule and reverse." A second amendment ratified in 1891, transformed the Court of Appeals into the Texas Court of Criminal Appeals, with jurisdiction over criminal cases only. Civil cases were finally left to the Supreme Court and this established the bifurcated Texas judicial system of two courts of last resort, one civil and the other criminal. By 1893, the newly reorganized Texas Court of Criminal Appeals appeared to have overcome many of the court's problems, actually affirming 110 criminal cases and reversing just 61 cases that year.[4]

THE FRONTIER BATTALION'S LAST ROUNDUP

Even before the end of the 1880s, the Frontier Battalion had fallen on hard times. Many of the more experienced rangers had left, and the number and size of the different companies had been reduced to where some ranger companies consisted of less than 10 men. The death of Captain Frank Jones, who was killed south of El Paso on June 30, 1893, can be blamed to a large extent on the limited number of men he led into a running battle with bandits that day. Suddenly, the most important advantages the earlier rangers had in their fight against Indians and outlaw gangs, were lost. One has to ask the question whether this would have happened, if John B. Jones had still commanded ?[5]

Over the decade of the 1890s, the Frontier Battalion individual companies reduced patrols and instead tried to locate their camps near where they thought they might be needed. One method tried was to follow in the wake of the building of the railroads. As a result, the ranger commands would time and again find themselves with less meaningful missions to carry out. They also oftentimes found themselves lacking sufficient men to effectively do some jobs and they finally became largely impotent, except for chasing prize fighters across the state and keeping the peace on the picket lines. To a large extent the Frontier Battalion had become what everyone had wanted to avoid when it was organized in 1874. They were now little more than another state police organization that some felt had outlived its usefulness.[6]

During the 1890s eight rangers, one more than had been killed in the line of duty in the 1880s, would loose their lives while trying to bring law and order to Texas. Looking at the deaths of those men tells us much about the ranger's work in the last decade of the nineteenth century. Six of those eight men were killed in far West Texas. One of the others, R. E. Doaty, was killed chasing Mexican bandits along the Rio Grande near Laredo, while the last, J. W. Woods, disappeared while doing undercover work on a number of cattle thefts in Menard County, and his body was never found.[7]

Four of those six rangers were killed in El Paso County. Captain Frank Jones lost his life while chasing Mexican bandits;

Ernest St. Leon was shot and killed while trying to quiet a disturbance; Charles Fusselman was killed while chasing cattle thieves and Joe McKidrict was murdered in downtown El Paso by a former ranger who was surly, drunk and at the time wore the badge of the U. S. marshals service. Of the last two rangers killed in far West Texas, J. F. Gravis was shot and killed by unknown persons at a party and dance in Shafter, Texas and T. P. Nigh was killed while trying to disarm a man near Pecos. All of the eight rangers killed in the 189Os were operating either alone or with no more than a couple of other rangers at the time of their death.

Law Enforcement In The 189Os

While eight rangers were killed during the 189Os, at least fifty-four elected and appointed lawmen in the various counties and municipalities around Texas would be killed in line of duty during that same 1O year period. The years, 1892, 1893 and 1898 during that decade turned out to be the most dangerous for lawmen. But the most dangerous single year in that 1O year period was 1892, when 15, or some 28 percent of the total killed would die. That many lawmen had never before been killed in line of duty in just 12 months, even in the 187Os. In contrast to the casualties in the Frontier Battalion in Far West Texas, only one member of an elected law enforcement agency would die during 1892 in line of duty in the western part of Texas, and that was almost 4OO miles east of El Paso. That man was Deputy Sheriff Brack Mitchell, who on Jan. 1, 1892 was murdered while transporting a prisoner to jail in Fisher County, just north of Sweetwater, Texas.[8]

In the 189Os a surprising number of those 54 lawmen-seven-were killed as a result of both family and job related feuds, including five who would be shot by other lawmen, none by accident. The remaining two lawmen, were murdered by those who harbored ill feelings toward them or their families. Even so, they were killed in the line of duty, for in each case the violence was directed toward them because they were a peace officer on duty. During the 189Os other lawmen were murdered during a jail break, while stopping a robbery, or shot during a chase. However, the most common time of death for peace officers was while making an arrest. The most unnecessary death must have been the murder of Constable John E. Adams in Erath County, who was shot in the back and killed while enforcing local option laws against the sale of liquor within the small town of Dublin. Breaking local option laws were offenses in Texas that were usually settled by paying a small fine, but the murderer of Constable Adams was sentenced to death and publicly hanged in the county seat two years later.[9]

Whereas the vast majority of lawmen in Texas did not consider law enforcement a life-time job, in 1890 a major exception occurred on Nov. 4, 1890, when James S. Scarborough was elected sheriff of Lee County for the first time. Jim Scarborough would serve three consecutive two year terms as Lee County sheriff. Then after a six- year break he would again be elected sheriff of Lee County on Nov. 4, 1902 and be reelected to four more consecutive terms, until the end of 1910. He stepped down that year and, W. D. Scarborough, was elected the new sheriff of Lee County.[10]

"MORE LIKE YOUR NEXT DOOR NEIGHBOR"

Whereas the profile of the average killer of lawmen in the 1880s has previously been described as being "more like your next door neighbor" than a professional gunman, there were several times during the 1890s when a few more desperate criminals were again making Texas a part of their itinerary.

On Dec. 8, 1893 a posse from the Hamilton County sheriff's department surrounded a house in the northeast part of the county near the small town of Fairy. They were after Jim Jones who had been in the area for a few weeks posing as a music teacher and preacher. But a recently received wanted poster from Missouri asked that he be arrested. Jones was not arrested that day, but shot his way out of the house, killing Deputy Sheriff Thomas J. Deaton during his escape. Jones apparently had some ambition in the pursuit of crime, for six years later, he and his brother John would hold up the Union Pacific train near Hugo, Colorado. After a running gun battle, John was killed by the posse and Jim killed himself rather than be captured.[11]

Almost a year later, on Nov. 24, 1894 in the northern Panhandle, Hemphill County Sheriff Tom McGee was called to the train station in Canadian, Texas to check on some suspicious activity. The sheriff responded quickly for he knew that the Burlington Northern and Santa Fe train was due to arrive with a large shipment of money for the Wells Fargo office. As he walked around the depot, he was fired on from several different directions and was badly wounded. He returned fire and drove off his attackers, but died from the wounds. A posse tracked and arrested the men and one of them, George Issacs, was convicted of his murder and sentenced to life imprisonment in the Texas State Penitentiary.[12]

DEACON JIM, A KILLER FOR HIRE

During 1894, "Deacon" Jim Miller would again be noticed by law enforcement in Texas. Miller and Mannen Clements daughter, Sallie, had been married since 1888, and Miller was said to have reformed and become a church member who attended Worship services in Pecos. He had also been hired as a deputy sheriff by a former Frontier Battalion ranger and now Reeves County Sheriff George "Bud" Frazer. Miller was later fired, after a prisoner died in the county jail.[13]

In late 1892, Frazer was running for reelection and Miller campaigned against him, but Frazer easily won. Miller then applied for the job as City Marshal of Pecos. He got the job, bringing Mannen Clements' son, Mannie, to Pecos as his night deputy. A few months later Frazer was warned that Miller, Clements and a third man planned to kill him. Sheriff Frazer wired his friend Captain John R. Hughes of the Frontier Battalion and Hughes came to Pecos and arrested all three conspirators. Not long after the arrest, the only witness against Miller and the others was shot and killed and the case was dismissed.

Frazer ran for reelection in November of 1894 but this time he lost. Then on the day after Christmas, Frazer and Miller had a confrontation in Pecos and the sheriff shot Miller in the chest several times. But the bullets did not hit Jim Miller, they bounced off of a steel plate Deacon Jim wore at times under his coat, and except for some terrible bruises he was not harmed. A few weeks later attorney John Wesley Hardin arrived in Pecos to assist his kin by filing a charge of attempted murder against Bud Frazer. Frazer asked for a change of venue to El Paso where the trial was held in April of 1895. It ended in a hung jury, four for acquittal and eight for conviction.[14]

The retrial took place a year later in May of 1896 in Colorado City, Texas, but Wes Hardin would not represent Miller, for he had been killed by Constable John Selman and buried in El Paso's Concordia Cemetery just four months after he had defended Jim Miller in court the first time. Bud Frazer was acquitted, but four months later not many miles west of Pecos in the small town of Toyah, "Killin Jim" hit Frazer with a shotgun blast while he was playing cards. Miller had chosen his location with some care, for he killed Frazer in a town where all knew of the earlier shootings. Jim Miller easily won acquittal by claiming self-defense.[15]

James B. Miller would, over the next 13 years murder at least 11 more men, many of whom he had been hired to kill. His most famous victim was Pat Garrett, who 27 years before he was shot from ambush by "Killin Jim," had himself shot and killed Billy the Kid while he was Sheriff of Lincoln County, New Mexico. Miller spent much more time in courts being tried for different murders than he did killing the men, yet he somehow managed to avoid any conviction and spent little time in any jail and no time in any penitentiary for his crimes.

Then on Feb. 26, 1909, outside of Ada, Oklahoma, Miller killed Gus Bobbitt with his favorite weapon, a shotgun. Bobbitt was a rancher that three other cattlemen had hired Miller to kill. Miller was recognized and fled to Ft. Worth after the murder. There he was arrested and soon brought back to Ada for trial. On April 19, 1909, Jim Miller and the three men who hired him were taken out of jail and, because there were too few hanging trees available, all were hanged from the rafters of a local livery stable.[16]

More than once conflicts would arise when there were jurisdictional disputes over who was in charge of chasing the crooks. On Jan. 19, 1891, the Rio Grande Railroad running through Cameron County in South Texas was robbed of the U. S. Mail and some $75,000 in cash. Cameron County Sheriff Matthew L. Browne formed a posse to chase the train robbers, as did Brownsville City Marshal Santiago Brito, a long time sheriff of Cameron County, who had been defeated by Browne just a year before.

Marshal Brito was obviously outside of his jurisdiction, but because of his long time in law enforcement investigations in the county, he soon found a tool used to derail and stop the train and traced it back to the man who had it made at a local blacksmith shop. He arrested the man and his accomplices, but refused to turn them over to the Cameron County sheriff. John M. Haynes, the U. S. Marshal who had final jurisdiction over the case as it involved the U. S. Mail, solved that problem when he took custody of the prisoners, and lodged them in the only secure jail in the county, that of Sheriff Browne. Much of the money taken during the robbery was never recovered and two of those arrested died in jail. Less than a year later Browne was shot from ambush while rounding up cattle and Brito was shot and killed a few months later in Aug. of 1892.[17]

During the 1890s, two new counties in the state would be organized, while three would be abolished and their territory incorporated into other nearby counties. Texas would also lose its claim to Greer County, an area which officially reverted to the Indian Territory in the United States. Greer had been claimed by Governor Sam Houston in 1860 as a part of Texas after the Red River had been declared the northern boundary of the State. At the time Texas recognized that boundary as the North Fork of the Red River and the United States claimed the South Fork as its boundary with Texas. This was finally decided 36 years later in 1896, when the U. S. Supreme Court ruled in favor of the United States. Texas would end the 1890s with 243 counties organized in the Lone Star State, just 11 counties short of the 254 counties in todays Texas.[18]

Wild West Texas—Again

A decade earlier, El Paso had been a part of a very lawless area in Far West Texas. The 1890s would be little different. As already noted, four rangers were murdered in El Paso County during this period. One El Paso lawman who had been involved in one of those shootings was Constable John Selman. Selman had shot and mortally wounded Baz Outlaw, a deputy U. S. Marshal, when he murdered lawman Joe McKidrict with the Frontier Battalion, and then wounded Selman on April 5, 1894. Years before, Selman had been a deputy sheriff in Shackelford County, Texas, and had been accused of cattle theft, but rode out of the county one night only a few hours in front of a vigilante mob which had just murdered the former sheriff who was also accused of cattle theft. Later Selman was arrested in 1880 by the Frontier Battalion because of several outstanding warrants for cattle theft, but when returned to Shackelford County, he was released and sent on his way. Then in 1888, all charges were dropped. Selman had moved to El Paso and then been elected Constable of Precinct #1 in El Paso County in 1892. He was a very visible and active lawman in El Paso during that time.[19]

By the time Constable John Selman shot Baz Outlaw in April

Co. D., Frontier Battalion at Realitos, Texas in 1887. Baz Outlaw, who murdered Ranger Joe McKidrict in El Paso in 1894, is standing second from left. (Author's Collection)

of 1894, El Paso was full of aging hard cases who made far West Texas their favorite watering hole. Many wore one badge or another and a few wore more than one. They were policeman, deputy U. S. marshals, Texas Rangers, constables, sheriffs and their deputies from various jurisdictions in Texas and New Mexico. There were also others who drifted through the area who were running from the law. But one famous gunman arrived in El Paso in March of 1895 , with a pardon in one pocket and a new license to practice law in the other. His name was John Wesley Hardin.

John Wesley Hardin had spent just over 15 of his 25 year sentence in the Texas State Penitentiary in Huntsville, before receiving a full pardon from the governor of Texas. After about four months in El Paso, during which time Hardin drank and gambled too much, threatened some by deed and reputation and finally turned to robbing a number of poker games, he made a big mistake when he threatened both John Selman and his son, John Jr., who was an El Paso policeman. After challenging Hardin to a gunfight that afternoon and being refused, at about 11 pm on the night of Aug. 19, 1895, Constable John Selman stepped through the open doors of the Acme Saloon and shot Wes Hardin

El Paso Constable John Selman, killer of Baz Outlaw in 1894 and John Wesley Hardin in 1895. (R.G. McCubbin Collection)

three times, killing him instantly.[20]

Two days later the "El Paso Times" began its comment on the shooting by saying, "The people of El Paso breathed a sigh of relief yesterday morning when they read in the Times the story of the killing of John Wesley Hardin—-". Selman was indicted and the first trial resulted in a hung jury, 10 for acquittal and two for conviction. The second trial never took place, for on April 5, 1896, Constable Selman was himself shot and mortally wounded in the alley behind the Wigwam saloon by Deputy U. S. Marshal George Scarborough. Although acquitted in the murder of Selman, Scarborough was forced to resign from the marshals service and soon left Texas for New Mexico.[21]

By 1897 there were only seven army forts left in Texas, including the headquarters at Fort Sam Houston in San Antonio. With the Indian menace gone, the army's strength in Texas had dropped to only 1,500 men. In 1898, because of the threat of war with Spain, the troop strength had more than doubled to 4,398 soldiers. Over the next two years the troop strength would then again drop significantly as many units would be deployed across the U. S. and overseas during the Spanish-American War and then the Philippine Insurrection. That would have little if anything to do with bringing the rule of law to the Lone Star State, for during most of the last decade of the nineteenth century the army's role in protecting individual Texans from harm was pretty well over. But that was not true for those in law enforcement.[22]

As the nineteenth century came to a close, gunfights and murder committed by well known outlaws was largely a thing of the past in Texas. The murder of Texas lawmen, however, appears to have noticeably increased in 1898 and remained high for the next few years until 1902. After that murder and general levels of violence across much of Texas appear to have remained low for several years. But it was only a fleeting glimpse at a time of less crime, for the twentieth century would again grow more dangerous and violence would again become more and more an everyday affair in the Lone Star State.

EPILOGUE

LOOKING AHEAD TO A NEW CENTURY

TEXAS RINGS IN A NEW CENTURY

Murders, along with violence in general, dropped to a point during the first decade of the twentieth century not seen in Texas since the 185Os and early 186Os. But this period of relative peace and tranquility would last but a short time and by 1911, the killing of Texas lawmen and level of violence particularly along the Mexican border, had risen to a level equal to that reached during the violent 187Os.

In 19OO, Texas was still mired in an economy maybe 5O years behind the times when compared with mainstream America. The state was also still struggling to bring the rule of law to Texas in what would prove to be a never ending battle. That battle had not been won by 19OO, but much had been accomplished in those first 55 years of the Lone Star State. The Texas court system had experienced some growing pains, but it had been firmly established and was so well grounded that there would be little change within the courts through much of the last century. Law enforcement in the state had also prevailed over an outbreak of murder, riots and other violence plus a multitude of other crimes, the likes of which had never before been seen in Texas. During the three decades following the Civil War, lawmen had killed, arrested and sometimes imprisoned the worst bunch of murdering riff-raff that had ever existed in the state's history.[1]

One continuing criminal justice problem was the Texas prison system, which was often beset with charges of corruption, mismanagement and the abuse of prisoners. Responding to criticism over the ever rising costs of the prison system, beginning in 1883 convicts had been leased to work for private contractors in the cotton and rice fields and on the railroads and rock quarries in Texas. Two years later in 1885 and extending into the twentieth century, the prison system also opened a number of prison farms in an effort to further reduce the cost of maintaining prisoners. While those measures did alleviate some short term problems, the prison system would remain troubled for many more decades, with a large number of escapees being the most obvious problem.[2]

During the first years of the twentieth century, the Frontier Battalion became a casualty of the type of lawyer that Texas courts would soon see in increasing numbers, as the legislative act passed 26 years earlier that gave only officers the power to arrest, was used to strike a death blow to the ranging service. The legislature would pass another act to overcome that problem, but the ranger command made its transition into the twentieth century a mere shadow of its former self. There were now less than 100 men assigned to four small ranger companies widely scattered across the state. With no Indians to chase across a disappearing frontier, they were now what most had tried to avoid after Reconstruction, a state police force, hated by an increasing number of racial minorities.[3]

Across the state, elected and appointed county and municipal lawmen still enforced the law in Texas. During the first 11 years of the twentieth century, just 34 lawmen were murdered in line of duty. That was a number smaller than in any decade during the previous 30 years. That was, however, only a brief respite to a period of heightened violence from 1910 to 1920, when more than double that number, or at least 85 lawmen would lose their lives while doing their duty. That number exceeded even those killed during those terrible days during the late 1860s and 1870s. The belief briefly held in the late 1870s that, the worst was over, had proven to be just wishful thinking.[4]

Looking back at the first 55 years of the Lone Star State, we now know that from the late 1860s to the early 1900s, a period of just over 30 years, all indications are that much of Texas was indeed a violent land. As discussed herein, where there is enough information to calculate the number and type of crimes, we know that estimated crime rates (the number of crimes calculated per 100,000 population) for much of that period often exceed those crime rates of the late twentieth century. On the other hand, the number of lawmen we now know that were killed in the line of duty after the Civil War does not reach the level of those killed later in the twentieth century.

Regardless, the number and rapid increase in murders and other types of violence during the 1870s is still very significant and foretells a sea change in the level of violence from that time. Information available as a result of this study also indicates that the number or volume of crimes committed were lower in the last thirty years of the eighteenth century than in a similar time during the twentieth century; however, when crime rates are calculated on the number of crimes committed per 100,000 population, those rates for short periods of time are often much higher in the nineteenth century. In addition, there continues to be abundant anecdotal evidence confirming high levels of violence in Texas following the Civil War.

Changing Face Of Crime In Texas

A closer look at those deaths among law enforcement definitely indicates something about the changing face of crime in Texas. During the last 20 years of the nineteenth century (1880-1900), just over 20 percent of those lawmen killed in the line of duty worked for a police department as either a city marshal or policeman. But, during the first 20 years of the twentieth century (1900-1920), the number of policemen killed on the streets of Texas large and small cities and towns, or in their saloons and back alleys would increase to some 35 percent of the total killed. Although Texas was still predominantly a rural state, more and more of the killing and crime would take place in and around urban areas. But there were other changes taking place in law enforcement in the Lone Star State.

By 1900, the hostile Indian was no more than a bad memory. But, during those first two decades of the twentieth century, bands of roving cattle thieves and bandits would ride out of Mexico into the Rio Grande Valley of Texas, reinstating not only a higher level of violence, but also strongly reviving that earlier sense of distrust along the border for Texas southern neighbor. In 1918, five Texas Rangers and a number of other lawmen were killed along the Rio Grande while fighting smugglers and stock thieves coming out of Mexico.[5]

More Violence On Blacks

Although it had begun again during the 1890s, there would be no let up in a new wave of racial strife that would sweep across Texas in the early twentieth century. The first of the Jim Crow Laws, to limit Blacks' access to public services was passed in 1891. That first law required railroads to provide separate accommodations for Blacks and whites. Vigilante justice had all but ceased by the mid-188Os, but an increasing number of lynchings began to take place in the 189Os. Some occurred as a more personal attempt at revenge after a court sentence of guilty was returned, but most occurred before any trial took place and named a guilty party. Most lynchings were of Black men, but a significant number of white men were also lynched by mobs. Twice during the early days of the twentieth century, Black army soldiers would also come into serious conflict with lawmen in Texas.[6]

In August of 19O6, a group of unidentified men ran through the downtown streets of Brownsville, firing weapons into stores and buildings which killed one man and wounded two others. Townspeople blamed the Black soldiers from the First Battalion, 25th Infantry, stationed in Fort Brown. Ranger Captain Bill McDonald and two rangers went to Fort Brown to conduct an investigation, which resulted in the issuance of arrest warrants for 13 Black soldiers. The Cameron County Grand Jury, however, was unable to return any indictments based on the evidence, and all were released. Soon after that, Fort Brown was deactivated and the enlisted men in all three of the companies stationed there during that incident were dishonorable discharged by order of President Theodore Roosevelt. Then, 11 years later, on Aug. 23, 1917, during the build-up to American entry into the war against Germany, more than 1OO Black soldiers of the 24th Infantry Division rioted over their alleged mistreatment by Houston city police officers. Five Houston policemen were murdered that day, but 116 soldiers were subsequently tried and 8O were convicted of murder.[7]

It is obvious that efforts to establish the rule of law in the Lone Star State would occupy the criminal justice system's efforts for the next century, and still fall short. In fact, seemingly major events in the twentieth century such as prohibition, the rise of organized crime, the Great Depression, labor unrest, wartime espionage, civil rights, the War on Drugs and now the War on Terrorism were all just speed bumps along the road leading to this goal. Lawmen, prosecutors, judges and the various branches of government are all big players in this effort, but the people themselves actually hold the key. A change in many of the poor personal choices that are sometimes made, or in overlooking criminal acts carried out by some, will do more to help establish the rule of law in the Lone Star State than any new law passed or other act of government related to law and order.

John Ringo. (Courtesy of the Arizona Historical Society/Tucson, AHS#78486)

APPENDIX "A"
A CLOSE LOOK AT TWO TEXAS GUNMEN

THE ADVENTURES OF SCOTT COOLEY AND JOHN RINGO

Because of those many men he so indiscriminately murdered, John Wesley Hardin is a difficult man to ignore in any examination of criminality in Texas. As a result, I have probably looked at Hardin closer than any other well known Texas outlaw. But, except for a fascination with the many murders he committed, his life and the motivations of that psychopathic killer are otherwise quite unexceptional. The profile of many of the other well known outlaws of the day pretty well mirrors that of Hardin. But there are a few exceptions, as shown in the following story. What follows then, is a close look at the adventures of two rather unlikely gunmen, Scott Cooley and John Ringo, and their confrontation with the law and the courts during a period of unbridled violence across much of Texas during the 187Os.

The reason for looking at the story of their involvement in a vendetta in Mason County, Texas, is to give the reader an opportunity to look closely at their motivations, and those others who also came in contact with law enforcement and the courts. This story also demonstrates some of the problems and the workings of the criminal justice system in several Texas counties during that period. But this is no ordinary tale of violence and crime, for woven through this story is an alleged "range war," a savage vendetta, wanton murder and personal revenge sought at all costs. Yet, when all the facts as we now understand them are examined, the "bad guys" are just not all that easy to identify.

Another interesting aspect of this story is that neither Ringo nor Cooley really appears to have been the typical outlaw during that period of the nineteenth century. We know that neither man ever robbed a bank, a stagecoach, or a train, nor is it likely that they ever stole a horse or any cattle. But both Cooley and Ringo gained significant reputations as violent killers, and they were either the cause of, or played a major role in at least five murders during that one terrible year in Texas, 1875. Both were well known feudists in Texas at the time, as they came to the attention of many people due to various stories in the newspapers. They were also often singled out and noticed by both lawmen and outlaws in a place and at a time when many other violent men walked the streets.

The center of that violence was in Mason County, Texas, during what has been represented as a local range war, with racial overtones emanating from the early days of the Civil War. I am not sure, however, exactly what those who claim that the "Mason County War" involved the theft of large numbers of livestock base their claim on. There are no court records showing large numbers of livestock theft indictments in Mason County before mid-1877, because the court house and the court records inside burned down in January of that year. The court records available after that time, do not support the allegation that a large number of livestock were actually stolen in Mason County by anyone. In fact, court records from nearby Lampasas, Gillespie and Burnet Counties for much of that same period, indicate a larger number of livestock stolen in those counties than in Mason. Furthermore, the climate and soil of much of Mason County never made cattle ranching an easy calling or allowed for large herds of cattle to be grazed. As a result, the motivation for the murders committed anywhere in this story do not appear to have taken place to simply protect property. The motivation always appears to have been just pure hate.[1]

Regarding the struggle between the German and Anglo factions, there was certainly bad blood between some of the German and Anglo families in the region. Some of those bad feelings are said to be because many of the lately arrived German immigrants in Texas had refused to support the Confederate cause in the late war. Mason and neighboring Gillespie Counties were the home of some of the most dedicated Unionists in Texas and both counties voted overwhelmingly against secession in 1861. Then in 1862, a German wagon train containing some of those who supported the Union cause was escaping Texas and traveling toward Mexico, when it was attacked by Texan Partisan Rangers. During the attack, 60 German settlers were killed for no other reason than for their Unionist sympathies. Remnants of those families and their friends who survived may have sought revenge for more than a decade. But whether that was a real consideration for the Mason County War, to me has always been nothing more than speculation. But, we will never know for even today, the families of those who participated are still guarded in their comments and only talk about the theft of cattle, not hate.[2]

Having said all that, neither John Ringo nor Scott Cooley were a party to any range war or ethnic feud, although both did come to Mason County with a similar agenda. Their missions were to avenge the recent murders of their own best friends who had been killed by the most visible members of the “German faction” in Mason County. The members of that faction appear to have been the same kind of people who in other areas of Texas where vigilante justice ruled, have often been called “the mob.” Both “the mob” and others in Mason County soon found out that they had never seen anything quite like what they had let out of the bottle when they killed good and close friends of Cooley and Ringo. It took them totally by surprise.

Mason County, Texas in 1874

Our story begins in Mason County in 1874, when Sheriff John Rufus Clark arrested a number of very reputable cattlemen from nearby Burnet and Llano Counties in September, during their fall roundup of cattle that had strayed into Mason County. They were thrown into the Mason County jail, and when released, they were “escorted” to the county line and all their cattle had been scattered. The drive had been led by M. B. Thomas from Burnet County, who was fined for driving cattle he did not own later that year when the case was heard in Mason County District Court. This example of Mason County justice occurred even though only two of the calves in the entire herd did not belong to Thomas. George Gladden was probably on that cattle drive and John Ringo may also have been, for both knew and sometimes worked for Thomas.[3]

We do know that John Ringo was already a respected citizen living in Burnet County and worked there, at one time or another for Thomas. Ringo was also a close friend of John and Moses Baird and their friends the Olneys and the Gamels, who all lived in Burnet County. These were all well-liked and respected citizens, who, for their own reasons, would participate in the violence in Mason County later in the 1870s.

Scott Cooley on the other hand, had only recently resigned from the Frontier Battalion, after spending some seven months in Company D and was also working in the area. Whether Ringo and Cooley knew each other in the beginning is not known, but it is likely, as they were about the same age and would seek similar type of work. What follows then is their story, much of it confirmed by information contained in various court records.

John Ringo, was born in Indiana in 1850 and the family moved to California after the Civil War, when he was fifteen years old. He would leave California to begin his adult life in Texas sometime in the early 1870s, having relatives already established in the state. By 1874, Ringo was living in Burnet County, Texas and on Christmas Day that year while celebrating, he shot his pistol in the air, across the town square. The act was observed by several people. No one was injured and life went on. But, four months later during the next term of the Grand Jury in Burnet County, John Ringo was indicted on April 5, 1875, for "disturbing the peace", as contained in District Court Cause # 854. Messrs M. B. Thomas and John W. Calvert, one of whom we looked at previously, agreed to act as bondsmen for John Ringo, who walked out of the Burnet County District Court arraignment after a $200 bond was posted.[4]

While Ringo had his first known run-in with the law in Burnet County, a few months before that on Feb. 10, 1875, violence in nearby Mason County got much more serious when Sheriff Clark and his posse arrested five men, including the Baccus brothers and an unidentified teen-age boy for suspected cattle rustling. While in Clark's custody a mob came looking for the prisoners. Clark and Frontier Battalion Captain Dan Roberts, who was in town to pick up supplies, put up no defense at all of the jailed men, who were taken from the jail and two were lynched. Another was shot and killed, but two managed to escape into the brush when townspeople came to the aid of the men.[5]

Then, three months later on May 13, a very close friend and mentor of Cooley was murdered in Mason County. That man was Tim Williamson, a well-known small rancher who can best be described as a father-figure, who had years before befriended a young Scott Cooley. Along with his wife, Williamson had helped raise Cooley after the young man's family were killed by Indians and Cooley escaped with his life.[6]

Mason County Sheriff John Clark had been elected sheriff on Dec. 31, 1873, and law and order went downhill rapidly. There was apparently bad blood between Tim Williamson and Sheriff Clark. In May of 1875, Clark ordered that Williamson be arrested by Deputy Sheriff John Wohrle on what is said to have been "suspicion of cattle theft," although Williamson was working for Charlie Lehmberg at the time. Some also suggest that even this charge was in itself bogus, for Williamson had apparently only been asked to come in on nothing more than a question about property taxes, for the sheriff was also tax assessor.[7]

While Deputy Wohrle was transporting Williamson to Mason, Texas on May 13, 1875, a vigilante group from the German faction in that County rode up on the two men. Wohrle, instead of either running with, or defending his prisoner, prevented an already disarmed Williamson from escaping the mob, by shooting his horse. Williamson was then murdered, with Wohrle either participating, or at least just looking on. Deputy Wohrle was already known to have been sympathetic to that faction, as was his sheriff, and the part he played in this incident, made him primarily responsible for Williamson's death. The murder of Tim Williamson, a well known local resident, rekindled much of the hate and fear of various factions and families in the region.[8]

Scott Cooley is said to have arrived in Mason County about three months later. He spent several days searching for the locations of those men that had been involved in the murder of his friend, Tim Williamson. Then, before noon on Aug. 10, Cooley rode up to the home of Deputy John Wohrle, where several men were working on a water well. He introduced himself and when Wohrle told him his name, Cooley pulled out his pistol, shot and killed him on the spot. He then leaned over Wohrle and with his knife cut along the hair line and scalped the man. He then shoved the bloody scalp into his pocket and rode away.[9]

That got the attention of both local citizens and law enforcement and the "German faction" fell apart. Sheriff Clark, who was himself an obvious accessory in the murder of Tim Williamson quickly found a good reason to go on a visit out of the county. Then on Aug. 19, Scott Cooley was alleged to have also shot and killed Karl Bader. Karl, however, was said to have played no part in the murder, but whoever killed Karl may have thought they were killing Karl's brother, Peter Bader, another of Williamson's identified killers.[10]

Events were moving very fast and within a week, Clark now

full of fear, had gathered a large group of men together and they spent much of their time by the river road as it approached town. They soon successfully ambushed George Gladden and Moses Baird, two friends of Scott Cooley. Baird and Gladden had only approached Mason after Clark had sent a man named Jim Cheyney or Chaney, to talk them into coming to town. Both were wounded in the ambush, and then Peter Bader rode up to the wounded Moses Baird, shooting him again and killing him. For an unexplained reason, perhaps because some may have felt it was the second most stupid thing they had done after murdering Williamson, they let severely wounded George Gladden go. But it is just as likely that they hoped he would suffer more before dying. But the wounded Gladden survived.[11]

It was probably at that time that Ringo travelled to Mason County to take revenge for the murder of Moses Baird, for he was a very close friend of the Baird family. Others, who counted Baird as their friend, would also soon drift into Mason County. At that same time John Ringo would have met, if he had not already known Scott Cooley before Baird's murder. Within five days of that shooting Jim Cheyney was murdered. Ringo was later indicted for the crime. Then on Sept. 29, three more of the German faction were in turn ambushed, during which time one of them, Dan Hoerster, who was County Hide Inspector and a part of the "inner-circle" of the mob, was killed.[12]

The Frontier Battalion Finally Responds

That burst of violence finally had the effect of having a Frontier Battalion command from Company A and D sent to Mason County, by the adjutant general. But, we can only wonder why the rangers had not been sent to Mason County over a year before, when the Baccus brothers were taken out of the county jail and hung by a vigilante mob, all the time being carefully watched by Sheriff Clark and Frontier Battalion Captain Dan Roberts. Perhaps the kindest thing that can be said about Roberts conduct was that at the time he did not understand that the Frontier Battalion had responsibilities as peace officers. Later, why were the rangers not sent to Mason County soon after Williamson's murder by another vigilante mob, back in May of 1875 ? It had been obvious for well over a year that the local sheriff was corrupt, and that violence in return or flight from Mason County was about all that had been left for those who had been disenfranchised. But the state was not protecting its citizens.[13]

By coincidence, Scott Cooley had also served in Company D of the Frontier Battalion for seven months, resigning just a little over a year before. Major John B. Jones, in charge of both the Frontier Battalion and also personally commanding this mixed command sent to Mason County, had apparently forgotten that some of the men still with Company D were Cooley's friends. After Jones realized that the pursuit of Cooley was going nowhere, he offered to release from the ranger service anyone who felt personal loyalty to Scott Cooley. Contrary to what has been written in many tales telling that story, Jones while in Mason County on Oct. 7, 1875, honorably discharged only two men (Sgt. N. O. Reynolds and Pvt. Jason P. Day of Company D), "because they cannot conscientiously discharge their duties". Then the Frontier Battalion command stayed in Mason County for only a short time, arresting no one for any violence committed, and to many seeming to be there only to protect Sheriff Clark during his last days in office during early October, 1875.[14]

Clark, who had not run for reelection, wasted little time leaving Mason County after the election. He was replaced by James A. Baird, a former deputy of Sheriff Clark. James Baird was elected sheriff on Oct. 2, 1875, and was said to be no relation to Moses Baird who had recently been killed by Clark's posse. The role that he must have played as the new County Sheriff in reducing the violence, however, has not been recognized in previous accounts examining the violence that occurred in Mason County. But Sheriff James Baird, who served a little over four months as sheriff of Mason County, and the man (Jesse W. Leslie) who replaced him in February of 1876, both played pivotal and significant rolls in this drama. There had now been a total of 11 men murdered and others wounded in just eight months in Mason County, beginning with the Baccus brothers. After Clark was replaced as sheriff, the violence involved in the so-called "range war" declined significantly.[15]

It is inconceivable to imagine that such violence would have almost stopped without different people heading Mason County's law enforcement, for the hate felt by all sides was still there. Baird may have been a deputy of Clark, but he was apparently a friend of Tom Gamel and is said to have met Cooley, Ringo and others at Loyal Valley in Mason County before being elected sheriff. This would suggest that he was, in fact, some kin to John and the late Moses Baird from Burnet County, all good friends of John

Ringo. Regardless, the activities and direction of Mason County law enforcement efforts changed completely from the time Baird was elected sheriff and much of the violence associated with hate killings began to fade away.

About Christmas time, and exactly a year after John Ringo had first been arrested for "disturbing the peace" in Burnet, Texas, he and Cooley were back in that town together. On Dec. 27, 1875, they were arrested by Burnet Sheriff John Clymer and Deputy J. J. Strickland after the two men had allegedly threatened Clymer and his deputy with bodily harm. Soon after Ringo and Cooley were arrested, a large crowd arrived at the local jail and threatened to break them out of jail. Knowing the Burnet County jail was not escape proof, both men were moved to the more secure Travis County jail a week later. But down in Llano County the war continued. On Jan. 13, 1876, John Baird and the recovered George Gladden, finally caught up with and killed Peter Bader, who was known to have killed Baird's brother Moses, and who had also been positively identified among the killers of Tim Wilkinson.[16]

Cooley and Ringo were soon brought back from the Travis County jail to Burnet County for arraignment, and on Feb. 1, 1876, the grand jury returned two indictments, each jointly charging both men with "seriously threatening to take the life of (Clymer & Strickland) a human being." They pled not guilty to those charges. The next day Ringo pled not guilty to the year old charge of disturbing the peace and when convicted paid a $75.00 fine. Two days later, on Feb. 3, 1876, both of the new cases were removed to Lampasas County in a change of venue, because the court probably agreed that a fair trial might be difficult to get in a county where you were charged with threatening the life of the local sheriff.

On Feb. 4, bonds for Ringo and Cooley on the two new indictments were filed. As if to demonstrate their good standing in Burnet County, an interesting group of local citizens raised the now, $1,000 total bond by pledging $200 each from, J. H. Stapp (the City Marshal), Swifts Ogle (the jury foreman in Ringo's short trial two days before for disturbing the peace), John Clyman, William Prince and a Miss M. McGuire. Back in Mason County, James A. Baird resigned as sheriff after serving only a little over four months. Jesse W. Leslie was elected the next sheriff on Feb. 15, 1876. Like Sheriff Baird before him, Sheriff Leslie was not allied with the German faction and he served two and one-half years, during which time all of the fight just went out of the "Mason County War".[17]

In the 187Os, Lampasas County was a sometimes violent county and in 1877, it was one of the most violent places to be in the Lone Star State. Its so-called long history of violence, however, is mostly a myth, if court records are used to examine that violence. However, there is no indication that either Cooley or Ringo played any part in that violence during the 187Os. After the two indictments in Burnet County were removed to Lampasas, those charges were renumbered in the new District Court, with Cause #38O for Ringo and #381 for Cooley. Scott Cooley and John Ringo were held in the Lampasas County jail. In the March, 1876 term of the District Court, Ringo was tried and convicted of the charge of threatening the life of another person, but appealed his conviction. He then was denied bail and sat in jail for several months awaiting the results of his appeal. Long before the results of the appeal were known, however, several of their "friends", probably led by Joe Olney and John Baird, broke Ringo and Cooley out of the Lampasas jail in May of 1876, and they rode south toward Llano and later to Loyal Valley in Mason County.[18]

Neither of the two indictments brought against Ringo and Cooley in Burnet County in February of 1876 were particularly heinous or unusual for the time and place. While serious, there was no act of violence connected to those two indictments, only the threat of same. But the two gunmen had made a name for themselves and the jail break just added to it. It had been but a little over a year since Ringo's first known arrest for disturbing the peace, and a little over two years since Cooley had resigned from the Frontier Battalion. Yet in that short time both had become well-known gunmen, and the pair had possibly killed as many as four men. But if some considered them outlaws, they had no problem in raising bail money, being broken out of jail, hidden from the law, or being called by a considerable number of people in the area as their friends.

Scott Cooley Gives Up The Fight

Not long after they escaped jail in Lampasas, Scott Cooley apparently gave up the fight. It is said that he rode off toward Fredericksburg and his fate is somewhat uncertain, although he is apparently buried in Miller Creek Cemetery in Blanco County,

Texas, where a tombstone records his death only as "1876." The most repeated story is that he died in the Esquire D. Maddox home in Blanco County of "brain fever." Other stories have Cooley dying of a dose of poison after riding out of Fredericksburg, or living to be an old man somewhere in New Mexico. So during the summer of 1876, Cooley and Ringo parted, but John Ringo stayed in the area and still had the support of a number of those he could call his friends. John Baird, A. T. Taylor, George Gladden, John and Joe Olney and others would give John Ringo support just about whenever he needed it. His conviction in Lampasas District Court (Cause #380) was reversed in 1877, and the case would then be continued at every meeting of the District Court over the next three years, until finally dismissed in 1879.[19]

At the end of Oct. 1876, however, Gladden and Ringo were both arrested by a posse led by Llano County Sheriff J. J. Bozarth, his deputies and a few rangers from Company C of the Frontier Battalion. Both men were first transported to the more secure Travis County jail. John Ringo from the time he was arrested during October of 1876, would spend over a year in some county jail awaiting trial for the murder of James Cheyney in Mason County. In contrast, just over a month after his arrest, George Gladden was moved to Llano County for trial and on Dec. 7, 1876, he was convicted of the murder of Peter Bader and sentenced to 99-years. Texans have traditionally called a 99-year sentence, "life imprisonment" in the State Penitentiary.[20]

In November of 1876, John Ringo is said to have been brought back to Mason and indicted for the murder of James Cheyney. But, soon after, the Mason County court house burned down on the night of Jan. 21, 1877, and the district court records, including any records dealing with the indictment of Ringo and others, were lost in the fire.[21]

On May 18, 1877, some four months after the court house burned in Mason County, Ringo was indicted (Cause # 21) by the grand jury for the murder of James Cheyney. This indictment took place during the first district court term after the fire and may have been a reindictment, but the records do not provide such information. That it had taken District Attorney F. D. Wilkes six months to obtain an indictment, regardless of any fire and it would then take another 12 months to determine that his case against John Ringo was too weak to go to trial, was not a good sign for the courts in Mason County.[22]

Ringo (Cause #21) had been the fifth of six men indicted for murder in that district court term of May, 1877. Only one of the others indicted had anything to do with Cooley's or Ringo's vendetta and that was John Ringo's old friend, John Baird (Cause # 22), who was indicted for the murder of Peter Bader. Baird was, however, never arrested and his case was finally dismissed in the Nov. 1882 District Court Term, for "Defendant Baird (was) supposed to be dead—." But there were no indictments for the murder of Tim Williamson or Moses Baird, much less the Baccus Brothers and two other men who were later found dead, after being taken away by a posse of Sheriff Rufus Clark. A look at the district court records in Mason County in the two terms of the court during 1877 after the fire and at the next several years are even more revealing. At a time when some local citizens and the Frontier Battalion still claimed that a range war was "raging", only fifteen indictments were returned in 1877, for cattle theft and three for the theft of a horse. Not much of a "range war," as Lampasas County that same year had twenty-one indictments for livestock theft and Burnet County had forty-five indictments.[23]

On Jan. 11, 1878, after being held in jail for over a year, John Ringo was released on a writ of habeas corpus and his bond was fixed at $2,500. As had happened previously, a number of very responsible citizens and cattlemen went his bond. As David Johnson wrote in his book, "John Ringo," that, "If ever there was a time to run, it was now." But to his credit Ringo did not run out on his bondsmen.[24]

John Ringo's Indictment Quashed

Four months later, on May 15, 1878, having spent over eighteen months attempting to gather witnesses and testimony, District Attorney Wilkes in Mason County moved to dismiss the case against John Ringo because, "testimony can not be procured to make out the case." Contrary to what appears in several books on John Ringo regarding jail sentences as a result of being "convicted of a Mason County murder," Ringo was never convicted of any murder in Mason County. He was not even tried, because the only case against him was dismissed. He was, therefore, not sentenced, nor did he spend any time in the Texas State Penitentiary.[25]

Not only was John Ringo neither tried for murder, nor sentenced to the Texas State Penitentiary, six months after the case against him was dismissed, on Nov. 15, 1878, he ran for and was elected constable in Precinct #4, in Mason County. Precinct #4 included a large rural area in southeast Mason County, along with the community of Loyal Valley located on the road to Fredericksburg. There is, however, no indication that Ringo ever served as constable, as his date of qualification and commissioning are not included in the election returns. But, neither are the other four constables elected that same date in the other Mason County precincts. This most likely indicates that either none of those elected ever qualified and served, or that a recording error occurred.[26]

Ringo never appeared in Lampasas District Court the second time to defend against the charge of "seriously threatening to take the life of a human being." The charge would be dismissed on Nov. 12, 1879, almost four years after he was first indicted, "upon suggestion of (the) death" of John Ringo.[27]

He was however, very much alive for only a month after the Lampasas case was dismissed, and some eighteen months after his murder case was dismissed in Mason County, Ringo again came to public notice when on Dec. 14, 1879, he was arrested in Stafford, Arizona after the alleged attempted murder of Louis Hancock. Then only some 3-1/2 years after he left Texas, in July of 1882, John Ringo would take his own life in a lonely corner of the desert in Southern Arizona.

Some Closing Thoughts

History has not been very kind to either Scott Cooley or John Ringo. When Cooley is noticed, he is usually cursed and totally vilified. Yet his crime, that of participating in a vendetta to avenge the murder of true and good friends, sounds very much like what those men (the Earps and Holliday) who John Ringo later opposed in Tombstone, are praised for time and time again. Ringo has been called "antisocial," "alienated," a "back-shooter," "unhappy," "alcoholic" and "suicidal." Yet, in real life he was personally supported time and time again by a number of very respectable citizens of Burnet County over a number of years, even during times of trouble and after being indicted for serious crimes in several district courts.

Suicidal, Ringo certainly was by the time he reached Arizona, and likely a heavy drinker. But, antisocial, alienated and unhappy just does not seem to fit the John Ringo I looked at in

Texas between 1874 and 1879. For some reason, however, Ringo is never described in any biography as a "loyal and true friend", but there is little question that he was all of that to a number of people.

APPENDIX B
CRIME & VIOLENCE IN NINETEENTH CENTURY TEXAS

Included in this Appendix are important, diverse and thought provoking, but unrelated comments and observations on two broad subjects related to crime and violence in nineteenth century Texas. To have put them elsewhere, would have possibly hidden them from view in one chapter or another, when these comments actually touch on more than just one period of time. Because the sources of information are either self-evident, or they are included in the text, there are no end notes in this Appendix B.

MURDER, VIOLENCE AND OTHER CRIMES IN TEXAS

The information contained herein and in various other places in the book, is to my knowledge the first attempt to look seriously at the type of crimes committed, along with estimating violent crime and murder rates in a number of different counties in early Texas. This was done primarily to better understand and more accurately portray the level of violence in Texas during the first 55 years of the Lone Star State. If one chooses to rely on this data, no matter how imperfect it may be, it provides the first glimpse of statistical data calculated that tells just how violent Texas was over 100 years ago. As a result, some comments and background on the research presented herein follows.

On January 1, 1976, the State of Texas adopted the Uniform Crime Report (UCR) as the official statewide assessment of crimes. It is used for many different purposes, but most often as a guide to judge how dangerous the state and different areas in the state were during any reporting calendar year. It has also sometimes been used to grade the effectiveness of different law enforcement agencies across the state. The Department of Public Safety is responsible for maintaining this study. The latest available compilation is, "2000, Crime in Texas", published in 2002.

The information that is contained in "2000, Crime in Texas," gives the reader some uniform statistics across the state for so-called major crimes. To do this the Uniform Crime Report collects data from across the state on seven index crimes: murder, rape, robbery, aggravated assault, burglary, theft and motor vehicle theft. The first four are classified as violent crimes, those crimes where there is a confrontation between the perpetrator and victim. The last three are property crimes, where the crime committed is the attempt at, or the actual taking of property, most often during the absence of the owner. Of the total offenses reported in Texas during 2000, 11 percent of those crimes committed were violent crimes (assault, rape, robbery and murder), while 89 percent of those crimes committed were property crimes (burglary and theft, including motor vehicle theft).

Of importance is also the "clearance rate" of offenses, when the perpetrator is identified and taken into custody. In 2000, law enforcement cleared 46 percent of all violent crimes, but only 15 percent of all property crimes in Texas. That general level of arrests for those index crimes changes only slightly from year to year. The total value of all property stolen in Texas during 2000 was over $1.5 billion dollars and the crime rate was actually down from the previous year, and down more significantly from the 1980s, when violence was most widespread in Texas.

During the first 55 years of the Lone Star State there was no Uniform Crime Report, as practiced today to make sure government and citizen know how much crime and violence was actually taking place in their communities. There was also no Index Crimes to help track different criminal offenses, no Reporting Procedures to make sure there was a valid count of crimes, no hate crimes, little interest in family violence, and no Crime Rates were calculated to be able to understand exactly just how violent living in the Old West really was.

Furthermore, there probably never will be a collection of statistics or a report available on crime in nineteenth century Texas that all will accept. This is due to the problems involved not only with the collection of data, but more important it is due to the lack of an accurate, complete and unbiased data base. Many of these problems are mentioned in the manuscript, and without being too repetitive, the first problem is that some counties have lost their records to fires, floods, neglect and theft in years past.

While such a compilation appears unlikely covering the entire state, there is some hope that data from a large number of Texas counties can be collected and analyzed, if one is not a perfectionist. This is exactly what has been attempted in this book. For several years a number of selected Texas counties were visited to examine and collect data primarily from district, county and justice court records and where possible from sheriff's dockets and other records. The Texas State Library and Archives Commission and other libraries across the state were also visited and information from all these sources are a valuable part of the data base.

When dealing with nineteenth century records, there must be some compromises arrived at early in any analysis, and one of the first is that one must deal with grand jury indictments and not arrests. This makes it impossible to calculate the volume of crimes in different Texas counties during the nineteenth century as the "Crime Volumes" are calculated today, because the data base is tainted. There simply is little or no arrest data available from which to base any credible study. There is also little opportunity to know all of those who actually stood trial, were judged guilty or who went to prison; the information is just not always available in the court records.

Therefore, what is calculated herein are "Crime Rates" in various Texas counties for those already recognized violent Index Crimes (murder, rape, robbery and all types of assault), plus murder is also calculated separately. This data is based on a study and calculation of the number of indicted violent crimes and murders committed per 100,000 population. As a result, no matter what the population of the county, the resulting rates are comparable with the previous rate of those crimes in either the same county or in any other county in Texas. In addition, it was possible to use the information collected on other crimes committed, to both present some idea of the level of crimes committed and to round out the many comments and occasional opinions contained in the manuscript. By using this method, it was then possible to finally begin to develop a realistic understanding of the number and type of crimes that occurred, where and when they occurred and then have some way to compare the level of crimes committed in many of the years during the first fifty-five years of the Lone Star State.

The initial nineteenth century data on violent crime and murders in Texas used in this book can never reach the level of sophistication of current "Uniform Crime Report" statistics. They are, however, a giant leap ahead in determining just how violent and where Texas was most violent, than only relying on the collection of mostly anecdotal accounts of violence. Some will question these estimates, but surely they are better than anyone's "convictions," or "hunches."

Regarding certain types of crime and criminals, it is also worth noting that some observers have proposed that violence among todays teenagers is to a large degree the result of the violence young people have seen on television and in movies. This has been suggested because juvenile crime has increased in the last twenty years. During 2000 for example, 9 percent of all violent crime clearances and 18 percent of all property crime clearances in Texas involved the arrest of persons under 18 years of age. Do these crimes by teenagers in the late twentieth century really mean that the movies and TV play a large part in encouraging such violence? While that may have some effect, teenage violence is no new phenomena.

As with other crime data, there is little or no teenage crime statistics published for the nineteenth century. However, already mentioned in this text are a number of murders in the 1860s and 1870s that were committed by very young men, all under 18 years of age. Those young murderers are easy to follow, as four of them after they were adults, turned out to be among the most violent psychopathic killers in early Texas. A listing of those men and a conservative estimate of those each killed as both a teenager and as an adult, over 125 years ago included: John Wesley Hardin (11), (although Hardin personally claimed the number was closer to 40); Cullen Montgomery Baker (8); Bill Longley (11) and Jim Miller (12). As these numbers indicate, teenage crime is not a twentieth century phenomena. Young men violently taking the lives of others has been with us for a long, long time.

The following is a look at crime and murder in a number of specific Texas counties, during the late 1800s. A number of other Texas counties were also visited, but for a host of reasons that data is not included here.

BURNET COUNTY:

Located in the Texas hill country, by the 1870s it could no longer be considered a frontier county, with any danger of Indian raids. Its western boundary is the Colorado River and it is the next county west of Travis County, where the capitol of Texas is located in Austin. Burnet County supplied the granite for its construction and was organized in 1852. Its population in 1860 was 2,487, in 1870 it had barely grown to 3,668, but by 1880, it had nearly doubled to 6,855. Burnet County has long been given over to grazing land, and in 1887 there were just over 37,000 cattle and 49,831 sheep, but there were also 4,109 milk cows with an annual production that same year of almost 600,000 gallons of milk. Near the Colorado some farming took place, but away from the river, farming was not often attempted.

There were no significant or sustained periods of violence and murder in Burnet County after the Civil War. That should not, however, give the impression that Burnet County was crime free, for there were never less than some 26 felony indictments returned each year by the grand jury through the end of the nineteenth century. The years 1871, 1875, 1877, 1878 and 1885 were times when higher levels of livestock theft, unlawfully carrying a weapon and illegal gambling were charges for which most grand jury indictments were issued.

Livestock (cattle, horse & mule) theft became noticeable beginning in 1871 when 16 indictments were returned by the grand jury. In 1876 this had increased to 32 indictments and in 1877/78, a total of 41 indictments were returned for theft of livestock. For a number of years after that livestock theft dropped. Then in 1884, there were suddenly 33 indictments returned for unlawful carrying of weapons. While never quite that high again, eight years later (1893) there were still 13 indictments and in 1899, four were indicted for unlawful carry.

While there were always some violent crimes committed, violence was usually isolated and murder was even more rare. During some 30 years of court records reviewed, there were only two years (1870 and 1891) when as many as two people were indicted for murder in the county. During the remaining 28 years only 15 men were indicted for murder. With regard to crime rates of murder in Burnet County, with a population of only 3,668 persons in 1870, the two murders that year resulted in the highest murder rate (54.0 murders per 100,000) in Burnet County than in any other of the remaining 30 years of the nineteenth century.

Colorado County:

One of the original 23 counties in Texas, it was organized in 1836. The county was predominantly a farming area, with large fields of cotton once grown along the Colorado River which runs through the center of the county. Before the Civil War, because of that, there were large numbers of slaves living in Colorado County and cotton was the most important cash crop. The county had a population well over 7,000 in 1860, growing slightly to 8,326 by 1870 and then doubling in 1880 to 16,673. The county would grow to just over 22,000 in 1900 and then level off to between 17,000 and 18,000 during the remainder of the twentieth century. Because of the relatively large population in Colorado County after the Civil War, murder rates per 100,000 population were never as high as in some other counties, however beginning in 1867 there was a sudden increase in the amount of violence and five murders occurred that year.

In 1870 and 1871, that number had increased to eight murders in each of those two years, and the murder rate was 96.3 per 100,000 population, the highest murder rate in Colorado county during the nineteenth century. If the murder rate did not increase in the future as the population grew, the number of murders did. In 1874, 1879 and 1886, nine people were indicted for murder in each of those three years. In 1883, 14 people were indicted for murder, a nineteenth century record for the county, but because of the increase in population, the murder rate was still only 80.0 per 100,000 population, less than it had been in 1870/71. When the period from 1865 to 1874 is examined, there were 41 grand jury murder indictments issued, indicating a large amount of violence, mostly involving freedmen, both as victims and as perpetrators.

There were some hard men and women in Colorado County and a number distinguished themselves by being repeat offenders in a host of crimes from about 1851 to 1900. The most memorable of those were 21 men and women with a shared last name of Townsend. All were indicted one or more times during that period for offenses ranging from obstructing a public road to rape and multiple murders. Beth Townsend had five indictments for cattle theft between 1872 and 1875. But Moses Townsend was indicted 16 times, usually for illegal gambling but also a number of those times for aggravated assault and assault with intent to kill. He was also sometimes a victim of violence. In the 1890s, Constable Thomas L. Townsend died while investigating a disturbance when thrown from his horse, and Constable Moses Townsend was stabbed and killed by a prisoner in the Weimer jail.

Because of the long period of record keeping and the efforts of local historians to index crime statistics, looking at the level of violent crimes in Colorado County during that first ten years after the Civil War, indicates that without question Colorado County was a very violent and dangerous place to live. From 1866 to 1875, the various grand juries indicted 214 persons for violent crimes in the county, indicating a very dangerous level of violent crime. After 1875, murder rates dropped, but relatively high murder and violent crime rates returned to Colorado County during the 189Os.

LAMPASAS COUNTY:

Located just north of Burnet County and organized five years later in 1856, Lampasas western boundary is the Colorado River. Mostly suited to cattle and sheep raising, very little of the land was ever in cultivation. The county had a population of only 1,334 in 187O, grew to 5,421 in 188O and 7.584 in 189O, but by 191O had reached a population of 9,5OO and in the following years has never quite again reached that number.

Lampasas is a Texas county with what appears to have been a partially mythical reputation for violence, due almost entirely to the actions of one family, the Samuel Horrell's. Samuel Horrell had five sons and all but one lost his life in a violent death. The Horrell brothers helped kill four Texas State policemen in 1873, packed up the family and moved to New Mexico and only returned to Lampasas three years later, but were never tried in the courts for their part in those murders. In 1877 a feud between the Horrell and Higgins family and friends cast another shadow across the land and 14 indictments were returned for murder that year. That made Lampasas one of the most violent places in Texas that year, with an estimated murder rate of 333.3 per 1OO,OOO population and an estimated violent crime rate of 952.3 per 1OO,OOO population.

With the departure of the Horrell brothers to boot hill and "Pink" Higgins for West Texas, however, Lampasas soon settled down and only 18 murder indictments were returned by a grand jury during the following 22 years. During that same period, even assaults of all types dropped significantly, indicating that the wild old days ended in Lampasas at the same time as the Horrell brothers, in 1877. From 1877 to 1887, illegal gambling made up a large number of indictments in the district court. But the theft of cattle and horses was also significant, as in the four years between 1877 and 1881, there were 91 indictments for livestock theft. Even as late as 1884, 14 more indictments were returned for livestock theft.

Mason County:

In the mid-184Os German immigrants moved into Gillespie County, which almost a decade later the northern part of Gillespie would become a part of Mason County. They would still make up around forty percent of the population in the late nineteenth century. In 1851, the army established Fort Mason, in addition to Fort Martin Scott near Fredericksburg and those two army posts provided some protection against hostile Indian raids. But as late as 186O, Sheriff Thomas Milligan, the first sheriff of Mason County was killed on Feb. 19 of that year by an Indian raiding party after mules and horses in his care.

When Mason County was organized in 1858, hostile Indian raids into the county were not unusual. Because of the danger on the frontier and the sudden lack of adequate military protection during the Civil War, Mason County's population was almost the same in the census of 186O and 187O. Both census showed only some 65O people in the county. When the U. S. Army returned to Fort Mason after 1866, it again offered more protection along the frontier and the 188O census showed growth to a population of 2,655. Then in 189O the population reached 5,18O, but that is about where it remained level for the first half of the twentieth century. Mason County is cattle country, with some sheep, but little of the land was under cultivation.

Beginning in mid-1874, the ethnic German cattle raisers were said to have been pitted against the Anglo-Saxon cattlemen of the county in what has been called the Mason County War, a range war with allegedly large numbers of cattle stolen or killed by either side. But, between 1877 and 188O (the court house burned in January, 1877 destroying earlier records), there were only 35 indictments for cattle and horse theft. That range war started soon after Sheriff John Rufus Clark was elected with German backing and that story is told in some detail in Appendix A.

During a 12 month period in 1875 and 1876, at least 12 men were killed as a result of personal vendettas evolving out of the Mason County War. Only three men were ever indicted for those murders and only one of those was ever tried and convicted. But 12 murders in a county with a population of only 1,7OO people, results in a murder rate in Mason County of 705.8 per 100,000 population. During that period the law and the district court in Mason County failed time and time again to prosecute those known to have killed within the county.

That high a rate of murder during 1875/1876 is unparalleled in the Texas counties that were studied. In 1877 there were five new murder indictments in Mason County. Then between 1877 and 1885, there was very little violence in the county. In 1885 a new wave of violence swept through the county when six murder, 13 aggravated assault and 46 liquor violations topped the grand jury indictments. Luckily this show of violence was fleeting and there were no murders and the number of assaults dropped significantly during the next four years. Like most Texas counties about that time, liquor and gambling offenses made up most of the indictments between 1877 and 1900, however, from 1887 and 1893, there were 15 indictments for the theft of horses in Mason County. In 1886, violations of the unlawful carrying law were transferred to the county court, as were all liquor violations just two years later. Prosecution of gambling offenses stayed in the district court.

SHACKELFORD COUNTY:

Although created in 1858, Shackelford County was not organized until 1874, some seven years after Fort Griffin was established in the northeast part of the county. This long time frontier county, located some 120 miles west of Fort Worth is stock country, had only about 7,000 acres under cultivation in the 1880s. In 1870 the county only had a population of 455 people, increased to 2,037 by 1880 and then stayed near that same level through the remainder of the nineteenth century.

Before the county was organized, the only population center was outside of the army post at Fort Griffin, in what was called the flats, or Griffin. That community had a reputation as the center for gambling, drinking and whoring, as confirmed in various court records. After the county was organized, the citizens of the county formed a new town near the center of the county as the county seat and named it Albany. During the first term of the district court in 1875, three murder indictments were returned by the grand jury, but with a relatively small population among those counties studied, Shackelford county in that first court session had a murder rate of 250.0 per 100,000 population, a higher murder rate than was ever reached in Burnet or Colorado Counties during the nineteenth century, but less than half the murder rate in Mason County that same year.

Then during the 15 years between 1876 and 1890, indictments for murder and violent crimes never again reached that level, except in 1878, when three indictments for murder were again returned by the grand jury, plus one former sheriff, John Larn, was murdered in the county jail. Even with three indicted and one killed by vigilantes in 1878, the murder rate stayed the same as in 1875 because of the increasing population numbers. In addition to murders in Shackelford County, an amazingly high level of violence occurred in the county in 1875, although the grand jury returned just 17 indictments for violent crimes. With such a small population, however, this resulted in an estimated violent crime rate of 1,416.6 per 100,000 population.

In 1875 and 1876, a very effective vigilante committee is evident when reviewing Shackelford County District Court Minute Books. More than one defendants death was "suggested (to have taken place) and the court case was dropped." A significant number of bonds were forfeited when a defendant chose to ride out of town while still in good health, rather than await trial in the county. Charles McBride, a repeat offender, who was indicted for both the theft of a mare and aggravated assault in June of 1875, along with Joseph Watson who was indicted for assault with intent to kill, were also both suspected cattle thieves. The two men were lynched by vigilantes in 1876, before either was tried for any crime. In addition to vigilante justice, by the 1878 term of the district court, the court was regularly sentencing those convicted of livestock theft to 5 years in the State Penitentiary.

But most crimes in Shackelford County were misdemeanors, and beginning about 1877 many of those cases were handled in the county or justice courts. "Long Kate," "Minnie," Mollie McCabe, "Hurricane Bill," Lotta (not Lottie) Deno, Nancy Sharpe and "Sway backed Mag," were all charged at different times with keeping a house of prostitution. Mike Lynch and Doc Holliday were indicted for playing cards in a public place and "Curly alias Horace," was indicted for assault and battery, robbery, and discharging a pistol in Griffin.

Lizzie Harvey was charged with vagrancy and fined $1.00. W. M. Tate was tried and sentenced to two years in the state penitentiary for swindling $26.00, while Charles Musslemen, Stuart Wilkerson, Perry Miller and George Turner were all indicted for the theft of horses and all were tried and sentenced to five years each in the state penitentiary. Then W. H. Ledbetter admitted to discharging a firearm across a public street in the town of Albany on May 1, 1876, and he was fined 10 cents with a 15 cents docket fee. In Burnet County, John Ringo paid a fine of $75.00 for that same offense. By most standards, after 1878 Shackelford County appears to have abandoned its wild ways and between 1886 and 1899, there were no murder indictments filed.

YOUNG COUNTY:

Although organized in 1856, the loss of U. S. Army protection during the Civil War largely laid waste to this North Texas county from 1862 until 1866, because of significant Indian raids in the area during that period. The population in Young county was 592 in the 1860 census, but in 1870, there were only 135 people remaining in the county and all were forted up for mutual protection. As a result, a second organization took place in 1874 and a new county seat was selected in Graham, Texas. By 1880, the population had increased rapidly to 4,726; in 1890 it reached just over 5,000 and then increased to 6,540 by 1900. Cattle raising, in addition to attempts at farming took place in Young County. Because of the number of Indian depredations that occurred in the 1860s, Young County was classified as a frontier county until the late 1870s, making it legally possible to carry a firearm without being fined, somewhat longer than in other Texas counties in that area.

The district court returned to Young County in 1875, and within a few months Sheriff Richard Kirk was killed in a gunfight in February of 1876. The death of Sheriff Kirk occurred when he attempted to arrest a desperado known as "Buffalo Bill," on an out of county warrant and the two men killed each other in a gun fight in Holly's Store in Belknap. A second lawman, Deputy Sheriff Sam Murphee was killed and Deputy Dave Melton was wounded on New Years Day, 1881, when the three McDonald brothers who were already in the Young County jail on murder indictments (Cause #126, 127 & 128) attempted to escape. All three of the McDonald brothers were shot and killed outside the jail by local citizens.

From 1875 to 1900, except for problems that involved two other violent families, the McDonald brothers in 1881 and Marlow Brothers in 1888-1889, there was actually very little violent crime in Young County. During that 25 year period, Young County typically had no more than one or two murder indictments per year, and only twice were three and then four men indicted for murder. That largest number of murder indictments, four, were returned by a Young County grand jury in 1889, with two of those involving the Marlow Brothers. But, in addition to four murder indictments returned by the grand jury, three Marlow brothers, a guard and two of the mob who came to kill the Marlow's were shot and killed in 1889, making that a very deadly year in an otherwise rather peaceful county.

Brown, Fayette, Fort Bend, Llano, Navarro, Smith and Taylor Counties:

During the research for this book some records from the county and district clerks office in these Texas counties were also reviewed. For one reason of another, including but not limited to one court house that was burned which destroyed most of the pertinent criminal records, records lost to floods, or records for a number of reasons found difficult to interpret, caused the author to abort any further examination at these locations. Regardless, there is included information from some of these areas that make up a part of the story included herein. For that I want to acknowledge the assistance of those in the above listed courthouses and particularly the county and district clerk offices.

Brief Analysis Of Frontier Battalion Activities

During the research for this book, it became obvious that while there are numerous tales told of the adventures of different ranging companies, little effort has been spent analyzing those adventures, in order to know more about the operations of the Frontier Battalion when they took on law enforcement duties. As a result, the activities of the Frontier Battalion were examined in order to try and determine why they were so successful in their pursuit of Reconstruction outlaws and many groups of hostile Indians, but then sometimes failed to prevent or even show-up during some important periods of murder and mayhem in Texas.

In 1874, the Frontier Battalion, was a Texas state troop command organized primarily to supplement the army's efforts at protecting the frontier from hostile Indian raids. By the late 187Os, however, the Frontier Battalion was running out of hostile Indians to pursue and they began to operate more and more in the area of law enforcement, initially along what was still considered the Western frontier counties of Texas. As lawmen, the Frontier Battalion had its successes and failures, as did any law enforcement agency.

In fact, there is much to be learned about rural Texas law enforcement from those successes and failures of the ranging companies in post Civil War Texas. It is obvious that much of the Frontier Battalion's success in law enforcement after 1874 can be attributed more to their organization and to their command structure, than to their individual abilities as lawmen. Their organization and command structure required that they keep records of the criminals they chased or encountered and they often used the telegraph to quickly report on events the individual commands were involved in. As a result they were able to call for reinforcements, to be quickly sent to a new crime scene and to gain vital information on criminals and crimes committed across the state.

They also had methods in place for acquiring supplies in remote areas of the state and were able to press forward as required, seldom being delayed for lack of men or equipment. But most important, they did not have to rely on the goodwill or anger of local citizens to make up a posse to chase the bad guys; they initially had the men to do the job already in the saddle. That was a ranging companys biggest advantage.

Like U. S. Army detachments on patrol, the Frontier Battalion and most earlier ranger commands were also able to travel across lines of jurisdiction in armed posses, looking for and fully capable of handling most trouble brought about by individual or smaller groups of outlaws, Indians or bandits. In effect, the captains in the Frontier Battalion, at least until the 189Os commanded fairly large groups of well-armed and deputized lawmen, who, along with the rapidly evolving development of cartridge pistols and repeating carbines, gave them a tremendous advantage compared to either individual outlaws or to the small bands of criminals they chased.

These are very significant, but seldom discussed assets of state troops, for in comparison to elected lawmen, who had to first maintain the jail and guard and feed any prisoners, the ability of a rural sheriff or constable to rely on more than one or two deputies in the nineteenth century was indeed rare. It was only if the citizens in his county, due to the severity of the crime committed, then agreed to accompany a sheriff or constable in a posse, that they were ever able to arrest any but the most incompetent or badly wounded fleeing outlaws. Even then, chasing desperate men with inexperienced man hunters in the posse often brought death to those who had just been deputized, or to those who led them. Furthermore, the county lawman's ability and oftentimes his desire to go after most criminals, except when large rewards were offered, usually ceased at or near his county line.

Good detective work was, however, seldom learned while chasing hostile Indians and the occasional bank or stagecoach bandits on horseback. To his credit, Frontier Battalion commander, Major John B. Jones seems to have recognized that fact as his command became more and more involved in arresting outlaws, rather than trailing hostile Indians. As a result, the state sometimes hired already trained detectives to assist them in big cases. The arrest of John Wesley Hardin is perhaps the most significant case in which a Dallas city detective was hired and played a major role in the tracking down and capture of Wes Hardin.

As noted in Chapter IX, by the late 188Os the Frontier Battalion had fallen on hard times and the size of the organization and many of the more prominent rangers had left, some for other jobs in law enforcement. As a result, the ability of the individual companies to effectively uphold the law had been severely reduced. During the 189Os, there is a strong indication that the reduction in size of the ranger companies may have even contributed to the death of several men.

The Frontier Battalion companies now appeared to be understaffed and may had sometimes lost their edge against different bands of bandits and cattle thieves along the Rio Grande. Certainly the number and effectiveness of the activities conducted by the mid-189Os seemed to seldom produce the type of results they had in the 187Os.

ENDNOTES

All of the sources used in developing this story are cited in these Endnotes. As a result, there is no bibliography included, as it would only be a duplication of those sources already cited.

CHAPTER I
COLONIAL TEXAS AND THE REPUBLIC, 1821-1845

1. "Judiciary" Handbook of Texas Online, accessed May 5, 2000; John Tumlinson, Sr To Barron de Bastrop, March 5, 1823, Austin Papers, Vol I, 582-583.

2. "Spanish Law" Handbook of Texas Online, accessed July 12, 2000; "Law" Handbook Online, accessed July 22, 2001.

3. William R. Hogan, "The Texas Republic" (Austin: U. T. Press, 1969), 245-246; H. N. P. Gammell, "The Laws of Texas 1822-1897" (Austin: The Gammell Book Co., 1898), Vol I, 1074, 1077, 1255, Vol II, 124, 177-178, 262, 1294; "Constitution of the Republic of Texas" The New Handbook of Texas, Vol I, 292: "Spanish Law" Handbook of Texas Online.

4. John Coles to Stephen F. Austin, Jan. 31, 1824, Austin Papers, Vol II, 733; Alcalde's Court Docket 1824, Austin Papers, Vol II, 760.

5. Constable's Subpoena, May 13, 1824, Austin Papers, Vol II, 792; Forms and Writs, Form of Attachment, Form of Warrant, Form of Subpoena in Criml. Case, Form of Subpoena in Civil Suit, Form of Bail Bond, 1824, Austin Papers, Vol II, 792, 800-802; Gammell, "Laws of Texas," Vol I, Austin's Colonization Laws, 1.

6. William B. Dewees, "Letters from an Early Settler of Texas," compiled by Cara Cardelle (Louisville:Morton & Ghriswold, 1852), 32-36; John Tumlinson, Sr To Jose Felix Trespalacios, March 9, 1823, Bexar Archives # 074:0338-43.

7. Dewees, "Letters Early Settler," 34-35; Tumlinson to Trespalacios, March 9, 1823, Archives.

8. Dewees, "Letters Early Settler," 33-37.

9. Gregg Cantrell, "Stephen F. Austin, Empresario of Texas" (New

Haven & London: Yale University Press, 1999), 224-226; William A. DePalo, "The Mexican National Army, 1822-1852" (College Station, Texas A&M Press, 1897), 41-46.

10. DePalo, "Mexican Army", 43-45.

11. T. R. Fehrenbach, "Lone Star" (New York: American Legacy Press, 1983), 287.

12. "Journal of Amon Underwood, 1834-1838", Southwest Historical Quarterly, Vol XXXII, Oct. 1928, #2, 127; personal communication Marshall Kuykendall.

13. Gammell, "Laws of Texas," Vol I, 905-1060, 1069-1085.

14. Gammell, "Laws of Texas," 1277-1302; "Constitution of the Republic," New Handbook, Vol II, 292.

15. Fehrenbach, "Lone Star," 281; Everett Dick, "The Dixie Frontier, A Social History" (Norman & London, O. U. Press, 1993), 59.

16. Hogan, "Texas Republic" 9-10; Fehrenbach, "Lone Star," 319-320; Lorna Geer Sheppard, "An Editor's View of Early Texas", (Austin, Eakin Press, 1998), 139-140.

17. Seymour V. Connor, "Adventures in Glory" (Austin: Steck-Vaughn Co., 1965), 16-17; John Edward Weems & Jane Weems, "Dreams of Empire" (New York: Barnes & Noble, 1871), 111; Luke Gournay, "Texas Boundaries" (College Station: Texas A & M Press, 1995), 25-34; "Columbia" Handbook of Texas Online, accessed 12/15/01.

18. Hogan, "Texas Republic," 260-262; Gammell, "Laws of Texas", Vol I, 187-195.

19. William R. Hogan, "Rampant Individualism in the Republic of Texas" Southwestern Historical Quarterly, Vol 44, 454463; Hogan, "Texas Republic", 260-262; Bill Stein & Bobbie Elliott compilers, "Index to District Criminal Cause Files, 1837-1879", Nesbitt Memorial Library Journal, May, 1994, Vol 4, No 2, 92-95; Sheppard, "An Editor's View," 142, 143, 146.

20. Stein, Nesbitt Journal, May 1996, 71-74; Sheppard, "Editor's View," 155-156. The following newspaper article appeared in the Dec. 4, 1844 issue of "The Northern Standard," perhaps describing the typical escape from a jail at the time. "BROKE JAIL.-On Sunday night last John Chapman, who was charged with the murder of a man by the name of Barkley, and who was confined in the (Harrison) county jail for appearance at the next term of the District Court, quitted the snug walls of his chamber and took leave of the hospitable keeper. The outer door was forced by some persons from without and the pad lock broke by which the trap door in the floor was fastened, when the prisoner took leg bail and has not been heard of since."

21. Gammell, "Laws of Texas," Vol I, 137-195.

22. "Compiled Index to Elected and Appointed Officials of the Republic of Texas, 1835-2846," Texas State Library & Archives Commission, 1981, 1-134.

23. Jack Selden, "Texas Justice, The Life and Times of the Third District Court of Texas" (Palestine, Clacton Press, 1997), 64-78; "Judiciary," Handbook of Texas Online, accessed 12/03/01.

24. Sheppard, "Editor's View" 145-148; Bill Stein, "Consider the Lily: The Unguilded History of Colorado County, Texas," (Columbus, Nesbitt Memorial library Journal, May, 1996, Vol 6, #2, 85-87.

25. C. L. Sonnichsen, "Ten Texas Feuds" (Albuquerque, U of New Mexico Press, 19957), 51-55.

26. Joseph M. Nance, "After San Jacinto, The Texas-Mexican Frontier, 1836-1841" (Austin: U. T. Press, 1963), 45-65; Jan Hutson, "The Chicken Ranch" (Cranbury: A. S. Barnes & Co., 1980), 21-40.

27. "John V. Morton" Handbook of Texas Online, accessed 06/20/00; "The Morton Family" Southwest Historical Quarterly, Vol 3, January 1900, 225.

28. Gournay, "Texas Boundaries," 31-36.

29. "Compiled Index of Officials," State Library, 1-134.

30. David M. Horton & Ryan K. Turner, "Lone Star Justice" (Austin, Eakin Press, 1999), 146-147, 157-158; Selden, Texas Justice," 20-76. It is difficult to follow the work of judicial districts in the early days of the Republic, because more than one county made up each district and the counties making up the judicial districts also changed every few years. Because district court records are maintained in the county courthouse to which the district court belonged and not in any files maintained by the judicial district, to look at the work of a single judicial district in early Texas, requires visiting a number of counties.

31. Selden, "Texas Justice," 86-87.

32. Walter Prescott Webb, "The Texas Rangers" (Austin: U. Texas Press, 1935), 29-32.

33. Gammell, "Laws of Texas," Vol I, 274-275.

34. Rena M. Green, editor, "Memoirs of Mary A. Maverick" (Lincoln & London: U. Of Nebraska Press, 1989), 24.

35. Weems, "Dreams of Empire," 161-168.

36. Green, "Maverick Memoirs," 25-31; Ronald G. DeLord, editor, "The Ultimate Sacrifice" (Austin, Peace Officers Memorial Foundation, 2000), 39. During the writing of "Texas Constables, A Frontier Tradition," on page 29, I wrote that there was no Sheriff in Bexar County during the Republic and the only lawman was a constable. Since that time I have come across information that corrects those ear-

lier statements in that San Antonio and Bexar County both had law enforcement officers during the days of the Texas Republic, including not only a constable but also a sheriff and his deputies.

37. Donaly E. Brice, "The Great Comanche Raid" (Austin: Eakin Press, 1987), 27-65.

38. Frederick Wilkins, "The Legend Begins" (Austin, State House Press, 1996), 74-76, 117-135.

39. Sonnichsen, "Ten Texas Feuds," 60.

40. Sonnichsen, "Ten Texas Feuds," 12-29.

41. Sheppard, "Editor's View," 148-152; Sonnichsen, "Ten Texas Feuds," 20-21, 30, 38-39, C. L. Douglas, "Famous Texas Feuds" (Austin, State House Press, 1988), 22-61.

42. Semour V. Connor, "Adventure in Glory" (Austin: Steck-Vaughn Co., 1965) 218-221; Horton, "Lone Star Justice," 32-33; Sheppard, Editor's View," 148-152; Sonnichsen, "Ten Texas Feuds," 51-55.

43. "Gone to Texas" Handbook of Texas Online, accessed April, 23, 2000.

44. "Augustine Hardin," Handbook of Texas Online, accessed 11/20/00. This family only shares the name of Hardin with, but is no relation to a well known outlaw family which included John Wesley and Joe Hardin.

45. Stein, "Index Colorado Cause Files," 87-89.

46. Sheppard, "Editor's View," 70-73.

47. Hogan, "Texas Republic," 253-254.

48. "Compiled Index of Officials." State Library, 121.

49. Selden, "Texas Justice," 12-15; Andrew Forest Muir, "Augustus M. Tomkins, Frontier Prosecutor," Southwest Historical Quarterly, Vol LIV, #3, 316-321.

50. Muir, "Tomkins, Frontier Prosecutor," SWHQ, Vol LIV, #3, 316-319.

51. Hogan, "Texas Republic," 250; Muir, "Tomkins, Frontier Prosecutor," SWHQ, Vol LIV, #3, 318-321.

CHAPTER II
THE LONE STAR STATE, 1846-1855

1. John S. D. Eisenhower, "So Far From God" (N. Y.: Doubleday, 1989), 63-68.

2. Wilkins, "Legend," 199; Charles D. Spurlin, "Texas Volunteers in the Mexican War" (Austin: Eakin Press, 1998), 60-67.

3. Spurlin, "Texas Volunteers," 141-254.

4. A. A. Bender, "Texas Frontier 1848-1861," Southwest Historical

Quarterly, Vol 38, #2, October, 1934, 135-145.

5. "Constitution of 1845," New Handbook, Vol I, 278-288; "Law," New Handbook, 114-115; "Judiciary," Handbook Online, 01/05/01.

6. Gammell, "Laws of Texas," Vol II, 85, 92-93, 127-128, 257-259, 261-269; "Texas Almanac, 2002-2003" (Dallas: The Dallas Morning News, 2001), 45.

7. "Law" New Handbook, Vol 5, 114-119; "Judiciary" Handbook Online, accessed, 06/21/00.

8. Selden, "Texas Justice" 120-121.

9. Gournay, "Texas Boundaries," 54-56; Fehrenbach, "Lone Star," 288-291.

10. "Register of Elections & Appointments, State & County Officials, 1846-1848" Reel 3498, Texas State Archives and Library.

11. Gammell, "Laws of Texas" Vol III, 219-232.

12. Dick, "Dixie Frontier," 229-234.

13. Thomas T. Smith, "The Old Army in Texas," (Austin, Texas State Historical Assn., 2001), 14-15.

14. Smith, "Old Army," 6-21, 53-87.

15. John Boessenecker, "Gold Dust & Gunsmoke" (N. Y.: John Wiley & Sons, 1999), 3-4.

16. "John Coffee Hays," Handbook Online, accessed 05/30/01.

17. Boessenecker, "Gold Dust," 22-28.

18. Boessenecker, "Gold Dust," 250-265.

19. Texas Almanac, 1978-1979, "Texas Population, 1850-1970," 184; Fehrenbach, "Lone Star," 309-313.

20. Randall B. Campbell, "A Southern Community in Crisis: Harrison County, Texas, 1850-1880" (Austin: Texas State Historical Assn., 1983), 22-27, 119-122.

21. James L. Haley, "Texas From Frontier to Spindletop" (N. Y. : St. Martin's Press, 1985), 120, 132; Fehrenbach, "Lone Star," 309-311; Texas Almanac, 2002-2003, 45.

22. Fehrenbach, "Lone Star," 296-299, 323.

23. "Declaration of Revolutionary War Pension of John Hargrave, Sr.," dated October 1832 in Union County, Illinois, from family papers of Allen G. Hatley.

24. Fehrenbach, "Lone Star," 319-322.

25. Gournay, "Texas Boundaries," 68-72; Smith, "Old Army," 53-89.

26. Smith, "Old Army," 14-48.

27. Smith, "Old Army," 14-19.

28. Webb, "Texas Rangers," 141-143; Smith, "Old Army," 26-138.

29. Smith, "Old Army," 135-138.

30. W. J. Hughes, "Rebellious Ranger" (Norman, O. U. Press, 1964),

88-98; Smith, "Old Army," 137-139.

31. Charles M. Robinson, "The Men Who Wear the Star" (N. Y. Random House, 2000), 110-115; Smith, "Old Army," 26-27.

32. Webb, "Texas Rangers," 130-146.

33. "Indian Reservations" Handbook of Texas Online, accessed, 11/22/00. A league of land equaled 4,428 acres. Jefferson Davis, while Secretary of War would also approve an experiment using camels to aid the army's ability to go on extended patrols in semi-arid parts of Texas. In 1861, that same Jefferson Davis would become President of The Confederate States of America. In 1854 Texas took a symbolic and fascinating step in paying off some of its public debt. An "Act to Provide for Ascertaining the Debt of the Late Republic of Texas" was approved on Feb. 7, 1853. On the 2nd day of December 1854, the TSL&A Commission, James S. Shaw Comptroller, officially recognized David Crockett's claim as # 6127 Second Class "B" Certificate of Public Debt, and the heirs of David Crockett were paid the sum of $24.00 for Crockett's service at the Alamo in 1836.

34. "Indian Reservations," Handbook of Texas Online, accessed, 11/22/00.

CHAPTER III
THE FRONTIER MOVES EVER WESTWARD, 1855-1861

1. Ophia Smith, "A Trip to Texas in 1855," Southwest Historical Quarterly, Vol LIX, #1, July, 1955, 24-33.

2. Smith, "Trip to Texas," 30.

3. Barry A. Crouch & Donaly E. Brice, "Cullen Montgomery Baker, Reconstruction Desperado" (Baton Rough & London: L. S. U. Press, 1997), 26-33.

4. Crouch, "Cullen Baker," 34-36.

5. "Cullen Baker" The Handbook of Texas Online, accessed 7/23/00.

6. DeLord, "Ultimate Sacrifice," 40.

7. Gourney, "Texas Boundaries," 74-83; Selden, "Texas justice," 140-141; Smith, "Old Army," 17. The quote, "They must be pursued, hunted, rundown, and killed," is taken from remarks made by George W. Kendall, who was a member of the Texas Republic's ill-fated Santa Fe Expedition in 1841. He later played a major role in developing and promoting the sheep business in Texas.

8. John Salmon Ford, "Rip Ford's Texas" (Austin: U. Of Texas Press, 1963), 223-225; Webb, "Texas Rangers," 151-160.

9. Ford, "Ford's Texas," 223-232.

10. Hughes, "Rebellious Ranger," 153-157; Ford, "Ford's Texas," 247-249, 266. Judge N. W. Battle of the 19th Judicial District ordered Ranger Captain John S. Ford in 1859, to arrest a number of men accused of murdering seven Indians from the Brazos reservation. Captain John S. Ford refused to carry out that order, basing his refusal on the fact that he was a military officer and not subject to the orders of civil officials. Ford was criticized for his refusal to act on the District Judge's order, as well he should have been—if as some contend the rangers were lawmen at the time. In fact, Ford was legally correct, as the rangers would not take on the duties of a peace officer until the formation of the Frontier Battalion in 1874.

11. "Juan N. Cortina" Handbook of Texas Online, accessed 04/15/00.

12. "Juan N. Cortina" Handbook Online; DeLord, "Ultimate Sacrifice," 41-42.

13. DeLord, "Ultimate Sacrifice," 41-42; "Texas State Gazette," January 4, 1861. On April 20, 1860, R. E. Lee, Lieutenant Colonel Commanding the Department of Texas advised Governor Sam Houston that he had no authority to receive volunteers into the service of the United States and that he was "unable to retain the Squadron of Rangers on the Rio Grande upon the conditions proposed". By that time, Cortina had been defeated, a Civil War was rapidly approaching and the U. S. Army had no desire to finance more Texas volunteer troops, who might soon be used against them. Letter dated 20 April, 1860 from R. E. Lee to Governor Sam Houston, # C 3-1-1, Inv# 5123, Texas State Library & Archives Commission.

14. Fehrenbach, "Lone Star," 334-336; Texas Almanac, 2001-2002, 46.

15. Fehrenbach, "Lone Star," 287-288; Stein, "Unguilded History," September, 1996, Vol 6, #3, 41.

16. Stella G. Polk, "Mason and Mason County: A History" (Austin, Pemberton Press, 1966) 29

17. Fehrenbach, "Lone Star," 335-338.

18. James Smallwood, "The History of Smith County, Texas" Volume I, (Austin: Eakin Press, 1999), 151-156; James Martin, "Texas Divided:Loyalty & Dissent in the Lone Star State, 1856-1874" (Lexington, U. of Kentucky Press, 1990), 6-9.

19. "Texas Troubles" Handbook of Texas Online, accessed 05/07/01; Fehrenbach, "Lone Star," 337-340.

20. Smallwood, "Smith County," 151-155; Martin, "Texas Divided," 13-17.

21. Fehrenbach, "Lone Star," 343-344; Texas Almanac, 2001-2002, 46.

CHAPTER IV
CIVIL WAR & RECONSTRUCTION, 1861-1870

1. Jeffrey M. Roth, "Civil War Frontier Defense Challenges in Northwest Texas" Military History of the West, Vol 30, #1, Spring, 2000, 21-22. On Feb. 23, 1861, when Texas voted to secede, there were 154 counties of which 30 were still unorganized and did not vote and two, McCulloch and Presidio were not heard from. In all 122 counties who voted, twenty voted against and the rest voted for secession. The aggregate vote was 60,826 of which 46,129 voted for secession and 14,697 voted against.

2. Roth, "Frontier Defense," 24.

3. "First Regiment, Texas Mounted Riflemen" Handbook of Texas Online, accessed 06/22/01; Roth, "Frontier Defense," 24-42.

4. Selden, "Texas Justice," 124.

5. "Military History" Handbook of Texas Online, accessed 6/22/00.

6. "Great Hanging at Gainesville" Handbook of Texas Online accessed 03/30/01.

7. DeLord, "Ultimate Sacrifice," 42.

8. Carl C. Rister, "Fort Griffin" West Texas History Assn. Yearbook 1, June, 1925, 16; Marilynne Howsley, "Forting Up on the Clear Fork" (Abilene: McWhinney Press, 2000), 145-193; Fehrenbach, "Lone Star," 369, 523; Texas Almanac, 1978-1979, 185-193. In the 1860 census there were 592 people in Young County. Ten years later in the 1870 census, only 135 people could be counted. Young Counties drop in population was not unusual, for Wise County's population over that same period decreased from 3,160 to 1,450, as a result of Indian raids during a period of little or no military protection.

9. DeLord, "Ultimate Sacrifice," 43.

10. "Brownsville, Texas" Handbook of Texas Online, accessed 02/06/01.

11. DeLord, "Ultimate Sacrifice," 43.

12. William L. Richter, "The Army in Texas During Reconstruction" (College Station, Texas A & M Press, 1987), 129-136; Smith, "Old Army," 104-106.

13. William B. Holberton, "Homeward Bound" (Mechanicsburg: Stackpole Books, 2001), 81-83.

14. Holberton, "Homeward Bound," 87-96.

15. Randolph B. Campbell, "Grass-Roots Reconstruction in Texas, 1865-1880" (Baton Rouge, L. S. U. Press, 1997), 8-11.

16. Sonnichsen, "I'll Die Before I'll Run" (Lincoln, U. Of Nebraska

Press, 1988), 35-37; DeLord, "Ultimate Sacrifice." 43.

17. Charles W. Ramsdell, "Reconstruction in Texas" (Austin, U. T. Press, 1970), 145-170; Campbell, "Grass-Roots," 11-40; Richter, "The Army in Texas," 97-115.

18. Richter, "The Army in Texas," 133-136, 161-166; William C. Nunn, "Texas Under the Carpetbaggers" (Austin: U. Texas Press, 1962), 177-209; Martin, "Texas Divided," 129-138; Smith, "Old Army," 104-109; Roth, "Civil War Defense," 41.

19. Robert Wooster, "The Military & United States Indian Policy, 1865-1903" (Lincoln & London: U. Of Nebraska Press, 1995), 128-132.

20. Smith, "Old Army," 17, 150-152; Roth, "Civil War Defense," 41-44.

21. Wooster, "Military Indian Policy," 45, 150-158.

22. Arthur M. Schlesinger, Jr., "The Business of Crime" Introduction to Inspector Thomas Byrnes, "1886, Professional Criminals of America" (New York: The Lyons Press, 2000), xiii-xxvii.

23. Candy Moulton, "The Writer's Guide to Everyday Life in the Wild West" (Cincinnati: Writer's Digest Books, 1999), 69-72.

24. Roth, "Civil War Defense," 31.

25. Crouch, "Cullen Baker Desperado," 32-33.

26. Richter, "The Army in Texas," 145-146; Crouch, "Cullen Baker Desperado," 62-68, 90-92.

27. Bill O'Neal, "Encyclopedia of Western Gunfighters" (Norman: University of Oklahoma Press, 1979), 31-32.

28. Crouch, "Cullen Baker Desperado," 32-33, 124-125; "Cullen Baker" Handbook of Texas Online, accessed 7/23/00.

29. Richter, "The Army in Texas," 136-139, 144-153; Smith, "Old Army," 107-111.

30. O'Neal, "Encyclopedia of Gunfighters," 4-6, 192; Miller, "Bloody Bill," 4-14.

31. Miller, "Bloody Bill," 15-25; Leon Metz, "John Wesley Hardin, Dark Angel of Texas" (El Paso, Mangan Books, 1996),12-16.

32. Miller, "Bloody Bill," 16-30.

33. Miller, "Bloody Bill," 22-28. Rick Miller, who wrote a very entertaining and well-referenced book, "Bloody Bill Longley", provided a valuable insight into the personality of Bill Longley's brother-in-law John Wilson, when he summed up Wilson's relationship with Longley's dead and departed sister Francis. He did this by quoting the following passage out of the Longley Family Bible, which stated that, "This was not a happy union")

34. "1872 Elected & Appointed Officials", Reel 3502, Texas State Archives & Library; Ernest Wallace, David M. Vigness, George B. Ward,

"Documents of Texas History" (Austin, State House Press, 1994), 213-216.

35. "1872 Elected & Appointed Officials", Reel 3502, Texas State Archives & Library; Campbell, "Grass-Roots," 20.

36. Wallace, "Documents," 214; DeLord, "Ultimate Sacrifice," 44-45. After the Civil War, problems sometime occurred with the distortion of court and other records by partisans of all stripe. As a result, some law enforcement and court records from the period during the initial military occupation of Texas and later during Reconstruction must be viewed with some caution, for they are sometimes both incomplete and distorted.

CHAPTER V
A TIME OF INCREASED VIOLENCE
1870-1873

1. Texas Almanac, 2002-2003, 48.
2. DeLord, "Ultimate Sacrifice," 45.
3. DeLord, "Ultimate Sacrifice," 46.
4. Nunn, "Texas Under Carpetbaggers," 29-38; Gammell, "Laws of Texas" Vol 10, 179-182; Robert M. Utley, "Forgotten Rangers" Journal #1, The Texas Ranger Dispatch, The On-Line Journal of Texas Ranger History, 2-4.
5. Gammell, "Laws of Texas," 185-190, 193-194.
6. "State Police" Handbook of Texas Online, accessed 06/20/00.
7. Ann Patton Baenziger, "The Texas State Police During Reconstruction: A Reexamination", Southwest Historical Quarterly, Vol 72, #4, April, 1969, 470-476; Gammell, "Laws of Texas," Vol VI, 185.
8. "State Police Roster," Box #401-1059, State Police Records, Texas State Library.
9. Box #401-864, State Police Records, Texas State Library; District Court Records in various Texas counties.
10. Box #401-864, State Police Records, Texas State Library.
11. "Report of Arrests" Box #401-1001, State Police Records, Texas Archives; Baenziger, "State Police," 474-476.
12. "Jack Helm" Texas Handbook Online, accessed 23/02/11, Sonnichsen, "I'll Die," 35-60.
13. Sonnichsen, "I'll Die," 43=46, 69-70; Delord, "Ultimate Sacrifice," 49.
14. "Report of Arrests" Box #401-1001, Texas State Library; Chuck Parsons & Marianne E. Hall Little, "L. H. McNelly Texas Ranger" (Austin: State House Press, 2001), 55-56.
15. "Report of Arrests" Box # 401-1001, Texas State Library;

"Military History" Handbook of Texas Online, accessed 12/08/00; Parsons, "McNelly," 159-172.

16. Edgar P. Sneed, "A Historiography of Reconstruction in Texas" (Southwestern Historical Quarterly, Vol 12, #4, April 1969), 444-447.

17. "Riots" Handbook of Texas Online, accessed 10/10/00: "Report of Arrests" Box# 401-1001 and Box #401-1002, Texas State Library. Although those who originally prepared the two Ledgers named them "Report of Arrests", when the contents are examined, this list of those arrested, might more accurately have been named a report of offenses or crimes, rather than arrests. This is because a single arrest in many cases actually resulted in clearing more than one criminal case. This happened because the arrest of someone who had three offenses charged against them in this report, would close the search for the man who was charged with all three of those crimes, but would result in only one arrest. As a result, the number of those arrested by the State Police was actually somewhat less than the actual number of crimes closed by each arrest.))

18. Baenziger, "State Police," 483-485; "State Police," Handbook Online. In late 1872, Adjutant General James Davidson, while on a mission to New York City, boarded a ship and sailed away to Europe as a fugitive from justice. After he had left Texas, it was discovered that Davidson had stolen some $37,000 of state funds. His whereabouts in Europe were unknown, and if he ever returned, it was not made public in Texas.

19. Parsons, "NcNelly," 97; Metz, "Hardin Dark Angel," 73-75; DeLord, "Ultimate Sacrifice," 47.

20. Barry A. Crouch, "Captain Thomas Williams, The Path of Duty," Published in "Human Traditions in Texas" (Wilmington: SR Books, 2001), 80-82; Parsons, "McNelly," 122; Sonnichsen, "I'll Die," 125-128. Sonnichsen on page 123 of that book writes that Lampasas Sheriff Denson had been killed five days before this gunfight, but that comment is not accurate as the sheriff was very much alive; he did not, however, take any part in the gunfight.

21. DeLord, "Ultimate Sacrifice," 48-49; Crouch, "Path of Duty," 82-84; "Adjutant Generals Roster Files, Box # 401-1059, Texas Archives; Metz, "Hardin Dark Angel," 305; Cause # 148, #151, #159, Lampasas District Court Records.

22. Frederick Nolan, "The Life & Times of the Horrell Brothers" (Stillwater: Barbed Wire Press, 1994), 25-28; Frederick Wilkins, "The Law Comes to Texas" (Austin: State House Press, 1999), 21-22; Sonnichsen, "I'll Die," 128-133.

23. Cause # 160, #162, #163, #164, Lampasas District Court

Records. As noted earlier, with many of the records originating during or just after Reconstruction, there are several versions of some events. An example is an interesting story of two black State Policemen charged with murder committed in December of 1871, in the Linn or Lynn Flat community in Nacogdoches County. The efforts made by Adjutant General Davidson to turn over those two men to local law enforcement, while protecting them from a possible lynching is interesting and it is not unusual during this period of Texas history that two different versions are available. One is included in my book, "Texas Constables, A Frontier Heritage," pages 49-51 and the other in Barry Crouch's story of "Captain Williams," pages 75-77, published in Ty Cashin's book, "The Human Tradition in Texas."

24. "Report of Arrests" Box #401-1001, Box # 401-1002, Texas State Library.

25. "Report of Arrests" Box #401-1001, Box # 401-1002, "State Police Correspondence for April, 1873," File #864-19, Texas State Library; Metz, "Hardin Dark Angel," 109-111. The State Police Records in the Texas State Library and Archives Commission provides for the researcher one of the few valuable sources of correspondence and records of crime across the State of Texas immediately after Reconstruction. While the State Police may be tainted in several ways, that information is very valuable but seems to have seldom been tapped. Not only did those specific records noted herein add valuable information to this research, numerous miscellaneous comments and observations on crime, criminals and law enforcement contained in the State Police correspondence files gave me greater insight into a number of events occurring in the state and helped me to better understand the incidence of crime and the criminal justice system active at that time in Texas.

26. Miller, "Bloody Bill," 42-53, 64-65.

27. DeLord, "Ultimate Sacrifice," 48.

28. Fehrenbach, "Lone Star," 206-207.

Chapter VI
THE TAMING OF THE FRONTIER
1874-1876

1. Texas Almanac, 1978-1979, 184; Jent, "Browsers Book," 24.

2. Fehrenbach, "Lone Star," 108-109, 433-434, 605.

3. Gammell, "Laws of Texas," Vol 8, 86-91; "Oath of John B. Jones to raise a "Battalion for Frontier Protection," signed May 19, 1974, and notarized in Navarro County, Texas State Library & Archives

Commission; Parsons, "McNelly," 139-159.

4. Wilkins, " The Law Comes to Texas," 26-30.

5. William M. Osborn, "The Wild Frontier" (N. Y.: Random House, 2000), 228-229.

6. Smith, "Old Army," 16-17, 39-40, 113-115, 156-161.

7. Smith, "Old Army," 64; Joe McCombs, "On the Cattle Trail & Buffalo Range", Lawrence Clayton, editor, "Tracks Along the Clear Fork" (Abilene, McWhinney Press, 2000) 172-185.

8. Haley, "Texas From Frontier," 219-222; Gournay, "Texas Boundaries," 95-105; Hatley, "Texas Constables," 98-118.

9. Fehrenbach, "Lone Star," 206-207.

10. Gammell, "The Laws of Texas," Vol 8, 330; District, County and justice court records from various Texas counties.

11. O'Neal, "Encyclopedia Gunfighters," 150-154; Robert K. DeArmant, "Alias Frank Canton" (Norman: U. Of Oklahoma Press, 1996).

12. Sonnichsen, "I'll Die," 128-134.

13. Bill O'Neal, "The Bloody Legacy of Pink Higgins" (Austin: Eakin Press, 1999), 32-33.

14. Stephen Jent, "The Browser's Book of Texas History" (Plano: Republic of Texas Press, 2000), 181; Parsons, "McNelly," 132-133; Metz, "Hardin Dark Angel," 127-130.

15. Walter Clay Dixon, "Richland Crossing" (Ft. Worth: Peppermill Publishing Co, 1994), 257-259; Metz, "Hardin Dark Angel," 129-136.

16. Metz, "Hardin Dark Angel," 132-140; Dixon, "Richland Crossing," 260-264.

17. Dixon, "Richland Crossing," 265-266; Metz, "Hardin Dark Angel," 141-143.

18. Metz, "Hardin Dark Angel," 143-147, 161-169.

19. Fehrenbach, "Lone Star," 110-111.

20. Paul I. Wellman, "Death on Horseback" (Philadelphia & N. Y.: J. B. Lippincott Co., 1934), 150.

21. DeLord, "Ultimate Sacrifice," 50-52.

22. Parsons, "McNelly," 274-275; DeLord, "Ultimate Sacrifice," 50-52. The names of those lawmen killed in the line of duty in Texas before 1900, are at best just being collected and my figures may prove at a later date to be too few, but they are the latest and most accurate list made to date.

23. Richard F. Selcher, "Hell's Half Acre" (Ft. Worth: T. C. U. Press, 1991), 20-39.

24. Selcher, "Hell's Half Acre," 68-114.

25. Eugene Cunningham, "Triggernometry" (N. Y. : Barnes & Noble

books, 1999) 2O3-218.

26. "Government" Handbook of Texas Online, accessed 1O/1O/OO; Fehrenbach, 'Lone Star," 434-442; "Constitution of 1876" The New Handbook of Texas, Vol I, 289-291.

27. Fehrenbach, "Lone Star," 434-442; "Constitution of 1876," The New Handbook of Texas, Vol I, 289-291.

28. "Judiciary" Handbook of Texas Online, accessed O6/2O/OO; "Texas State Constitution of 1876," Sections 3 through Section 8, The New Handbook of Texas, Vol I, 289-291. In 1891, a constitutional amendment would establish an intermediate level of appeals for civil cases. This new court of appeals was given jurisdiction over most civil appeals for the district and county courts. Further review of civil cases by the supreme court was then made discretionary. That court of appeals which was established in 1876, renamed the Texas court of criminal appeals in 1891, finally established two levels of appeals and the second court of last resort in the judicial system of Texas.

Chapter VII
END OF THE ROAD FOR MANY TEXAS OUTLAWS 1877-1879

1. Metz, "Hardin Dark Angel," 162-166.
2. Metz, "Hardin Dark Angel," 167-169.
3. Metz, "Hardin Dark Angel," 167-169, 186.
4. "Index to Records of the Texas State Penitentiary," Book 1998/O38-15O. Texas State Library and Archives Commission, 143. John Wesley Hardin was received into the Texas Prison System as Prisoner #71O9. On page 212 of the Convict Record, Hardin was described as 26-years old, 5'9" tall, fair complexion, hazel eyes with dark hair and married. He was noted to have the following marks on his body: "wounded scars" on the right knee, left thigh, right side, on the elbow and shoulder and on the back. He used tobacco, was "temperate" in his habits, had a "common" education and his occupation that of a "laborer." His residence was shown as "Gonzales County."
5. "Index to Records of the Texas State Penitentiary," Book 1998/O38-15O, Texas State Library, 143.
6. "Index to Records of the Texas State Penitentiary," Book 1998/O38-15O, Texas State Library, 14O-145.
7. Metz, "Hardin Dark Angel," 155-156.
8. Miller, "Bloody Bill," 117-118.
9. Miller, "Bloody Bill," 117-12O. Rick Miller explained that Constable June Courtney was apparently so good at detective work that

only a month later, he became suspicious of another man newly arrived in his precinct named Collins. It seems that Mr Collins was actually wanted for a 1876 murder in Tarrant County, Texas and Courtney received an additional $400 reward for that arrest.

10. Miller, "Bloody Bill," 126-173.

11. O'Neal, "Encyclopedia of Gunfighters," 154-160; Sonnichsen, "I'll Die," 145-149.

12. Ty Cashion, "A Texas Frontier" (Norman: U. Of Oklahoma Press, 1996)230-231.

13. Sonnichisen, "I'll Die," 167-187.

14. Nyle H. Miller & Joseph W. Snell, "Great Gunfighters of the Kansas Cowtowns, 1867-1886" (Lincoln: U. Of Nebraska Press, 1963) 47-64; Hatley, "Texas Constables," 105, 108-112.

15. Smith, "Old Army," 161.

16. Smith, "Old Army,"55-60, 116-117.

17. Webb, "Texas Rangers, " 346-348.

18. Much of the information on the Salt War is derived from the following excellent sources. For a full account, see, "El Paso Troubles in Texas," (U. S.) House Document No. 93, Forty-Fifth Congress, Second Session, Serial No. 1809; Charles F. Ward, "The Salt War of San Elizario, 1877", M. A. Thesis, University of Texas, 1-184.

19. "Salt War of San Elizario" New Handbook of Texas, Vol 8, 783; Webb, "Texas Rangers," 345-367. That most of those opposing Howard and those rioting in San Elizario were Mexican-Americans, does not mean that all the Mexican-American citizens in the area took part in the riots. Two of Charles Howard's bondsmen were MexicanAmericans as were five of the rangers who fought to protect him in the siege. Others in the area hoped to settle the question of the salt deposits by peaceful means, but it obviously was not.

20. Wilkins, "The Law Comes to Texas," 137-140; Webb, "Texas Rangers," 354-356.

21. "Salt War of Sam Elizario," Handbook of Texas Online, accessed 10/10/00.

22. Webb, "Texas Rangers," 352, 358-362; Wilkins, "The Law," 142; Personal Communication with writer Paul Cool, 12/03/01.

23. Robinson, "The Men Who Wear the Star," 227-229; DeLord, "Ultimate Sacrifice," 52; Personal communication with writer Paul Cool, 08/27/01.

24. Almost seventy years ago Walter Prescott Webb in his book, "The Texas Rangers," and Charles F. Ward, who even longer ago wrote "The Salt War of San Elizario, 1877," a well-researched Masters Thesis at the University of Texas @ Austin, best documented this fascinating

and violent chapter of Texas frontier history. Later, C. L. Sonnichsen's book, "Pass of the North", also looked at this episode in Texas history. But that was some thirty years ago, and current work by writer Paul Cool on this subject may soon make this whole incident much clearer. I include this account in order to examine those troubles from a law enforcement perspective, for if it had happened in the late twentieth century, a host of lawyers, the Justice Department and some law enforcement agencies would have attempted to label the actions taken against Charles Howard during the Salt War as a "hate crime." One of the most telling bits of evidence confirms that they would have been correct in labeling this a "hate crime," otherwise why were only the Anglo-American bondsmen of Charles Howard murdered while the Mexican-American bondsmen were ignored and allowed to go their own way?

25. "Sam Bass" Handbook of Texas Online, 06/12/01.

26. Rick Miller, "Sam Bass & Gang" (Austin: State House Press, 1999), 149-232.

27. Miller, "Sam Bass," 1, 43-45, 115-175, 241-262; Delord, "Ultimate Sacrifice" 53.

28. O'Neal, "Encyclopedia of Gunfighters," 73-74, 107-109, 263-264.

29. Allen Hatley, "Cap Arrington, Adventurer, Ranger and Sheriff," 50-56, Wild West Magazine a Primedia Publication, June 2001, 50-56.

Chapter VIII
THE VIOLENCE RETURNS
THE 1880s

1. "Forgotten Texas Census: first annual report of the Agricultural Bureau of the Department of Agriculture, Insurance, Statistics and History, 1887-'88" by L. L. Foster, originally published: Austin, Texas: State Printing Office, 1889; republished: (Austin: Texas State Historical Assn., 2001), xlvi; Stein, "Consider the Lilly," Vol 10, #3, June 2001, 135-149; Fehrenbach, "Lone Star," 596-597; Texas Almanac, 1978-1979, 184.

2. DeLord, "Ultimate Sacrifice," 51, 54, 55, 61; Texas Almanac, 1978-1979, 184-193.

3. Texas Almanac, 197801979, 184-193.

4. Fehrenbach, "Lone Star," 600-601.

5. Court records of Brown, Burnet, Cherokee, Colorado, Lampasas, Mason, Shackelford, Smith, Young Counties.

6. Court Records of Burnet, Colorado, Lampasas, Mason,

Shackelford, Smith, Young Counties. Eighty-seven separate indictments for gambling offenses in Burnet County in 1881 may not sound significant until it is pointed out that the number of indictments result in a crime rate for that offense of 1,242.8 per 100,000 population. That is a most significant number in any crime rate calculation in this book, and is, for example, equal to three times the arrest rates in Texas in 1999 for Driving Under the Influence (DUI) of either liquor or drugs. Only the number of arrests for some type of theft and larceny (3,065.6 per 100,000) in Texas in 1999 exceeds the crime rate based upon those indictments for gambling offenses in Burnet County in 1881.

7. Foster, "Forgotten Texas Census," 293-294; "2000 Crime in Texas, The Texas Crime Report" (Austin: Texas Department of Public Safety, 2002).

8. Foster, "Forgotten Texas Census," 293-294. Although we are able to calculate the murder rate based upon the indictments issued by the grand jury's across Texas for the years 1883 through 1887, no such breakdown of information is available on which to estimate the total level of violence (assaults, rapes, etc) during that period. The author is impressed with the information provided in this compilation by the Attorney General's office for 1883-1887, as it provides us with a surprising insight into the handling of murder cases for that period. This data is discussed in more detail in Appendix B. During that same five year period, 33 Texas lawmen are now confirmed to have died in the line of duty. Information from most of the district court records examined, also confirms that the three years from 1884 through 1886 were a period of heightened violence in much of Texas.

9. Texas Almanac, 1956-1957: The Encyclopedia of Texas" (Dallas, A. H. Belo Corp., 1955), 342-343.)

10. Gournet, "Texas Boundaries," 103-106; Robinson, "Panhandle Pilgrimage, 167-171; Texas Almanac, 1978-1979, 185-193.

11. Leon Metz, "Pat Garrett: The Story of a Western Lawman," (Norman, U. Of Oklahoma Press, 1974), 96-117; Robinson, "Panhandle Pilgrimage," 171.

12. Webb, "Texas Rangers," 403-405.

13. Robinson, "Men Who Wear the Star," 224; Smith, "Old Army," 164; Webb, "Texas Rangers," 425. Webb on page 425 of "The Texas Rangers," claimed that "—never again was an Indian to scalp a settler or burn his cabin" (in Texas). That and similar statements in other books, were not really accurate statements as noted in this chapter.

14. Webb, "Texas Rangers," 425-426; Smith, "Old Army," 10, 119-126.

15. Foster, "Forgotten Texas Census," xliv, 293.

16. District Court records in Burnet, Colorado, Lampasas, Mason, Shackelford, Smith and Young Counties.

17. Lawrence M. Friedman, "Crime and Punishment in American History" (N. Y.: Basic Books, 1993), 110-111.

18. DeLord, "Ultimate Sacrifice," 54, 55, 61.

19. DeLord, "Ultimate Sacrifice," 51, 54.

20. DeLord, "Ultimate Sacrifice," 54, 55, 61.

21. O'Neal, "Encyclopedia of Gunfighters," 230-231; Metz, "Hardin Dark Angel," 217.

22. O'Neal, "Encyclopedia of Gunfighters," 64, 65, 231.

23. O'Neal, "Encyclopedia of gunfighters," 231-232.

24. Metz, "Hardin Dark Angel," 97-117.

25. Wilkins, "The Law Comes to Texas," 235; Robinson, Men Who Wear the Star," 244.

26. Foster, "Forgotten Texas Census." 124, 198, 249, 294, 295.

27. Webb, "Texas Rangers," 395-406; Robinson, "Men Who Wear the Star," 241-145.

28. Bill Stein, "Consider the Lily," Vol 10, #1, January 2000; Metz, "Stoudenmire," 24-35. Although allegedly involved in shooting incidents in Colorado County, Texas before moving to El Paso, there are no records of such in any court appearances, nor notices in the newspapers in Colorado County. Dallas Stoudenmier's name is spelled "Stoudenmire" by most all of those who have written stories on the man. The spelling of his family name, however, on his own marriage license issued in Colorado County, and the spelling of his brother's name, Colonel S. Stoudenmier, on both of his court records in Colorado County and on his tombstone in Llano, Texas, is as I have spelled the family name herein, Stoudenmier.

29. Leon Metz, "Dallas Stoundnmire El Paso Marshal" (Norman: Norman, U. Of Oklahoma Press, 1969), 39; Hatley, "Texas constables," 62-69.

30. Fred R. Egloff, "El Paso Lawman G. W. Campbell" (College Station: Creative Publishing Co., 1982), 88-89.

31. Metz, "Dallas Stoudenmire," 35-44; Egloff, "ElPaso Lawman," 74-94. Depending on the source, those doing the killings somewhat differ, but I have chosen to use Fred Egloff's version as it includes statements by several eyewitnesses describing the actual gunfight. Leon Metz' version is also equally credible and he credits Stoudenmier with the killing of Hale and not Krempkau. Either is possible.

32. "Missouri-Kansas-Texas Railroad" Handbook of Texas Online, accessed, P9/19/01.

33. "Stoudenmire" Handbook of Texas Online, accessed 06/12/01.

34. DeLord, "Ultimate Sacrifice," 56.

35. DeLord, "Ultimate Sacrifice," 57.

36. O'Neal, "Encyclopedia of Gunfighters," 315-321.

37. Webb, "Texas Rangers," 426-437; Frank Collinson, "Life in the saddle" (Norman: U. Of Oklahoma Press, 1997), 222-230; Robinson, "Panhandle Pilgrimage," 187-188.

38. DeLord, Ultimate Sacrifice," 57; J. H. Rainey v The State of Texas, #1980, Court of Appeals of Texas, 20 Texas Ct. App. 455; 1886 Texas Criminal Appeals LEXIS 68, March 3, 1886; J. Elmer Rainey v The State of Texas, #1981, Court of Appeals of Texas, 20 Tex. Ct. App. 473: 1886 Texas Criminal Appeals LEXIS 69, March 3, 1886.

39. DeLord, "Ultimate Sacrifice," 57-58.

40. Foster "Forgotten Texas Census," 288-291.

41. DeLord, "Ultimate Sacrifice," 57-58.

42. Robinson, Panhandle Pilgrimage," 180-182.

43. DeLord, "Ultimate Sacrifice," 59.

44. DeLord, "Ultimate Sacrifice," 60.

45. Index to Criminal Court Papers, Young County District Clerk File, Charles Marlow, Indictment for murder, Cause# 386, Box CR-8, 1889; Sonnichsen, "I'll Die," 194-198.

46. Sonnichsen, "I'll Die," 199-202.

47. Index to Criminal Court Papers, Young County District Clerk File, Eugene Logan, Indictments for murder, Box-8, Cause#385, 1889, Cause#400, 1890. Cause#426, 1891; Sonnichsen, "I'll Die," 203-204.

48. File Box 15, Case #1, County Clerks Office, Potter County Courthouse; Hatley, "Texas Constables," 118-122; Robinson, "Panhandle Pilgrimage," 280-286.

49. Della Key, "In the Cattle Country: History of Potter County" (Wichita Falls: Nortex Offset Publications, 1972), 50-60; Hatley, "Texas Constables," 120-122.

50. Pauline Yeldman, "The Jay Birds of Fort Bend County" (Waco: Texian Press, 1979), 51, 60; Sonnichsen, "I'll Die," 232-240.

51. Sonnichsen, "I'll Die," 240-253; Yeldman, "The Jay Birds," 69. Carry Nation's husband was a sometimes minister who also wrote a column for the "Houston Daily Post" . He had earlier arrived in Texas from Kansas and married Carry. In 1889 he was severely beaten by the Jay Bird followers and run out of Fort Bend County, largely because of some of the contents of his newspaper columns and his Republican Party sympathies. Carry Nation, who would later gain a worldwide following as a crusader against alcohol and saloons, was at the time the local postmistress and operator of the National Hotel, before they both departed for Kansas in the spring of 1889.

52. Sonnichsen, "I'll Die," 255-259.

53. Yeldman, "The Jay Birds," 97-98; Sonnichsen, "I'll Die," 259263.

54. Sonnichsen, "I'll Die," 265-27O; Yeldman, "The Jay birds," 1O4.

55. Sonnichsen, "I'll Die," 17O-177.

CHAPTER IX
THE END OF AN ERA
THE 189OS

1. Fehrenbach, "Lone Star," 611-615.

2. Fehrenbach, "Lone Star," 617-623.

3. Horton, "Lone Star Justice," 32-51; Fehrenbach, "Lone Star," 623-625.

4. Friedman, "Crime & Punishment," 256-157; Foster, "Forgotten Texas Census," 292-293; "Government" Handbook of Texas Online, accessed 1O/1O/OO. The Railroad Commissioner of Texas would later also take over the jurisdiction of regulating oil drilling, production and royalties and would become a very powerful and visible elected post in Texas State government.

5. Wilkins, "The Law Comes to Texas," 3O6-313.

6. John Miller Morris, "Private in the Texas Rangers" (College station, Texas A & M Press, 2OO1), 3-12; W. J. L. Sullivan, "Twelve Years in the Saddle With the Texas Rangers" (Lincoln: U. Of Nebraska Press, 2OO1), 3O-32, 146-148.

7. DeLord, "Ultimate Sacrifice," 62-68.

8. DeLord, "Ultimate Sacrifice," 62-68.

9. DeLord, "Ultimate Sacrifice," 62-68.

1O. Sammy Tise, "Texas County Sheriff's" (Albuquerque: Oakwood Printing, 1989), 313, 33O. The James S. Scarborough family are surely the record holders of both the total number of years spent as a Texas sheriff, but also their ability to stand for and be elected to office, which by my count was a total of 22 times. Between the three Scarborough men who served as sheriffs in Lee and Kleberg Counties, they would serve a total of more that 83 years and some eight months as a Texas Sheriff in two different counties. After his retirement in Lee County in 191O, Jim Scarborough moved to Kleberg County in 1911, where he was first associated with a real estate agency. Then with the support of the owners of the King Ranch when Kleberg County was created, he would first be appointed Sheriff in August of 1914, and then first be elected to that office on Nov. 3, 1914. He would be reelected several more times and serve as sheriff until he was defeated by Tom Mosley in

Nov. 1922. Another son, James S. Scarborough Jr, who had been Chief of Police in the county seat at Kingsville for 13 years, was appointed sheriff of Kleberg County on Aug. 5, 1935, after Sheriff Tom Mosley resigned. James, Jr, would then be elected sheriff and serve thirty-seven years, four months and twenty-five days until the end of 1973. James Junior's son, James S. Scarborough III, ran for sheriff in Kleberg County in 1972, was elected and then reelected to four additional consecutive four year terms as sheriff of Kleberg County, serving until the end of 1989. A brother of James Scarborough III, Dan, was also elected a constable in a Kleberg County Precinct on Padre Island.

11. DeLord, "Ultimate Sacrifice," 65.

12. DeLord, "Ultimate Sacrifice," 64.

13. Metz, "Hardin Dark Angel," 218.

14. Metz, "Hardin dark Angel," 219.

15. Metz, "Hardin Dark Angel," 219-221.

16. O'Neal, "Encyclopedia of Gunfighters," 232-233.

17. "Santiago A. Brito" Handbook of Texas Online, accessed 23/O9/O1.

18. Gourney, "Texas boundaries," 29, 83, 113-123.

19. Leon Metz, "John Selman Gunfighter" (Norman, U. Of Oklahoma Press, 198O), 12O-124; Collinson, "Life in the Saddle," 95-1OO. Shackelford County District Court Minute Book B, page 265, dated May 5, 1888, notes that the nine indictments against John Selman for suspected cattle theft were dismissed at the request of the district attorney due, "not sufficient evidence to be obtained to secure a conviction."

2O. Hatley, "Texas Constables," 77-79; Metz, John Selman," 168-181.

21. Metz, "John Selman," 182-2O3.

22. Smith, "Old Army," 13O-133.

Epilogue
LOOKING AHEAD TO A NEW CENTURY

1. Fehrenbach, "Lone Star," 633-634.
2. Horton, "Lone Star Justice," 217-224.
3. Webb, "Texas Rangers," 457-458.
4. DeLord, Ultimate Sacrifice," 68-85.
5. DeLord, "Ultimate Sacrifice," 82-84.
6. Horton, "Lone Star Justice," 32-51; Texas Almanac, 2OO2-2OO3, 49.

7. Webb, "Texas Rangers," 466-469; Robinson, "Men Who Wore the Star," 265-266; DeLord, "Ultimate Sacrifice," 81.

APPENDIX A
A CLOSE LOOK AT TWO TEXAS GUNMEN

1. District, County & Justice Court Record & Minute Books from Burnet, Lampasas, Llano and Mason Counties.

2. James Marten, "Texas Divided, Loyalty & Dissent in the Lone Star State, 1856-1874", (Lexington: University Press of Kentucky, 1990).

3. Steve Gatto, "John Ringo, The Reputation of a Deadly Gunman," (Tucson: San Simon Publishing Co, 1995), 19-21.

4. Burnet County District Court Minute Book "B", Cause #854, p 124; Gatto, 9-15.

5. Gatto, 21-22.

6. Margaret Bierschwale, "The History of Mason County", (Mason: Mason County Historical Comm. 1998), 138; David Johnson, "John Ringo," (Stillwater, Barbed Wire Press, 1997), 71; Stella G. Polk, "Mason and Mason County: A History", (Austin: Pemberton Press, 1966), 48-60.

7. Texas State Library & Archives Commission, Texas Election Results, Reel #6, 1874-1878, Mason County; Bierschwale, "History of Mason County", 138; Jack Burrows, "John Ringo, The Gunfighter Who Never Was," (Tucson: University of Arizona Press, 1996), 133.

8. Gatto, 25-27.

9. Johnson, 72-73.

10. Johnson, 74, Burrows, 135.

11. Johnson, Ringo, 74-82; Gillett, 46-50;

12. Burrows, 134, Johnson 74-82; Gillett, 46-50)

13. Polk, 48-59; James B. Gillett, "Six Years With the Texas Rangers," (Lincoln & London: University of Nebraska Press, 1976), 46-50; Burrows, 132-133; Bill O'Neal, "Encyclopedia of Western Gunfighters", (Norman: University of Oklahoma Press, 1979), 73, Johnson, 64-65.

14. Burrows, 133-135; Bierschwale, 143-144; Sammy Tise, 357; Gillett, 46-51. Gillett, who was almost always mistaken in his comments on Ringo and Cooley, says 15 men resigned over this problem, however, Special Order # 47, Frontier Battalion Records, Box 401-1158, at the Texas State Library and Archives Commission, names only two men who resigned; also Sheriff John Clark did not just depart Mason County, he did not run for reelection that month, and departed Mason County.

Burrows on page 135 says that John Ringo and Cooley were arrested in Lampasas soon after James Cheyney's murder, but I found no record of that arrest. I suggest that Cooley and Ringo's arrest in Burnet County (not Lampasas), around Christmas Day in 1875 for threatening the life of a human being, and the change of venue to Lampasas was what Burrows was referring to. Also I am unaware that the Frontier Battalion arrested anyone for any violent offense in Mason County, as they apparently made only a few arrests for suspected cattle theft while they were in Mason County in late 1875.

15. Texas State Library & Archives Commission, Texas Election Results, Reel #6, 1874-1878, Mason County; James A. Browning, "Violence Was No Stranger," (Stillwater: Barbed Wire Press, 1993), 50; Johnson, 80; Tise, 357; Tom Gamel is truly a tragic figure in the Mason County War. Unable to support his fellow Germans when they murdered the Baccus brothers and others, he spent years in constant fear of violence, without real friends, but with plenty of enemies. Yet, he was an important figure, for without his writings we would be less knowledgeable on events in Mason County.

Several have written that the rangers were only in Mason County to protect Sheriff Clark, who was replaced on October 2, 1875, by newly elected Sheriff James A. Baird. John Rufus Clark would die just 27-months later after returning home to nearby Llano County. He was only 28-years old and is buried in Llano County next to his father and mother, who both outlived him by more than a decade. If there are stories of Scott Cooley being poisoned that some believe, then the death of 28-year old John Clark should also spark a cottage industry of similar stories.

Few seem to have recognized and appreciated the role Sheriff James Baird or the man who replaced him just four months later, Sheriff Jesse W. Leslie played in reducing the violence in the county. Burroughs mentioned neither man in his book, while Johnson only mentions their election to office, but does not speculate as to either mans role in possibly reducing the violence in Mason County. Gatto ignores both, while Sonnichsen who did not mention Sheriff Baird, only mentioned Leslie, but did seem to recognize his good work as Sheriff.

16. Johnson, 84; "Austin Daily State Gazette" Jan. 4, 1876; "Dallas Weekly Herald," Jan. 8, 1876. As an example of the notoriety that Ringo and Cooley received at the time, while both were incarcerated in the Travis County jail at the end of January, 1876, the U. S. Army Assistant Adjutant General, Department of Texas, San Antonio, Texas, sent a "Telegram" to Fort Sill, Oklahoma on January 28, 1876, stating that, "John Cooley and John Ringo are in jail at Austin reported to have

killed soldiers at (Fort) Griffin asks if evidence can be procured against them." There is no known answer to this query, nor were Ringo or Cooley known to have ever been near Fort Griffin. Thanks to Diron Ahlquist of Oklahoma City for this information.

17. Texas State Library & Archives Commission, Texas Election Results, Reel #7, 1878-1880; Sammy Tise, "Texas County Sheriffs," Albuquerque:Oakwood Printing, 1989), 357; Gatto, 23; Burnet County District Court Record Book "B", Winter Term, 1876, Cause #925 and #926, page 175-180. John Ringo, is sometimes written or referred to as "Ringgold" in newspaper articles and in James B. Gillett's book, "Six Years with the Texas Rangers", who claimed to have met Ringgold. But Ringo's last name was always spelled "Ringo" in the records of the District Courts in Burnet, Lampasas and Mason Counties during the 1870's.

His and Scott Cooley's two joint indictments are contained in Causes #925 and #926, in the Burnet County District Court Record Book "B", Winter Term, 1876, p 175. The result of Ringo's trial on February 2, 1876, after pleading guilty to disturbing the peace is found on page 192 of the same book. John Calvert, who together with M. B. Thomas had stood bail for John Ringo when he was indicted for disturbing the peace in 1875, was shot and killed on his own porch by several unidentified men on Feb. 16, 1876, just days after Ringo was bonded out on his second offense in Burnet County. It is unknown if that was a cause for the shooting.

18. Gatto, 44-46; Johnson, 86-87. Ringo was tried and convicted on the charge of threatening the life of Clymer and Strickland in the Lampasas District Court during the March, 1876 Term, however, his conviction was appealed and was finally overturned in 1877.

19. Lampasas County District Court Minutes, Volume 3, Cause #380 and #381; Metz, 184; Browning, 57. Although jointly indicted in Burnet County in two Causes, when removed to Lampasas County, the indictments were separated into different indictments for each man, with Ringo as sole defendant in Cause #380 and Cooley as sole defendant in Cause # 381. Numerous continuances granted in Cause # 380 brought against John Ringo are a part of the Lampasas County District Court records on Sept. 25, 1877, March 27, 1878, July 27, 1878, and in May of 1879.

Scott Cooley apparently rode away from the area in mid-1876. Although there are several versions of what happened to him, the June 27, 1876 issue of the "Galveston News" stated that Cooley, "died this morning about one o'clock at the house of Esquire C. Maddox, nine miles north of Blanco, of brain fever." The tombstone on the grave in the nearby Miller Creek Cemetery bears the inscription, "Scott Cooley, 1852-1876, Texas Ranger." Chuck Parsons, who has seen the gravestone, described it to me as "more contemporary than anything dating from the 187Os."

A year later in the Minutes of the Lampasas District Court Criminal Docket, Cause #381, The State of Texas vs Scott Cooley, was dismissed on March 28, 1877. No explanation is given for this dismissal in the Criminal Docket. The District Court Minute Book covering that period of the court was lost when those records were burned on the court house square.

2O. Johnson, 95-97; The lack of any jail, much less a secure one was a way of life in post-Civil War Texas. Prior to the war few people were locked up for more than a day or two prior to a trial, and rarely for punishment. After the war, both the number of those requiring incarceration and the violence capable of many placed in the local jails, worked against holding them in most county jails for long. The Travis County jail, located near the Texas State Capital was relatively close to Burnet and Lampasas Counties and was one of the most secure county jails in the state.

21. Burrows, p 135; "Mason County War", The Handbook of Texas Online, Accessed 6/12/O1 . Perhaps it was this burning of the court house in Mason County that also inspired a similar burning of just the District Court Records in Lampasas County most likely by the Horrell Brothers only a few months later. No doubt both of those fires were lit in an effort by some to rid themselves of their court records. In fact, the burning of court houses, or certain records kept in Texas court houses during the first two decades following the Civil War was commonplace, and the reason was usually an effort to destroy the records of civil suits and land records, in an effort to hide false testimony, illegal transactions or improper surveys. But criminal records also played a part in some of the fires.

22. Mason County Minute Book, Vol 2/3, p 19, Cause #21

23. Mason District Court Minute Book, Vol 2/3, page 19, and Court Records from Lampasas and Burnet Counties.

24. Johnson, 99.

25. Mason County District Court Minute Book, Vol 2, page 58; List of Prisoners in Texas State Penitentiary; James B Gillett says on page 51 of his book that George Gladden and John Ringgold were arrested and that Ringgold "received a life sentence", while Gladden was "sent to the penitentiary for twenty-five years". Burroughs on page 135, wrote that George Gladden "was sentenced to ninety-nine years in the penitentiary", and that "there is no apparent record of the length of Ringo's

sentence." Neither Gillett nor Burroughs' statements are entirely accurate for Ringo was never tried for murder in Mason County and, therefore, was not sentenced to any time in jail.

26. Texas State Library & Archives Commission, Texas Election Results, Reel #7, 1878-188O, Mason County, 66O-661. There were five constables elected in Mason County on Nov. 5, 1878, including John Ringo, but none are noted as having been "qualified" or "commissioned." In Texas the lack of "qualification" usually means that whoever was elected was unable to serve because he could not raise the money to be bonded, even thought elected in a general election. The other possibility is that there was a clerical error in never posting that information. The inability to raise a bond seems doubtful when examining Ringo's past ability to obtain bail bonds for several criminal offenses. I suggest that he never tried to obtain such a bond and soon moved on.

27. Leon Metz, "John Wesley Hardin Dark Angel of Texas" (El Paso, Mangan Books,1996), 184. On Nov. 12, 1879, the case against John Ringo in Lampasas County was finally dismissed almost four years after the indictment, "upon suggestion of (the) death" of John Ringo. The rumor of Reno's death may have come to the attention of the Lampasas District Court because of a letter written by Wes Hardin to Mannen Clements in July of 1879, saying he had heard Ringo had been killed. At that time he was alive and living in Arizona.

INDEX